Latino Pentecostal Identity

Religion and American Culture

The Religion and American Culture series explores the interaction between religion and culture throughout American history. Titles examine such issues as how religion functions in particular urban contexts, how it interacts with popular culture, its role in social and political conflicts, and its impact on regional identity. Series Editor Randall Balmer is the Ann Whitney Olin Professor of American Religion and former chair of the Department of Religion at Barnard College, Columbia University.

Michael E. Staub, *Torn at the Roots: The Crisis of Jewish Liberalism in Postwar America*

Amy DeRogatis, *Moral Geography: Maps, Missionaries, and the American Frontier*

Latino Pentecostal Identity
Evangelical Faith, Self, and Society

ARLENE M. SÁNCHEZ WALSH

Columbia University Press   New York

Columbia University Press
Publishers Since 1893
New York   Chichester, West Sussex

Copyright © 2003 Columbia University Press

Library of Congress Cataloging-in-Publication Data
Sánchez Walsh, Arlene M. Latino Pentecostal identity :
evangelical faith, self, and society / Arlene M. Sánchez Walsh
p.   cm. — (Religion and American culture)
Includes bibliographical references and index.
ISBN 0–231–12732–4 (alk. paper) — ISBN 0–231–12733–2 (paper : alk. paper)
1. Hispanic American Pentecostals. I. Title. II. Religion and American culture
(New York, N.Y.)

BR1644.5.U6S26 2003
289.9'4'08968073—dc21
                                        2003044012

Columbia University Press books are printed on permanent and
durable acid-free paper.

Printed in the United States of America

c 10 9 8 7 6 5 4 3 2 1
p 10 9 8 7 6 5 4 3 2 1

Para Soledad, la gracia y paz del Señor todos los dias

Contents

Illustrations

Figures

Maps

Preface

The first encounter I had with Latino Pentecostals occurred when I was very young, around six or seven I would guess. I was sitting on a sofa in the living room of my great-grandmother's house, and I saw what appeared to be a band of people in white with tambourines marching down the street. They were going door to door and handing out tracts. Not knowing who they were or what they wanted, I ran to the door to see these people all dressed in white, something not normal in my East Los Angeles neighborhood. As soon as I approached the door, my mother picked me up and hid me underneath the sofa, away from the leering eyes of the Pentecostal missionaries. I was quite upset, because even at that early age their dress, their demeanor, held some interest for me. I stayed hidden safely until they left. I remember my mother and great-aunt telling the missionaries, thanks but no thanks. A little while later, the Catholic Church gave my family an anti-proselytizing placard that they still have on the front of their door near the doorbell. I asked my mom why she hid me; what I remember of the conversation revolved around the fact that the "aleluyas" often came around from one of the two Pentecostal churches that were around our block and that they were particularly interested in children, so my mother, doing her duty, hid me away.

Years and years of driving past the "Gospel Temple" on Townsend Avenue and sneaking away to get a peek at "El Aposento Alto" on Michigan and Hicks Avenues only whetted my appetite about who these strangers were. The women wore long skirts, often no makeup, and looked very severe; the men wore suits and ties, and everyone, including children, carried a Bible. The music was loud; often I could hear sermons preached at a fever pitch. I kept these memories and did little with them until I was in graduate school years later. I needed a topic for my dissertation, and, furthermore, I needed to think about specializing in a field so I would be marketable as an academic. Never did I imagine writing about this subject for so long, speaking to audiences about it so often, and having it become part of my life, if quite by accident. It seems that those missionaries who arrived on our doorstep nearly thirty years ago ended up capturing more than just my interest.

One of my early undergraduate mentors, Clay Drees, said that he studied history to learn more about himself. I, too, believe that this work is an attempt to find out about myself. Never adept at any field that would earn me quick money, history was the only path I knew well. Religious subjects were always part of my interests. I can remember my mother's bemused look as she took me to the library so that I could research my first paper in junior high school, the transmigration of souls in Hinduism. I was that kind of child. Perhaps that is why Dr. Drees suggested that when I look into graduate schools I consider his alma mater and give this religious history field a try.

While at Claremont Graduate University I met my next mentor, who, probably since our first class together, had plans to convince me to stay in school long enough to get my Ph.D. Vicki Ruiz, an esteemed historian of Latina labor history, and someone I had heard about in my brief acquaintance with academia, became the guiding force behind my decision to stay at Claremont and finish my degree. She also recommended that I abandon my first choice for a dissertation topic (a biography of nineteenth-century New Thought writer Warren Felt Evans) for something that both the academy and publishers would deem a sexier topic. With that, I began interviewing Latino Pentecostals of all stripes to see what I was trying to find out about their faith lives, their lives as Latinos in the United States, and how they melded the two.

Latino Pentecostals are an interesting lot. Many of them have been dismayed that I would waste my time in the academy when the Lord's work was waiting for me. Many have been proud to be represented by someone whom they view as their own. I cannot say that I agree with everything I captured on tape and in my notebooks—many ideas, especially those that appeared to be steering Christianity into one political camp or another, distressed me. The legalism and often blind allegiance some had to particular movements and individuals struck me as quite a heretical cult of personality; I was often left wondering about those many passages in the Bible that warn of being led astray. One thing you learn from speaking, worshiping, visiting, and following Pentecostals around for years is that they are people of extraordinary faith and that faith makes some extraordinary claims. How those claims reflect on the social, cultural, and political lives of my brethren is the focus of this book.

Through this book I hope to pry into Pentecostal lives and move beyond the superficial, the God-talk, to compel them to analyze their faith lives not simply as a litany of pat biblical verses but as a holistic part of their constructed selves. In doing so, it is my goal to illuminate Latino Pentecostal lives for the rather suspicious secular academy that often views evangelical faith as something to be avoided. One of my graduate school cohorts once said to me that she was glad I was studying "them" because "we" needed to know "what the enemy was up to." Little did she know that I was "them." It would serve the academy well to note that such hyperbole about hidden enemies and dichotomies about us and them are not the sole property of a narrow-minded evangelical Christian Right; it is language that often has a comfortable home in their hallowed halls. This one book cannot dispel the mutual suspicion that Pentecostals have of "humanistic" professors and academics have of "extremists," but it is my hope that it will inspire a rethinking of assumptions.

Acknowledgments

I get the feeling that as long as I have been writing this book in one form or another, I should thank every librarian and library staff member at Honnold Mudd Library at the Claremont Graduate University, Fuller Theological Seminary, and especially Vanguard University for numerous requests, many reference questions, and patience with an often unwieldy project. I would also like to thank Randall Balmer for opening the doors for this manuscript to be read by the editorial department at Columbia University Press. At Columbia, I wish to thank Wendy Lochner and Anne McCoy for their work and especially Rita Bernhard, my copy editor, for making me sound more coherent than I often am.

I also want to thank the Flower Pentecostal Heritage Center, which houses the most incredible selection of Assemblies of God archives I know of. I still owe Joyce Lee a copy of my dissertation, and she will receive it with a copy of this book. Hidden away in plastic boxes at the Latin American Bible Institute (LABI) in La Puente, California, is a treasure of yearbooks and catalogues, which are all that is left of the written record of that most important institute. I thank the staff there who supported my many requests to sift through all their old books to re-create the history of LABI. There is a special place in my heart for library folk, since I worked my way through school as a library assistant. I want to thank them all for their often unheralded work.

Equally important was the financial support I received to research this work. I want to thank the Historical Society of Southern California, the Haynes Foundation, the Billy Graham Center at Wheaton College, De Paul University, the Center for Religion and Civic Culture at the University of Southern California, Chaffey College, and California Baptist University for providing funds in some cases and employment in others, all of which allowed me to start writing this book which had sat on the shelf far too long.

I have benefited greatly from the friendship of Vicki Ruiz, who more than anyone else was responsible for convincing me to take this road. Every graduate student and budding junior faculty member should be so lucky. I thank her for keeping issues and ideas before me that I often ignore. Perhaps the person who has heard every word of this book, read it over several times, and, as a staunch Presbyterian, often wonders what all the fuss is about is the anchor who has kept me still through ten years of marriage; Tim Walsh's often astute musings about Pentecostalism gave me the perspective I needed. Others who often wondered what all the fuss was about were my parents, Cora and Miguel Sánchez, and my brother, Michael, all of whom often wondered when I would ever be finished writing but supported me nevertheless and are always at the center of my life. This book is dedicated to our child, Soledad, whose perfect timing allowed me months of writing time and whose arrival completed the circle.

Scholarly societies were the stage where I tried out much of this material over the past five years. I am grateful for the support and dinner conversations with various colleagues at the Society for Pentecostal Studies, the American Academy of Religion, the American Society of Church History, and the Oral History Association. Of particular note have been the friendship of Dan Ramírez, whose work on Oneness Latino Pentecostals and illuminating prose has inspired me, and the many conversations about Latinos and the church I had with Dr. Enrique Zone of Azusa Pacific University, who was always open to my many questions. Portions of this book were published in the *Journal of Hispanic Latino Theology*, and chapters 4 and 5 were represented in *Gen-X Religion*, edited by Richard Flory and Donald E. Miller (London: Routledge, 2000). In all cases, presentations and writings have been revised for this book.

Finally, I want to thank the Assemblies of God, Victory Outreach, the Vineyard, and all those who shared their lives with me. This book would not have been possible without their cooperation. They would eschew such praise and give thanks to the Lord and, in keeping with that spirit, so shall I.

Introduction

This book begins, in chapter 1, with a broad overview of Assemblies of God work on the borderlands. Of particular interest were the ways that Anglo-American missionaries and Latinos interacted, viewed each other, and negotiated their faith lives. In examining the history of the Assemblies of God missionaries and their Bible institute, I found that a shift from Latino ex-Catholic converts to Latino Pentecostals had occurred and that, despite the earnestness of the evangelical mission, Latinos were, and still remain, in pockets of powerlessness in churches they helped to build. In exploring the cultural and social assumptions of Euro American missionaries, I could have easily placed them in the comfortable category of their particular social milieu—is that not how everyone viewed Spanish-speaking people? But when I examined the writings of Pentecostals like Alice Luce and became enamored with the Azusa Street mythology which claimed that the "color line had been washed away in the Blood," the historian I am took note of the socioeconomic reality in post–Azusa Street Pentecostalism and found that its claims of racial utopia were baseless.

Chapter 2 examines the work of the Latin American Bible Institute (LABI) and shows how this new religious identity is maintained through rigorous applications of pedagogy and spiritual exercises. It is my contention that what occurred at LABI was a turning away of Latino Pentecostals from the legalistic tendencies of their midwestern Holiness roots toward an intentional excursion into the often marginal social realities in which many urban Latinos grew up during the 1960s and 1970s.

When a teenager at a little league baseball game, my cousin handed me a flyer between innings. The flyer advertised a Victory Outreach play at La Puente Church. Believing that my cousin needed such activities whereas I, confident of who I was, needed no such thing, I ignored the invitation. Shortly thereafter I lost track of my cousin. I heard periodic reports that she was on the street, on drugs, and probably picking up men for drug money, and eventually that she was in prison. I knew that years ago she had contacted a drug rehabilitation ministry and now saw that it clearly had not helped her. Because my cousin was the "crazy" one, her leaving the Church was an acceptable conversion; after all, she was supposed to get help. I knew little about the groups profiled in this book before I began my study in 1997, but I was familiar with Victory Outreach. Of course my initial impression of that church was closely tied to my cousin—a wild drug addict, hopelessly caught in the abyss of drug abuse. I did not accept the idea that this ministry was an actual church. I firmly believed that a church in Latino culture must adhere to certain standards, and those standards were synonymous with the Roman Catholic Church.

Chapters 3 and 4 provide an in-depth examination of the Pentecostal social mission called Victory Outreach. The history and philosophy of this church demonstrates that a Latino Pentecostal identity is shaped by social impulses as much as spiritual ones. Of particular note is the focus Victory Outreach places on retaining its youth, since it is this constant reshaping and reinventing of religious identities that makes Pentecostalism the fluid faith it is.

I recall my first visit to a Victory Outreach men's home to conduct my interviews. I immediately took note of the lack of air conditioning, the used furniture and appliances, and especially the humble nature of the residents, who did everything possible to make me feel comfortable in the stifling heat of a Los Angeles summer. I thought of that flyer I had thrown away twenty years earlier and how I wished I had kept it for this work. Why had I been so certain that Victory Outreach was not for me? What stigma did my cousin wear that made her choice of church so distasteful? As I continued my fieldwork and interviews with the church, I tried to answer that question and, in effect, to place this unique ministry in the context of the classical Pentecostalism I had found in the Assemblies.

Victory Outreach reshaped Latino Pentecostalism by turning the focus of the experience with God to a therapeutic catharsis that revives the miraculous in the mundane world of addiction. It is a focused ministry with little interest in changing its nature, but I believe it will be compelled to change as it enters its fourth decade. Victory Outreach extends a hand to the dispossessed, the untouchable caste of American society, and provides them an entryway to Christianity that many of my informants tell me they would never have found without this church. My cousin's stigma was that she was one of those untouchables. I may even have passed her on the street one day and not have known it. As I see it, the greatest strength of Victory Outreach may be its greatest weakness. The church's narrow view of its mission, couched in prophetic rhetoric of loyalty, causes members to become intensely protective of their narrative, just as they are protective of their members. When my cousin gave birth to her second child, her family did not visit her in the hospital but church members did, hoping to see her return to the fold. Though she had been drug-free for months, Victory Outreach viewed her as one of its own. It is through the development of a second generation of leaders that the church will be forced to reconcile with its desire to secure its legacy or evolve its message to a different audience.

The final chapter of the book examines a charismatic denomination, the Vineyard, and shows how, through various models of ministry, this very suburban and Euro American church has been able to attract yet another generation of Latinos. As with Victory Outreach, particular attention should be paid to how the Vineyard seeks to create a space for Latino evangelical youth. An important moment in this research was when I met Ryan De la Torre, who best summed up what I had felt growing up wandering through various religious phases. I examined the Vineyard's different approaches to Latinos because religious identity is often at the mercy of cultural change, and the revolutionary nature of the Jesus Movement, though tangential, I was convinced, could be traced through the Vineyard. I also attended a Vineyard-like church whose pastoral staff reminded me of the tattooed, body-pierced youth pastor, Ryan De La Torre. Being a stranger to the evangelical subculture, I was uncomfortable during my interview with him, not because of anything he did but rather because of what I had failed to do years earlier. Ryan described his difficulties in leaving his Baptist church rather matter-of-factly, saying that he felt called to a more experiential relationship with God and that nothing would keep him from exchanging his religious identity for another. He also gave up a secular college education in business so that he could be a full-time minister. There is a freedom in living out one's faith that I had never known, and I envied his boldness. He knew the subculture—its jargon, its music, its cultural appropriations—and I felt like an outsider, an adoptee who would never fit in completely.

The Vineyard has opened up the field of the evangelical subculture to Latinos who are not interested in the legalism of Latin American Protestantism. Because of its fluid engagement with popular culture, it is attractive to young Gen-X and millennial Latinos. What happens, I wondered, when a new generation of Latino charismatics, Pentecostals, and evangelicals meets its Euro American counterpart? Has the Vineyard learned anything from its Pentecostal brethren? After examining the Vineyard's leadership structure, theological education opportunities, and churches, I wish to offer a qualified yes. The Spanish-speaking Vineyards are still under the leadership of the Euro American church and, though autonomous leadership for Latinos was supposed to be a reality by now, leadership changes during the post-Wimber period have postponed such occurrences. The most optimistic development is the Vineyard's Bible institutes, which offer bilingual classes, affordable tuition, and are soon to become accredited, which will secure for future Latino pastors some degree of educational credit in a seminary setting.

By the time I interviewed John Luna, I thought I had everything figured out. I was coming to terms with who I was and what kind of church I needed to live my faith to its fullest. I was troubled by some of the political positions many pastors I interviewed held; in fact, several sermons shocked me because of their lack of historical accuracy. Among these were sermons that tacitly accepted the subordination of women and the maltreatment of Native Americans, that expressed gross stereotypes of people of color, an unhealthy obsession with material success, and an idolatrous acceptance of nationalism. But I had just become comfortable in this new subculture and was willing to overlook these sermons simply because I wanted to. I thought I finally understood why so many people found this subculture so attractive. It was a subculture that was passionate about God, passionate about seeking an experience. What did it matter that I found their politics distasteful?

John Luna's ambiguous relationship with the evangelical subculture caused me to rethink the ease with which I accepted my own church. Though I had found some evidence that reorienting one's religious life, as in the case of Victory Outreach, sometimes could lead toward more conservative politics, I had never met anyone like Luna, a person in conflict over his religious identity and struggling to fit that identity with his strong political convictions and even stronger ethnic pride. So, I thought, perhaps I had accepted this evangelical identity too fast, perhaps I wanted to take a second look, once I considered Luna's predicament. I wondered if perhaps I am just like him, that sometimes I do not have that kind of faith.

An unintended consequences of searching for something may be that you will indeed find what you are searching for and then may be unable to ignore it. You may remain forever in its grasp, unable to separate yourself from your discovery. I began this work because I wanted to learn more about myself. I was searching for my own identity and wanted to craft a narrative around it so that my historical memory would not be as a convert from anything but as a believer in something. All the while I was warned that my academic peers would be more accepting of my work were I not so self-reflexive, and certainly not about my faith. But I decided to accept the risk that some academics might regard my work as hagiographic scholarship in the guise of critical inquiry. I trust that my peers who review this work will hold me to the highest standards. And I trust equally that all the storytellers who entrusted me with their deepest thoughts, emotions, and expressions of faith will also hold me to the highest standards in my retelling of their stories.

Latino Pentecostal Identity

1. El Aposento Alto

This book examines the interplay between religious and ethnic identity among Latino Pentecostals/charismatics for clues to how they negotiate their varied identities. The Assemblies of God, Victory Outreach, and the Vineyard are studied to determine how they have created their religious identity and how that identity has intermingled with their ethnic identity. Through fieldwork, oral histories, and surveys, this project found that Latino Pentecostals/charismatics have an ambivalent relationship with their ethnic identity. On the one hand, they tend to subsume their ethnic identity under the rubric of their religious identity for very specific reasons: (1) the feeling Pentecostals have that they are commanded to relinquish any identity that deters them from a religious one; and (2) ethnic identity has little to do with the experiential nature of Pentecostalism, and therefore adherents are loosed from their ethnic moorings through a revitalized spiritual life. On the other hand, Latino Pentecostals/charismatics bolster their ethnic identity by retaining their language, founding churches that cater to their constituencies, and teaching their children about their history. Sufficient evidence from the historical and contemporary records indicates that Latino Pentecostals/charismatics, if not overtly, subtly view their ethnicity as an important component to who they are as religious people, and they often use this ethnic link as one of many evangelism tools to reach their community.

Aside from the overarching theme guiding this work, another underlying theme illuminates my contention that there is indeed such a thing as a separate Pentecostal identity inscribed on adherents through varied means that separates them from the Latino Catholic community. Through theological education, spiritual experiences, and reinforcement of an evangelical moral code, Latinos have become grafted onto the larger evangelical world and, within that world, have carved out separate social, cultural, and religious spheres for themselves where they should not be referred to as Catholic converts but as Latino Pentecostals. Latinos have been becoming Pentecostal for nearly one hundred years; therefore to suggest that this is a recent phenomenon, as much of the popular media do, is simply not accurate. To paint this conversion phenomenon as strictly a problem the Catholic Church has to solve, as both the popular media and some academics do, does not account for the generations of Latinos who have never been Catholic.

The umbrella movement that Pentecostals have often reluctantly called home is a rather unwieldy network called evangelical Christianity. This movement's reach gives Pentecostals a larger measure of their material culture. This adoption of the material culture of evangelical Christianity is crucial to understanding how Latino Pentecostals/charismatics have been able to graft themselves onto this culture. Latino churches play worship music by such industry heavyweights as Hosanna Integrity and the Vineyard Music Group; Latino evangelicals buy books from the latest Christian authors. Latinos are also sending their children to evangelical summer camps and youth conventions, and buy the cultural accoutrements of the evangelical subculture for their children and for themselves, signifying that they are connected to the larger evangelical world. Youth have always been a difficult group for churches to reach and even harder to retain. For example, in the mid-1940s, "Youth for Christ" was fronted by an up-and-coming evangelist dressed in flashy clothes and day-glow socks. Billy Graham presided at hundreds of rallies that catered to teenage audiences with "snappy choruses, instrumental solos, magicians, and Bible trivia contests."[1] Graham would later ask youth of the 1960s to "tune into God." Graham's risky endorsement of the Jesus Movement in 1971 before the National Association of Evangelicals offered the paternal approval the movement never sought but accepted, because it symbolized a generational shift from Graham to hundreds of youth ministries today that are deeply engaged in trying to retain youth through the power of pop culture. It is a subtheme of this work that Pentecostal Christianity needed, and in fact co-opted, pop culture for its own evangelistic purposes, and, in doing so, a generation of Latinos has now been grafted onto a larger, unwieldy network of contemporary Christian music, merchandising, missions organizations, and other parachurch organizations that comprise the American evangelical subculture.

Partaking of and becoming Pentecostal not only includes adherence to theological certitudes; it includes making cultural choices that require study, another subtheme of this work. Before delving into the history of the Assemblies of God missions to Latinos, a few words should be said to place conversion in context both culturally and historically. Historically Latinos viewed conversion to Protestant Christianity as more than a decision to choose belief in Jesus. Conversion often meant casting aside culture and language to become Americanized. Becoming a Christian became equated with, and in some sense still means, becoming American. As historian Vicki Ruiz demonstrates in her examination of the Houchen Settlement House in Texas, Latino children were taught the rudiments of the Bible alongside the rudiments of dressing up like Pilgrims for Thanksgiving.[2] Even earlier, as historian Timothy Matovina's study showed, Euro Americans during San Antonio's early annexation years wondered why Tejanos insisted on keeping their holidays and were often not interested in celebrating the Fourth of July.[3] In examining specific examples of Pentecostalism's growth in the borderlands from the early twentieth through the twenty-first century, my argument is not that Pentecostalism broke away from that Americanization mode, but it did, in radical ways, allow for some measure of autonomy because its early missionaries to the borderlands, especially the Assemblies of God's Alice Luce, insisted on Latino leadership of the churches. Nevertheless, Luce was never able to resolve issues of maternalism and supervision, as will be seen in chapter 2, and, as a whole, many American-based Pentecostal denominations are still stuck in the missionary mind-set of supervision. Essentially Luce's problem was emblematic of many Protestant and Catholic missionaries, many of whom had genuine concern for the Latino population and sought to be facilitators of faith rather than supervisors. The question was, did missionaries trust sufficiently that Latinos could develop theological and spiritual lives on their own without slipping into what missionaries viewed as heretical teachings. That Euro Americans thought enough of their own spiritual grounding to be able to supervise Latinos says much about the dynamics of the missionary/convert relationship. Equally, that Latinos took it upon themselves to teach, preach, and train one another despite the lack of confidence displayed by their Euro American overseers says much about the liberating ethos that drives Latinos to become Pentecostal.

Examining the varieties of Pentecostal identity among Mexican and Mexican Americans in Southern California first requires laying several foundations. These include (1) the conditions Mexican immigrants faced in turn-of-the-century Los Angeles; (2) the prevailing religious atmosphere in the city; and (3) the origins of the Pentecostal movement in the United States and the relationship between Pentecostal leaders and Mexican immigrants. The goal of this chapter, and succeeding ones, is to argue for the creation and maintenance of a Latino Pentecostal identity among a variety of communities bound together by their choice to become Pentecostal and often bound by social location. This first chapter seeks to provide historical context for the religious marketplace that Los Angeles became, especially after the Azusa Street revival in 1906. This context is important because it will demonstrate that, despite being viewed as objects of conversion by both Catholic and mainline Protestant missionaries, Latinos made a conscious choice to convert to Pentecostalism and became some of the faith's most zealous evangelists. Furthermore, once they made the decision to convert, sufficient numbers decided to convert again to Oneness Pentecostalism. Latino Pentecostals, for nearly a century, have sought to carve out social, theological, and cultural spaces in this mostly midwestern and southern import for a variety of factors, which is the focus of the chapters to follow.

Before examining turn-of-the century Los Angeles, it might be wise to encapsulate the historical events that propelled Pentecostalism onto the evangelical stage, where, more often than not, it met with more than a chorus of disapproval; indeed, Pentecostals were often expelled from their brethren's churches.

The rupture that occurred at the beginning of the twentieth century, when the Pentecostal movement began to sift members away from several religious bodies, caused more than a momentary outburst—Pentecostalism shocked Protestant America. Pentecostalism was anti-intellectual, antirational, ahistorical, nonliturgial, and allegedly sensual, and therefore morally dangerous. Evangelicals, as a diffuse body of Christians, as historian Randall Balmer has described them, form part of a religious subculture. Evangelicalism had its own language, imagery, institutions, and expectations that could not accommodate Pentecostalism's spiritual tidal wave.

Evangelicals, writes Balmer, pulled away from American society during the half-century between the Scopes trial and Jimmy Carter's presidential campaign. The subculture—composed of warring factions of separatist fundamentalists, mainline evangelicals (from historical Reformed and Holiness traditions), and Pentecostals—provided a place of refuge for evangelicals who felt alienated from the larger society and its values. Disturbed by the social and intellectual trends of American society, evangelicals "devised their own universe of congregations, denominations, Bible camps, Bible institutes, colleges, seminaries, publishing houses, and mission societies."[4]

One must wonder what evangelicals thought when, over several decades from the late nineteenth through the mid-twentieth centuries, they faced, in succession, the industrialization of America, waves of largely Catholic and Jewish immigrants, and liberal Protestantism's challenges regarding the Social Gospel and biblical criticism. Compounding this history is that evangelicals rarely got along with one another, especially after 1906, when Pentecostalism posed yet another challenge to the crumbling cosmos of evangelical consensus. Historian Grant A. Wacker delineates the conflict between evangelicals and Pentecostals. Pentecostalism's antirationalist, anti-intellectualism aside, what stirred up evangelicals about Pentecostals certainly had a theological component. Wacker's work on early Pentecostals gives us greater insight into who they were, what they believed, and why they succeeded. This insight also helps to explain the evangelical/Pentecostal rift.

Pentecostals placed all their spiritual hopes on what the Holy Spirit did, and therefore they did not bother to produce any systematic theology until after the 1950s. Besides the absence of seminary-trained clergy, Wacker notes that one reason Pentecostals did not develop a specific theology was because the Holy Spirit would explain the Bible and thus no outside help was needed.[5] Spirit baptism was the central Pentecostal focus, and as long as they preached that message Pentecostals were convinced that they were doing what God had planned for the final days of time—continuing the outpouring of the Holy Spirit as a sign that God was almost ready to wrap things up. Evangelicals, whose many luminaries attended the best seminaries, saw Pentecostals as poor, misguided country cousins who let their emotions get the best of them. I would argue that a subtext of evangelical problems with Pentecostals lies in the role of women and the loosening of tightly proscribed boundaries of idealized feminine spirituality. This should be kept in mind when examining the role of moral codes at the Latin American Bible Institute (LABI), and indeed the values that tend to become privileged throughout the study of Victory Outreach and the Vineyard.

Pentecostal preachers, men and women, traveled together and worshiped together. Under a trancelike state, commonly referred to as being "slain in the Spirit," men and women fell to the floor together, "side by side . . . in the most unseemly and immodest way."[6] Wacker quotes an unnamed observer who was horrified that, at Pentecostal meetings, women fell in the most "indelicate positions." Pentecostalism's alleged carnality no doubt emerged from the fact that women spoke "in groans that words cannot express" (Romans 8:26). Piety, the glue that keeps evangelicalism together, became redefined, under the auspices of Pentecostalism, as submission to a supernatural force that affected both men and women, and risked democratizing the male-dominated offices of apostle, prophet, evangelist, pastor, and teacher.

The irony of these criticisms is that evangelicals define themselves by their willingness to evangelize—to preach the Gospel to anyone anywhere—but not if that meant risking the loss of the idealized Christian woman. This last event sums up this evangelical paradox. A delegation of California ministers lobbied the British government to ban Aimee Semple McPherson from preaching in Britain because she might cause an outbreak of mental illness.[7] The idea of allowing a Pentecostal woman, who founded her own denomination, wore makeup, bobbed her hair, and attracted thousands to her campaigns to preach the Gospel, certainly hit some evangelicals as heretical because they opposed her theologically, but the fact that Sister Aimee oozed modernity was certainly a reason, in some minds, to protect the British public.

Another subtext that influenced the evangelical/Pentecostal split is examined in greater detail in chapter 2, but briefly the issue of Pentecostalism's attraction to people of color and their potential mixing in churches caused more than discomfort for evangelicals, and eventually Pentecostals, who, despite the rhetoric emanating from Azusa Street that the "color line had been washed away in the Blood," have never reconciled feelings of Euro American superiority over their African American and Latino brethren. What can be said for now is that this evangelical/Pentecostal divide continued well into the late twentieth century until the charismatic movement shook Catholic and mainline Protestant churches and ameliorated evangelicals' suspicion of Pentecostals. We shall return to that period later as we examine the growth of the Vineyard. For now, we return to a growing city in the middle of what was once a desert, once inhabited by Native Americans, and in 1906 became the sacred ground many believed was to become the American Jerusalem.

Los Angeles at the turn of the century meant downtown Los Angeles. The social and economic life of the plaza encompassed the life of the entire city. The few Euro Americans who lived there called it home with a number of Mexicans, Asians, and African Americans. The native Mexican population was split in two: the remnants of the *Californios*, on the one side, and the immigrant working class—miners, laborers, and railroad workers escaping north from the *Porfiriato*—on the other. The successive waves of Mexican immigrants found work in construction or on farms.[8] Most Mexican immigrants and Mexican Americans were Catholics. Southern California was a frontier that stood as an exception to the patterns of religious pioneering in the United States. Evangelicals were leading the way in the march westward during the nineteenth century. As historian Michael Engh notes, "California and the Southwest were different. In these two regions, Roman Catholicism was historically strong."[9] One of the factors that kept Protestants away from the Latino population was their inability to speak Spanish. Until the arrival of Reverend William Mosher in 1871, no Protestant minister spoke Spanish. Mosher did not put his language skills to work full-time in a Latino ministry until 1876. Protestants remained isolated from the Latino community, content to preach to Euro Americans at their camp meetings. Not until the late nineteenth century would Protestants make inroads among the Spanish-speaking community.[10]

In 1848 the Latter-Day Saints established a presence in Los Angeles and broke up the religious hegemony of the Roman Catholic Church. Jewish, Episcopal, and Congregational bodies followed as the immigration flow to Los Angeles now included Jews from the East Coast, and Episcopal and Congregational churches from the Midwest.[11] Protestant bodies like the Northern Methodists, Baptists, and Presbyterians experienced little success in Los Angeles, faring slightly better in outlying areas like Lexington (El Monte) or Lordsburg (La Verne). Baptists were strongest in Lexington. The areas around Los Angeles imitated much of their earlier frontier experiences: rural surroundings and families attracted to the Baptist message.[12] No Protestant body had drawn Mexican audiences in the plaza. The plaza, according to historian George Sánchez, was a bustling commercial, social, and religious center, but it lost its religious nature with the takeover by U.S. forces in 1847. Presbyterians suffered the same fate as other Protestants when they attempted to set up missions in the center of the city. Repulsed by what they viewed as the vice-ridden lifestyles of Latinos, Presbyterians confined themselves to preaching to their own.[13] Though the lawlessness of the plaza might explain some of the Presbyterian distaste, the collision with a foreign culture of dark-skinned peoples certainly lent itself to equating "vices" like bull-fights, gambling, horse racing, and cockfights with Latino inferiority and, by association, Catholic inferiority. The plaza became isolated from the rest of the city but continued to provide living quarters for Mexican immigrants prior to World War One.[14] The first indication that Protestants met with success, which, for missionaries, meant converts, did not come until 1883.

The first recorded Mexican convert was a lay Methodist preacher named Antonio Diaz. Licensed to preach and eventually ordained as a Presbyterian minister, Diaz founded three small congregations: Misión Mexicana de Los Nietos in Whittier in 1883, Misión Mexicana de las Olivas in Los Angeles in the 1880s, and Iglesia Presbyteriana de San Gabriel in 1891.[15] Reverend Alexander Moss Merwin arrived from a Latin American mission in 1888 and helped found at least three more Presbyterian missions, in Los Angeles (1888), Irwindale (1889), and San Bernardino (1903).[16] Merwin's church on Sunset Boulevard northwest of the plaza became the first permanent, prominent Protestant presence in the solidly Catholic area. The religious dynamics of the plaza changed as Los Angeles grew and became tied to the rest of the West through railroads and immigration. But before the plaza lost its Catholic identity in 1848, the subtle struggle for religious identity began as the Catholic Church, having helped in removing any traces of indigenous religious life, sought to do the same to the *Californios'* religious world.

Bishop Tadeo Amat, a Catalan from Barcelona, Spain, arrived in Los Angles in 1856 with the bones of a Roman saint Vibiana and named her patroness of his diocese, replacing the Mexican patroness, Nuestra Señora del Refugio.[17] Amat rejected the abode-lined streets of the plaza in favor of a grand cathedral west of the plaza made of brick and limestone. Historian Michael Engh believes that these actions furthered the spiritual and physical isolation of Mexicans who lived on the east and south sides of Main Street, away from the Cathedral of St. Vibiana.[18] Additionally Amat pledged to make "every effort to see to it that one and the same discipline is everywhere observed." Engh continues: "Such insistence on ritual conformity insured a controlled uniformity of religious expression, but it denigrated the local spiritual heritage and neglected altogether the tragic issue of Hispanic loss of economic vitality and political representation."[19] Despite this appearance of isolation, Mexicans in Los Angeles remained at least nominally Catholic throughout the twentieth century, partly because Protestant missionaries discovered many of the same difficulties that Amat faced. With limited financial resources, few personnel, and a population practicing largely a form of popular Catholicism, Protestants were powerless to combat what they viewed as the "darkness" of Romanism. So they bolstered their ranks with former missionaries from Latin America (a practice that occurs to this day among most, if not all, evangelical groups). The appearance of Diaz's Presbyterian churches and his previously founded Fort Street Methodist Church (1879) established the presence of classical mainline denominations within the Mexican immigrant community. Within thirty years the city of Los Angeles became Protestant, and the Mexican community's religious choices expanded.

Historian Gregory Singleton's work examining the Protestant elite of Los Angeles at the turn of the century postulates that the classical mainline denominations—Methodists, Baptists, Presbyterians, Congregationalists, and a small group of others—spread a voluntaristic noblesse oblige on the public institutions and social services of their new cities. "The control of local institutions, including city government by 1907, was firmly in voluntaristic hands."[20] An example of the voluntaristic spirit of Protestants in Los Angeles was the work of the Methodist Church in the plaza. In the late 1890s the church instituted a program of training Mexican youth for nonagricultural jobs. The board of stewards later wrote: "If they are removed from the bean fields, and placed in more modern occupations, they may be more able to adapt the Protestant faith."[21] In 1909 seventeen Methodist churches in the area joined the plaza church to expand the program into the Industrial Training School for Boys.[22] The Presbyterians preceded their brethren by several years when Ida L. Boone founded the Spanish Mission School in 1884. Boone's comment on the hardship of administering the school echoes later Protestant workers in the field. "The parents are all Catholics, and when they think that the children are learning too much about the Bible, they are withdrawn. . . . It is a hard place in which to work, because the priests have such complete control of the Spanish people."[23] Despite these difficulties, Boone administered the school until financial troubles during the Great Depression closed its doors.[24]

Religious education was often masked as an attempt at Americanization, as the Industrial School for Boys demonstrates. The Houchen Settlement House in El Paso demonstrates a case of Americanization and focuses on the importance of children in the evangelization program of Protestants. The aforementioned Thanksgiving recital at the Houchen Settlement House was supported by lessons given to Latina women on setting a proper table, with utensils replacing tortillas, and of sewing as a proper occupation for the woman of the house. The prevailing idea at Houchen and at the Industrial School for Boys was that children who partook of these services would melt into the proverbial American pot by becoming American Protestants. The education of children under Protestant tutelage proved too much for many parents and for the local Catholic parish. Mothers who lived near the Houchen Settlement frequently allowed their children to play outside at the settlement's playground but did not permit them inside.[25] Catholic priests in the area "predicted dire consequences for those who participated in any Protestant-tinged activities."[26] The mutual suspicion that Protestants and Catholics held for each other aggravated their interaction in Houchen and other settings, to say the least. The confines of Houchen remained friendly as long as children played outside, away from the foreign sanctuary of a Protestant church. The sacred spaces Catholics and Protestants demarcated for themselves could not be breached without serious consequences to one's communion within their religious tradition. Pentecostals did not found settlement houses or industrial schools, but evidence suggests that Pentecostals did engage in modified forms of Americanization efforts. Finis E. Yoakum's Pentecostal mission in the Highland Park section of Los Angeles, called Pisgah House, included, in its mission to prostitutes, alcoholics, and the homeless, a mission school for Mexicans where the children learned English and performed for audiences singing gospel songs in English and Spanish. The adult women, along with their children, were taught to cook and sew their own garments.[27] Yoakum was one of Los Angeles's earliest Pentecostal leaders and, unlike other leaders, was of the professional class that made a substantial income (eighteen thousand dollars a year), working as a doctor who also taught at a medical college in Denver before opening Pisgah House.[28] One of the first converts at Azusa Street, Susie Valdez, volunteered at the mission, helping to translate for Spanish-speaking visitors.[29] Throughout this effort to define a Latino Pentecostal identity and to understand how it is created, the essential role of Latinas as transmitters of faith and their traditional evangelical role as helpmates should not go unnoticed. My interviews with contemporary Latina Pentecostals supports my contention that Latinas, more often than not, convert first and become active church members quicker than men, and, in keeping with the evangelical tradition of viewing women as helpmates and keepers of a sacred feminine holiness, Latina Pentecostals have been grafted onto that branch of American evangelicalism.

Potential converts, once having made the decision to enter a Pentecostal church, availed themselves of the services the church or mission offered, whether it was Pisgah House or Bible institutes, but a safe space remained outside church, outside the mission, where the suspicion both Catholics and Protestants had for each other remained safe as well. Sometimes this ancient suspicion has transferred over to those who chronicle the Latino encounter with Protestantism.

Sánchez describes the Methodist work in the plaza as having a deliberate, almost subversive nature. Mexicans are "enticed" to convert, and Methodists "lure" Mexicans away "from the faith of their fathers and mothers."[30] The assumption of Catholic parentage is a glaring problem in Sánchez's otherwise admirable work. Sánchez rightly states that 80 percent of the Mexican population remained nominally Catholic, but only 40 percent attended Mass.[31] He believes that the Church's lack of priests in Mexican areas like Belvedere and Maravilla Park partially account for the lack of adherence. These areas, he notes, shared three churches to serve the "fifth largest Chicano population in the nation as of 1932."[32] But Sánchez uses Samuel Ortegón's 1932 figures to measure the strength of the Protestant population. Ortegón's master's degree thesis research counted only eight churches. Clifton Holland's 1993 research found the following: four Mexican Baptist churches founded between 1905 and 1923; two Seventh-Day Adventist churches founded between 1905 and 1923; one Church of the Nazarene founded in the early 1930s; two Free Methodist churches founded in 1932; and three Assemblies of God churches founded between 1918 and 1934, including the plaza church, El Aposento Alto, founded by the British missionary Alice Luce in 1918 and never mentioned by Sánchez; one Concilio Latino Americano de Iglesias Cristianas church founded in 1923; and one Foursquare Gospel church founded in 1929.[33] By 1934 there were fourteen churches in the East Los Angeles area, representing six different denominations. These figures do not represent the churches of the plaza area. Eight churches representing the Presbyterian, Northern Methodist, Church of the Nazarene, Apostolic Assembly, and Free Methodist bodies meant that by the mid-1930s Mexican immigrants converted in sufficient numbers that missionaries planted more churches within the community, and, in the case of the Apostolic Assembly, a group with Mexican origins, Mexican missionaries converted their compatriots without the help of Euro Americans.[34]

Protestantism revealed itself to Los Angeles's Mexican communities in its classical mainline formulations: Presbyterianism, two varieties of Methodism, and Northern Baptist. For those who fell under the influence of the Holiness idea of perfection and sanctification, the Church of the Nazarene offered them sanctuary. For those seeking direct experience of this sanctification, Pentecostalism offered certainty—the promise of God's existence and salvific powers. Sánchez's assertion that "most Anglo Protestant congregations were proud of their homogeneity and did not look favorably on the introduction of reformed Catholic Mexicans into their churches"[35] is simply wrong if one examines the totality of Protestantism beyond the history of the earliest missionaries. Pentecostals, as it will be demonstrated, welcomed Mexicans into their churches, delivered the services in Spanish, and trained Mexican ministers to inherit the cause. There were more than twenty Protestant churches in Mexican neighborhoods, many founded by Euro Americans and inherited by Mexicans.[36] A diverse and evangelical lot, Pentecostals were prepared to offer Mexicans an experience and, in turn, an antidote to what they viewed as debilitating Catholicism.

The Protestantism Mexicans encountered in 1906 Los Angeles began to resemble more the Holiness advocate's faith devoted to temperance, pure living, and evangelism. Holiness's roots lay in the nineteenth-century preoccupation with perfection and the belief that all who abandoned their sinful behavior could attain certainty of salvation. Methodism's changing theological character throughout the nineteenth century did not hurt its growth. By 1840 Methodism was the largest Protestant denomination in the United States. By 1857–58 the desire for perfectionism caused revivalists like Charles Finney and Phoebe Palmer to preach, write, and teach sanctification. The post–Civil War years brought a change in the character of Holiness's demographic makeup. Formerly rooted in the middle to upper middle classes of the East Coast, by the 1880s the Holiness movement was populated by a lower- to middle-class southern and midwestern population. Bodies like the Church of the Nazarene (founded in Los Angeles) and the Fire Baptized Holiness Church (founded in Iowa) became representatives of Holiness congregations. These churches grew independently at first, then began losing members to the "come-out" movement.[37]

The chief difference between Holiness and Pentecostals is that Holiness advocates who claimed to be baptized in the Holy Spirit now found their baptism insufficient for Pentecostals who believed no one received the baptism until they spoke in tongues.[38] Carrie Judd Montgomery represented this movement. Montgomery, a famed Pentecostal healer, former matron of the Faith Rest Home in Buffalo, New York, and a member of the Holiness group, Christian Missionary Alliance, "came out" of her congregation and became a faith healer. Being an alliance member, Montgomery came under the influence of the Higher Life teachings of Alliance founder A. B. Simpson. Montgomery's colleague, Charles Cullis, shared his faith healing experience with her. But the Azusa Street revival changed her life as she converted to Pentecostalism—this to the dismay of Simpson, who never supported Pentecostalism despite the sincere protestations of "come-outers" in the Alliance that he declare his support.[39]

Early leaders in the Pentecostal movement have been viewed as being predominantly from rural areas of the Midwest and the South, and mostly poor. Because of their "disinherited" background, these leaders sought refuge in Pentecostalism to make sense of their world.[40] Because we now can examine Wacker's corrective work alongside Anderson's, we can see that Pentecostals were not very different from the rest of American society, and, in fact, some of the early leaders had the financial or educational means or both to seek out a more "respectable" religion not wedded to poor rural folk. Montgomery, Yoakum, A. J. Tomlinson, and others, however, found solace in a movement that, on the surface, did not suit their social location.

Some of the "come-outers" found homes in churches where they identified themselves as believers in the "Apostolic Faith." To these Pentecostals, their movement restored the faith of the Apostles.[41] One of the first advocates of the faith was Charles Parham of Topeka, Kansas. His Beth-El Bible School experienced a Pentecostal revival with speaking in tongues and healings in 1901.[42] Parham's growing movement spawned another school in Houston, Texas, in 1905. One of these students was William Seymour, former Baptist preacher and slave born in Louisiana. Despite Parham's reluctance to allow blacks into his school, he allowed Seymour to attend, provided he sit outside the classroom. Seymour learned about the Pentecostal faith, the importance of tongues, and initial evidence of the baptism of the Holy Spirit, and he became a preacher under Parham's tutelage. Fellow Holiness advocate Neeley Terry persuaded a breakaway congregation in Los Angeles to invite Seymour to be associate pastor at the future Azusa Street mission that began tarrying for its own Pentecost in 1906. The Azusa Street mission was formerly located in a house on Bonnie Brae Street, just outside Los Angeles, in what is now the MacArthur Park area. The mission moved to larger quarters months after Seymour arrived.

The mythic representation of the mission has caused scholars to take another look at the significance of Azusa Street. One of the more perceptive critiques from historian Joe Creech surmises that "Azusa became the central mythic event for early Pentecostals because they perceived it to be the location where God initiated an eschatological plan for the restoration of the church."[43] When first-generation scholars, many of them Pentecostals, took this perception as fact, they helped perpetuate the idea that Azusa Street's spiritual revival was the genesis of Pentecostalism. These historians relied on what Creech calls the "Azusa stream" model where the revival in Los Angeles sparked revivals throughout the nation and the world. Those who mentioned other revivals in Topeka, Cove Creek (North Carolina), India, and Chicago, along with Azusa, developed a "many fires" model where revivals occurred independent of Azusa Street.[44] Creech demonstrates, through an examination of recent scholarship on Pentecostalism, that the reliance on the original histories cloud even the most adept scholars, who have either used the "Azusa stream" model or have placed interpretations on Azusa Street that Creech views as unwarranted. As examples he cites theologians Harvey Cox, Iain McRobert, and Douglas Nelson, who have attempted to refocus the legacy of Azusa Street as an event that tore down racial, class, and gender barriers.[45] Creech does not see enough evidence to support those conclusions since very few of the early Pentecostals supported racial and gender equality. Azusa Street's mythic role as the "American Jerusalem," like many historical events, receives an affirmative reaction when interpreted by believers, and less so by nonbelievers. Believers in the Azusa Street of biblical proportions find reaffirmation in tracing every Pentecostal revival back to the mission. Those with a more dispassionate interpretation note its importance but, like Creech, cannot ignore the significance of other revivals from which varieties of Pentecostalism arose. I agree with Creech that Azusa Street's dominance of Pentecostal historiography limits the view that scholars have of other revivals and movements. Further, as will be demonstrated in the succeeding chapters, to make a case that Azusa Street represents an epiphany in racial and gender relations relies more on romanticism than reality: Latinos, by most accounts, were considered coworkers for the cause but only if they played a subservient role to their Euro American overseers, and an even more subservient position applied to Latinas, who were viewed as little more than helpmates for their pastor-husbands. Despite the overreliance on Azusa Street as a beacon of Pentecostal history, it remains my focus since it recorded one of the first conversions of Mexican immigrants to Pentecostalism.

One of the ideas I wish to impart throughout this work should be reiterated—the Pentecostalism to which Mexicans and Mexican Americans converted experienced theological struggles from the very beginning; varieties of Pentecostalism from Trinitarian to Unitarian were but two choices Mexicans had in their search for a new religious identity. To delineate the idea of a religious marketplace and how it worked among Latinos in Southern California, it is important to note the work of sociologists Rodney Stark and Roger Finke.

By the time Pentecostalism began to challenge mainline Protestantism in Southern California, mainline Protestantism had become the religion of the elite, developing a monopoly among the political, educational, and cultural institutions of the area. When examining the Latino community, mainline Protestants had made certain inroads, but the Catholic Church was the dominant faith. According to Stark and Finke, wherever a religious monopoly exists, those religions that are viewed as "old mainline" tend not to be able to cope with the introduction of new religious movements. Hence the Catholic Church was unable to cope with Protestants of any stripe, mainline Protestants were unable to cope with Pentecostals, and, even further, Trinitarian Pentecostals were unable to cope with Unitarian Pentecostals. The strength of this theory for historians is that this sociological study of colonial America has other historical and contemporary examples. To explain how this religious marketplace theory works in our context, it is helpful to examine Stark and Finke's original work.

The religious marketplace idea found that the "decline of the old mainline denominations were caused by their inability to cope with the consequences of religious freedom and the rise of a free market religious economy."[46] Their examples were the old mainline denominations—Congregationalists and Episcopalians, whom they call "losers" because of their failure to react to the upstart "winners," the Methodists and Baptists. Such labels are not to be taken in a derogatory manner; it is simply a way for the authors to note which denominations grew and which did not.

When one examines why these denominations succeeded or failed, one is struck by the similarities to the Latino Catholic/Protestant/Pentecostal relationship. Before examining that directly, I shall briefly highlight Stark and Finke's findings. Congregationalists and Episcopalians suffered from a lack of democratic congregational life. Their clergy were professionally trained and from a genteel class. Baptists and Methodists were common folk with little education, their clergy received little pay, and they spoke the language of common people. The hierarchical nature of Congregationalist and Episcopalian polity left little room for such free-flowing activities as camp meetings and small groups. It was at these small groups where the behavior of the congregants could be monitored. Such monitoring proved important since it was the Methodists, of the Holiness persuasion, who stressed behavioral modification as a sign of sanctification. Finally, among clergy, Methodists and Baptists often stressed the calling of the ministry, whereas Congregationalists and Episcopalians emphasized a message of erudition.[47]

When colonial Americans had a choice, and when religious groups competed for congregants, those groups with a more evangelically oriented mission won out, displacing religious groups who either had a monopoly on their geographic region (Puritan Commonwealth of Massachusetts) or whose appeal could not suit the needs of one "market segment" without sacrificing its appeal to another.[48] In examining the religious choices Latinos had in Southern California, parallels can be made to Stark and Finke's work. First, and probably most important, it was the common folk who became Pentecostal, and even if they were from the middle class, they did not preach like they were. There was almost a complete lack of seminary training among Pentecostal preachers. Those who did choose to set up shop and compete for the large share of the Latino market usually spoke Spanish. The Catholic Church's hierarchy did not allow for autonomous churches or programs that did not fit outside the established liturgy. Further, the Catholic Church's dominance of Latinos' religious life in the Southwest could parallel the geographic monopoly of Puritan Massachusetts.

Among Protestant groups, what made Pentecostals stand out was their reliance on the Holy Spirit as the central experience from which one could partake to equip oneself to lead the sanctified life Methodists talked about, and to modify one's behavior as other conservative Protestants stressed. When faced with the choice of Unitarian-Trinitarian Pentecostalism, the marketplace became more competitive. In this case, Pentecostals were pitted against Pentecostals, including the Oneness groups willing to compete fiercely for congregants. Oneness Pentecostals offered similar spiritual experiences but stressed that their baptism in the Holy Spirit was just as efficacious as Trinitarians—meaning that believers spoke in tongues as evidence of the Spirit's indwelling. Oneness Pentecostals stressed that their baptismal formula of baptizing in the name of Jesus was correct, because there was a biblical verse and an Apostle who appeared to have baptized in that way (Acts 10:48). Oneness Pentecostals competed successfully for Latino congregants because they ministered to them where they were, as will be seen later; on a theological level, they convinced a sufficient number of people that their view of the Pentecostal outpouring and view of God was as biblically orthodox, if not more so, than their Trinitarian brethren. The significance of these parallels are that religious choice existed, and was partaken of, on a regular basis; the Pentecostal faith continued a long line of Protestant faiths that Mexicanos adhered to and promoted. Within the larger framework of Pentecostalism, the choices included the Unitarian-Trinitarian bodies, and later the movement led by famed evangelist Francisco Olazábal.

Here I shall turn our focus to the early years of the movement at the Azusa Street mission, to the breaking away of Oneness Pentecostals, and, finally, to the institutionalizing processes of the Assemblies of God.

Azusa Street's worshippers were a diverse population, some of whom spoke no English, but, as William Seymour expressed in his *Apostolic Faith* (hereafter, *AF*), that did not matter:"It is noticeable how free all nationalities feel. If a Mexican or German cannot speak English, he gets up and speaks in his own tongue and feels quite at home for the spirit interprets through the face and people say amen."[49] Pentecost broke down linguistic barriers. For Pentecostals, Azusa Street was part of a continuum, since the day of Pentecost marked the beginning of the Christian Church. From its inception, this revival became a worldwide phenomenon. Frank Bartleman, a Pentecostal missionary, wrote: "Pentecost has come to Los Angeles, the American Jerusalem. Every sect, creed, and doctrine under heaven . . . as well as every nation is represented."[50] Both Seymour and Bartleman noted the diversity among people at the mission. This diversity worked in favor of the evangelist Seymour who received instruction from Charles Parham on the importance of speaking in tongues; language was now a gift from God, regardless of one's original language. This experience allowed the Spanish speaker to communicate with the German speaker, with the English speaker, and so on.

The revival began in house church gatherings held by Seymour. Eventually, their tarrying for an outpouring of the Holy Spirit was answered when, on 6 April 1906, Pentecost descended on Seymour and his followers, in keeping with the biblical pronouncement of spiritual outpouring.[51] Speaking in tongues, healing, prophecy, and other signs brought in crowds so large that Seymour rented a larger church on nearby Azusa Street. The revival continued for three years, and converts at the mission exported the revival to the Midwest and southern United States.[52]

One of the few accounts of conversion among Mexicans came from A. C. Valdez, who was ten years old when his mother brought him to Azusa Street. Valdez's mother, Susie, converted from Catholicism and became Yoakum's helper at his Pisgah House mission for prostitutes and alcoholics. Valdez writes of his family's early years of evangelism from 1906 to 1916, a time he describes as the worst years of persecution. He tells of being thrown in jail while others were horsewhipped, clubbed, or stoned. He claims that some Pentecostals were martyred.[53] Other sources corroborated Valdez's accounts of harassment and violence, but I have found no evidence of martyrdom. Aside from Susie Valdez's work with Yoakum, A.C. did not record another time when he or his family ministered to Spanish speakers. This was not the case with other Azusa Street converts.

Historian Mel Robeck's important work on Latinos at Azusa Street places their roles in the context of Pentecostal history of the early twentieth century. Abundio López and his wife, Rosa, converted to Pentecostalism at Azusa Street and became emissaries of the Pentecostal faith to other Mexicans. It seems that the Lópezes had embraced the Protestant faith before Azusa Street as the Reverend Alexander Moss Merwin, pastor of the Spanish Presbyterian Church, officiated at their wedding in 1902.[54] They attended the revival on 29 May 1906, and converted the following month. Rosa was not mentioned in the Los Angeles City Directory, but Abundio was listed in the 1920 edition. He is listed as the pastor of the Apostolic Faith Church, a Spanish-speaking congregation that doubled as a Euro American church named Victoria Hall on Spring Street. The "Apostolic Faith" was the first name given to the nascent Pentecostal movement at Azusa Street.[55] The couple's ministry caught the attention of Seymour, who wrote about their work at the mission: "There are a good many Spanish-speaking people in Los Angeles. The Lord has given them language, and now a Spanish preacher, who, with his wife, are preaching the gospel in open air meetings on the Plaza, having received their Pentecost."[56] One month later the Lópezes became Seymour's helpers. "Brother and Sister López, Spanish people who are filled with the Holy Ghost, are being used of God in street meetings and helping Mexicans at the altar at Azusa Street." The Lópezes eventually left Los Angeles to minister to Mexicans in the borderlands.[57] The specter of a Mexican preaching in the open-air plaza of Los Angeles, which, at the time of Azusa Street, contained within the plaza eleven Catholic churches, adds another important dimension to the creation of a Pentecostal identity. Pentecostalism liberated immigrants from language, and also from the enclosed sacred spaces of the plaza that, for decades, symbolized the Catholic Church's strength within the Mexican community. Protestants contested that space by building churches and training their Spanish-speaking ministers in the plaza as early as the 1880s. Pentecostals like the Lópezes zealously sought converts and did so in the heart of Catholic Los Angeles. To the eventual (and continuing) dismay of the Church, they succeeded.

Language for the Pentecostal took on a sacred meaning that other Protestant denominations working in Mexican communities did not have. The following report from Seymour demonstrates what spiritual language did for the convert. On 11 August 1906, a native Mexican from Central Mexico interpreted the language of a German woman to be his own. "He understood, and through the message that God gave him through her, he was most happily converted. . . . All the English he knew was Jesus Christ and Hallellujah."[58] The Pentecostal baptism, according to converts, gave them the ability to transcend language barriers and proved key to gaining converts who did not speak English. Speaking in tongues transcended the temporal boundaries of human language and introduced the mostly working-class Mexican immigrant population to the ethereal world of the Spirit. Many reports describe what Wacker termed *missionary tongues* during the early years of the Pentecostal movement. This gift centered on the ability to speak in the language of the mission field so that the gospel could be preached all over the world in native languages. Wacker notes that no evidence of such a gift existed, aside from personal testimonials filling the pages of Pentecostal magazines and pulpits. He views missionary tongues as a pragmatic strategy employed by Pentecostals to continue their worldwide missionary efforts. Missionary tongues were needed, Pentecostals reasoned, because Jesus was coming soon, the "heathen" was perishing without the gospel, and it was not too far-fetched to assume that the Holy Spirit would give Pentecostals this gift to meet a practical need,[59] another example of the pragmatic approach to seeking converts.

Another key to conversion efforts lay in the places where Euro American evangelists sought converts—homes, social missions, plazas, and jails—sites where a marginal population might find themselves in early twentieth-century Los Angeles. A lay missionary in jail in Whittier began ministering to the Mexican population, and, as he described it: "The Lord gave me their tongue, the Mexican language. . . . I did not have that tongue, until I went into jail . . . most of the men are Mexicans, the men in jail asked me where the mission was, and they were going to come down as soon as they get out."[60] Pentecostals, then as now, have never been intimidated by the often dour and dark surroundings of prisons, migrant field houses, and the modest homes of working-class Mexicanos. In the same issue of *AF*, another unnamed missionary offered insight into the motivations behind this conversion strategy after the initial Azusa Street revival in April 1906: "I bless God that it did not start in any church in this city, but in a barn, so that we might all come and take part in it. If it had started in a fine church, poor, colored people, and Spanish people would not have got it."[61] Pentecostals recognized the segregation that comprised much of churchgoing in Los Angeles, cognizant that had the revival occurred anywhere else, people of color would have been excluded.

Azusa Street initiated the Mexican population into the evangelical world of Pentecostals. This revival and the ensuing push to convert others signified something more than the beginning of a new religious movement. The Protestant Los Angeles Singleton, found in 1907, now included a zealous and growing movement whose characteristics included more than a voluntaristic impulse. Pentecostalism delivered a message to the burgeoning immigrant population that extolled the virtues of a spiritual experience offering certain salvation. But almost as soon as Azusa Street waned, around 1909, Pentecostalism's discordant voices began to give way to schism.

A new theological issue casting doubt on the Trinitarian nature of God split the small but growing Mexican convert population.[62] The nascent Mexican Pentecostal movement experienced its first theological division, and, with that, Oneness Pentecostals felt the urge to spread their new message to their own. The significance of this break lies in the fact that the Mexican converts established churches and spread the Oneness message independently of the larger, Euro American Oneness group that separated from the Assemblies of God in 1914. Even more significant, for the purposes of unfurling the layers of a Pentecostal identity, is the establishment of a Mexican Oneness Pentecostal movement in Los Angeles by 1909 and its growth to the borderlands and Mexico by 1912. The first known Apostolic church (Oneness churches are still commonly referred to as Apostolic), the "Spanish Apostolic Faith Mission," opened on Alpine Street in 1912, pastored by Genaro Valenzuela.[63] Mexican converts began to challenge the established norms of Trinitarian Pentecostalism, and, within three years of their initiation, a separate Pentecostal identity began to take shape. The origins of the Oneness movement are not entirely clear. The movement began in house churches in and around Los Angeles, ministered by Mexicanos, who converted Azusa Street converts like Luis López and Romanita Valenzuela.

Romanita Carbajal de Valenzuela gathered followers in Los Angeles and rebaptized them in the name of Jesus. She returned to Chihuahua and converted her family. The church she established, La Iglesia Cristiana Espiritual (the Christian Spiritual Church), became one of the largest Protestant bodies in Mexico. The U.S. counterpart, La Asamblea Apostólica (Apostolic Assembly), spread quickly throughout southern California and the Southwest. Valenzuela also did work along the border of California, Texas, and Arizona.[64] Though there is little biographical information on him, Luis López was baptized at Azusa Street in 1909. The revival also produced evangelist Juan Navarro. López and Navarro were rebaptized in the name of Jesus later that year.[65] They established a mission and converted many of the future leaders of the Asambleas Apostólicas. One convert, Antonio C.Nava, copastored a small Apostolic church in Los Angeles, on Angeles and Aliso Streets, one of the denomination's first churches in Los Angeles.[66] By 1919 Apostolics had established churches in Watts, Oxnard, Los Angeles, San Fernando, San Diego, San Bernardino, and Riverside, usually establishing missions among migrant farm workers.[67] By 1925 there were at least twenty-three churches and twenty-five pastors scattered from Baja, California, to New Mexico.[68]

As Daniel Ramírez notes, the preponderance of the Apostolic Assemblies churches were planted among migrant labor camps of southern California. Ramírez contends that the movement which began in the plaza area of Los Angeles became increasingly rural and focused its attention on farm workers: "A nucleus of farm worker converts in the Coachella Valley proved key in subsequent evangelization work in Mexico."[69] The dire surroundings facing Apostolic Assembly members, and indeed most laborers in the fields, caught the attention of a rival missionary, Assemblies of God minister John Preston, who wrote of conditions in the Imperial Valley in 1918. "This is a very needy place. . . . There is absolutely nothing being done for the Mexicans on either side of the line by any of the Protestant churches, and so it is all over the Imperial Valley, the Mexicans are neglected."[70] Judging by the requests missionaries made for donations, the remedy for this neglect focused not so much on a social mission but on a spiritual mission offering laborers a better life through Pentecostalism with fellow laborers leading the way, establishing churches and bringing laborers out of the fields they plowed together. The ease with which church members crossed the border to evangelize and create churches ceased with the deportation of many Apostolic members during the 1930s. During their stay in Mexico, Apostolic members spent their time evangelizing and building churches.[71] Oneness Pentecostals established a separate identity from their Trinitarian brethren as early as 1912. Their desire to build on that difference is demonstrated by their commitment to evangelize their fellow immigrants and their former homeland. What attracted them to Oneness? To Pentecostalism? The spiritual gifts of tongues and healing were and remain two of the most important phenomena feeding the desire to become Pentecostal. In the pages of *AF* and in the experiences converts describe, several clues are provided.

What did Azusa Street represent to those who visited the mission? What did the emerging Oneness movement represent to the convert? What happened at the mission that so impressed people that they chose to adopt Pentecostalism, even for only a moment but often a lifetime? Two feats, in particular, appealed to visitors of Azusa Street: speaking in tongues and healing. Abundio López, Rosa López, Brigido Pérez, Luis López, Juan Navarro, and the unidentified native Mexican all experienced the baptism of the Holy Spirit. Both the native Mexican and Abundio López reported that they had been given the gift of healing or were healed themselves. The native Mexican laid hands on a woman at the mission, and she reported being healed of tuberculosis,[72] "de almas y de cuerpos" (of soul and body).[73] Information on early Oneness converts is scanty, revealing only that they claimed to experience Spirit baptism. Antonio C. Nava, on an evangelism tour of Yuma, Arizona, prayed for his sister, and she was reportedly healed of cancer. This resulted in the entire family converting to Oneness Pentecostalism.[74] Like the native Mexican, healing facilitated the opening of Pentecostalism to others who sought the same experience. This is not to suggest, however, that Pentecostalism introduced religious healing to the Mexican community. The desire to alleviate physical suffering by means of divine intervention has a long tradition among Mexican immigrants, who, years before they entered the

Azusa Street mission, visited the homes of curanderas like Teresa Urrea and took the prescriptions of curanderos like Don Pedrito Jaramillo.

Urrea brought her healing powers to the Mexican population of Los Angeles in 1902 in exile. "The halt, the blind, the inwardly distressed, paralytics almost helpless, and others ravaged by consumption, are helped to her doors each day by friends, and relatives and none go there without the belief that by the laying on of her magic hands, they will be cured."[75] Urrea purchased a home in Boyle Heights on Brooklyn Avenue and State Street, and, according to the *Los Angeles Times*, a continual stream of "invalids" visited her. Urrea's exile began when she became a larger threat to the Mexican government, who did not appreciate the moral support she gave to native Mexican uprisings. Faith healer Don Pedrito Jaramillo, the healer of Los Olmos, ministered to the Mexican population of southern Texas and northern Mexico from 1881 until his death in 1907. Jaramillo wrote unusual prescriptions for his followers, as the patients informed his assistant of their symptoms.[76] During one engagement in San Antonio in 1897 between March 24 and April 11, Jaramillo received and prescribed cures for 11,583 people, sometimes sending telegrams as far away as New Orleans.[77]

There are significant differences and a few similarities between the healing arts legacy within the Mexican community of Urrea and Jaramillo and the Pentecostal healing converts at Azusa Street experienced. Both the Pentecostals and Urrea used the laying on of hands to transmit healing. Both Urrea and Jaramillo became associated with the Latino Catholic lexicon of folk saints, a lexicon Pentecostals reject as having any part in their healing. For example, Tomochic rebels attempting to invade Mexico on behalf of Santa Teresa wore her picture on their person to help ward off bullets from Mexican government soldiers.[78] Don Jaramillo's grave became a pilgrimage site.[79] Pentecostals, implicitly if not explicitly, tried to remove any hint of popular Catholicism from the healing experience. Although similarities exist between the trance possession curanderos report when channeling spirits and the Pentecostal act of being "slain in the Spirit," Pentecostals diligently discourage any theological link to practices of folk religion in an attempt to create boundaries of orthodox/heterodox religion. Another experiential similarity exists between the healing tradition of Spiritualists and Pentecostals—both claim the supernatural ability to speak in tongues. Though this phenomenon has been recorded by both curanderos who are *espritualistas* and U.S. Spiritualists, it is again relegated outside the boundaries of orthodox religious practice.

While the healing traditions of the curanderos and santos have ancient roots among Mexicanos, the healing tradition brought to them through Pentecostalism bears little resemblance to the healing traditions of the past. The chief and, for Pentecostals, most important difference is their claim that their tradition receives its supernatural commandments from the New Testament's injunctions to use the power Jesus gave to heal to the Apostles as part of their reclaiming of the Apostolic tradition. Pentecostals would disavow any linkages—cultural, spiritual, or otherwise—to any healing traditions outside Christianity.

The power of Pentecostalism is in its immediacy and the implicit acceptance of the miraculous. God mandated the end of the exclusiveness of language by making spiritual language available to all who asked for the Spirit baptism. Among those who accepted the baptism, a handful of Mexicanos became evangelists for a new faith. Problems for these evangelists and for their new faith were not far behind. One of the problems, according to Robeck, was culture: "When Hispanic Pentecostals such as Lopez, Pérez, or the Valdez families did choose to share their personal testimony with other Hispanics and encourage them to seek the same thing thereby evangelizing them, have they actually violated their own culture?"[80] Does preaching for Pentecostalism mean preaching against Catholicism? Did that, in turn, mean a betrayal of the cultural marker of Catholicism imbued so deeply that its loss signified a cultural death? Some of the more introspective analysis on Latino Pentecostals and the question of ethnicity and culture have come from Catholic priest/scholar Allen Figueroa Deck.

> The thoughtful Hispanic will view evangelical efforts to convert Hispanics as a particularly vicious attack on his or her cultural identity. Even though the Hispanic American may not be active in practicing the Catholic faith, he or she perceives that the culture is permeated by a kind of Catholic ethos and symbols that revolves around a rich collection of rites and symbols. Many of these rites and symbols are imbued with a certain Catholic spirit. The evangelical penchant for reducing the mediation between God and humanity to the Scriptures is antithetical to the Hispanic Catholic tendency to multiple mediations. . . . Hispanics have often experienced serious family divisions when a member becomes Protestant. In Hispanic culture, this is not just a religious matter. It is a profound cultural, social, and familial rupture.[81]

Examining Figueroa Deck's words explicates the dilemma that early Pentecostal converts experienced and, to some extent, still do. As Figueroa Deck described in another work, it is the reactionary impulse of the Catholic Church and the indifference of mainline Protantism to the "Hispanic shift" toward Pentecostalism that has given rise to a culture of suspicion and animosity. All sides that have failed to understand the shift toward Pentecostalism feed this culture, ascribing to a premise based more on the proprietary concern of the Catholic Church and its desire to be seen as the Mother Church. Add to this the lack of attention Latino Protestants received in mainline Protestant churches, where, for nearly two centuries, becoming a Christian has been equated with becoming Euro American.

Although Figueroa Deck writes more about contemporary conversions than does Robeck in his historical analysis, the former recognizes the profound tensions created around conversion, but his insistence on placing it in a Catholic context does not help us ascertain how a Pentecostal identity is created among mainline Protestant or agnostic converts who have never been Catholic. In my research for the succeeding chapters, I interviewed many converts who did not have ties to Catholicism before conversion, and to suggest, as Figueroa Deck does, that Latinos have an innate Catholic ethos requires rigorous examination. If Figueroa Deck limits his scope to Catholic converts, then the problem becomes, of course, how these converts work out their faith life as an ex-Catholics, who may or may not still be involved in popular Catholic practices, and how they deal with familial tensions. But if we want to examine the larger picture of Latino converts, we cannot assume a Catholic ethos for non-Catholics nor even for nominal Catholics. However, we may be able to assert a symbolic religious identity for Latino Catholics, who are nonpracticing and are quite ambivalent about the Church but would never think of leaving.[82] By this I wish to suggest that Latino Pentecostals developed a historical memory and religious identity separate from Catholicism and that, by maintaining certain faith traditions, these Pentecostal identities continue to this day, operating separately from Catholicism's historical memory and religious identity. Ruiz posits another perspective on ethnicity and religious identity called "cultural coalescence." "Immigrants and their children pick, borrow, retain, and create distinctive cultural forms. There is not a single hermetic Mexican or Mexican American culture but rather permeable cultures rooted in generation, region, class, and personal experience."[83] If there is no single culture, then presumably there is no single religious heritage informing the faith lives of Latinos. Assumptions anchoring scholarship about Latinos and religion need reconceptualization. The permeability of cultures certainly finds support in the Pentecostal experience of Latinos, who not only chose their religious identity but also began forming it early on as they sifted through varieties of Pentecostalism. Sociologists Rubén Rumbaut and Alejandro Portes offer another theory that does not deal explicitly with religious identity but may help to explain why Latino immigrants, especially Mexican immigrants, enter into the acculturation process and form identities at different rates than other immigrant groups.

Portes's and Rumbaut's segmented assimilation idea suggests that a host of factors determines how second-generation immigrants, in particular, acculturate effectively into American society. The two describe three levels of acculturation based on their findings.[84] Unfortunately, like most sociologists who do not deal with religion, there is no factor attached to this topic. In fact, in their entire book on second-generation immigrants, Portes and Rumbaut make only one reference to religion, and it focuses narrowly on Chinese immigrants and Buddhism. Nevertheless, this and other theoretical models are helpful in contributing to an understanding of the larger picture of Mexican immigration and how Pentecostalism figures into the acculturation process. Certain questions should be kept in mind as the story continues: Does Pentecostalism offer anything with regard to human capital? Does it ease modes of incorporation? Does it buffer family structures? How does Pentecostalism help successive generations of Latinos acculturate, and what does that do to their identity as Latinos? To answer these questions, we continue.

The very nature of Pentecostalism as an independent faith would be the cause of its unraveling within a few years of its inception. The evangelists would then have to organize churches, build Bible schools, and solidify a Pentecostal identity among the Mexican communities from California to Texas. In order to maintain our focus on the institutionalization of Pentecostalism within Mexican communities, attention here shifts to the Assemblies of God, one of the most productive of Pentecostal groups, who, by 1918, had missionaries committed to Latinos in the United States despite the breakaway movement of the Mexican healing evangelist, Francisco Olazábal.[85]

Olazábal, born in El Verano, Sinaloa, Mexico, on October 12, 1886, was the mayor's son. After his mother converted to Methodism, he was sent to the United States to study for the ministry. After a stint at the Moody Bible Institute in Chicago, Olazábal worked at the Glad Tidings Tabernacle in San Francisco and then pastored at Misión Mexicana de Pasadena, founded in 1907. During that time he founded a cooperative laundry for Mexican immigrant women in Pasadena. Olazábal's Pentecostal conversion occurred under the ministry of Carrie and George Montgomery.[86]

The Montgomerys worked in Arizona and California. Their Pentecostal lineage is not traced to Azusa Street but to the "come-out" movement within the Holiness denominations at the turn of the century. The Montgomerys "came out" of the Christian Missionary Alliance, a denomination particularly rife with contention over the alleged unsavory character of Pentecostalism. For years, Holiness converts to Pentecostalism tried unsuccessfully to win approval from the Alliance founder A. B. Simpson, who never accepted the more elaborate doctrines of Pentecostalism, especially speaking in tongues.[87]

Carrie's fame as a healer-evangelist grew within the Holiness community as her husband, George, funded her nationwide revivals with the profits of his northern Mexico mining business. On a trip to Los Angeles, they visited Misión Mexicana in Pasadena and met Olazábal, who told George that his own conversion to Pentecostalism came through George's healing experience which he had read about in a Spanish Bible tract.[88]

Olazábal was one of the first Mexican Pentecostal leaders to leave any written record of his ministry. Not only do his writings piece together the early history of the movement but they also provide clues to the creation of a Latino Pentecostal identity. Olazábal demonstrated a typical nineteenth-century Protestant education in a speech before the Methodist Epworth League in Gardena, California, in May 1913,[89] his predisposition to anti-Catholic sentiment having been set years before he became Pentecostal.

> In the critical moments through which my country is passing, when nearly the entire world considers my people to be barbarous and uncivilized because of the fratricidal war that is desolating the fields and cities of Mexico . . . I do not believe in the armed intervention of your country because it is not what we need and you can bear it to us: the intervention of the Gospel and of Christian love.[90]

The Mexican, according to Olazábal, would prefer death rather than be subject to armed intervention.[91] In an ironic twist, Olazábal's nationalism echoed what conservative Mexican Catholics said at the time on the need to respect the sovereignty of the Mexican nation.[92] The obvious difference was that nationalist Catholics viewed Protestant missionaries in Mexico as part of the U.S. invasion, not as part of the solution to the nation's problems. Catholic detractors accused triumphant revolutionaries of Protestantism. Historian Deborah Baldwin believes that conservative Catholics saw the revolution as "culturally incongruous," since being both Protestant and Mexican was unacceptable.[93] Not only did Olazábal see no incongruity in conversion, he encouraged the continued conversion of Mexican and Mexican Americans.

Olazábal, the Methodist, blamed the Catholic Church for Mexico's misfortunes. He explained: "I was born in that faith, and the first instruction which I received was Roman Catholic."[94] Olazábal echoed a familiar refrain at the end of his speech, the idea that Catholicism was not Christian. "When Mexico shall come to be a Christian country, which it surely will be if we do our part, let its best friend be the U.S."[95] Ruiz's contention that cultures permeate and create identities from various sources finds strength in Olazábal life. Olazábal, the Mexican nationalist Protestant with strong ties to the American Protestant community, pleads for the United States not to invade Mexico militarily but, instead, to invade Mexico with more American missionaries. Another ironic twist to this story is that the Americans who heeded similar calls from Olazábal and others to "save" Mexico turned out to be missionaries like Henry Ball—an Assemblies of God pastor whom Olazábal would break away from over allegations of racism.

Olazábal continued working for the Misión Mexicana Church in Pasadena until 1916 when he moved to Texas and began to work with the Assemblies of God mission to Mexicans. Olazábal was ordained into the Assemblies of God on 24 September 1916, and soon afterward moved to El Paso to pastor.[96] Within three years the mission was in financial trouble, and Olazábal wrote to Montgomery for support. In response, Montgomery sent him forty-five dollars toward a new church building. In thanking him, Olazábal asked for prayer and more workers for his growing mission. The El Paso mission flourished in the midst of revival but not without repercussions. Olazábal described the difficulty of operating in a Catholic stronghold: "We had to fight against the powers of the Catholic Church. The tent was stoned, threatened to be set on fire, etc."[97] Along with Spirit baptisms, the members reported healings, visions of Jesus and the Second Coming, and prophetic utterances regarding the future of the church.[98] Olazábal concluded his column by asking for support for his ministry and hinting about a Bible school for Mexican men and women preparing for the ministry.[99] In 1921 an unknown writer pleaded Olazábal's case to the readers of *Pentecostal Evangel* (hereafter, *PE*), the weekly magazine of the Assemblies of God. The writer notes the lack of workers for the masses of Mexicans who attend services in El Paso in a church that needs expansion to accommodate the crowds.[100] During the first three years of his ministry with the Assemblies of God, Olazábal appeared to receive support and encouragement for his work. Apparently, however, as his ministry continued to grow and require more donations, his fund-raising activities on behalf of the church made the Assemblies of God uncomfortable. Depending on which version of the story one chooses to accept, Olazábal was either asked to leave or he resigned.

In January 1923 J. R. Flower, the Assemblies superintendent, wrote a column in *PE* describing Olazábal's situation. According to Flower, Olazábal's attempts to begin a school in El Paso failed so badly that Flower, Ball, Olazábal, Luce, and the missionary to Mexico George Blaisdell attended an emergency meeting in December 1922. According to Flower, the El Paso school was too far away from Mexicans to be effective. He also cited the poverty of the Mexicans of El Paso as a reason why the school failed. Flower said, quoting Olazábal: "He agreed that he would devote his time and energies to the ministry rather than to attempt to build up a school or other institution which would take him from the field."[101] Flower moved the efforts to build a school to San Antonio and placed it under the supervision of the Missionary Commission of the General Council of the Assemblies of God. Ball took charge of the administration of the school, and Luce took charge of the faculty.[102]

According to Miguel Guillen, the official chronicler of Olazábal's story and former minister with the Texas mission of the Assemblies of God, Olazábal did not leave the denomination voluntarily but was asked to leave because of problems related to his fund-raising for the school, which caused the leadership concern. According to Guillen, the Assemblies of God was intent on not allowing Olazábal any position of leadership and terminated his ministry in an effort to silence his powerful presence amid the growing Mexican Pentecostal community. In 1922 the Mexican members of the Texas Assemblies of God voted to start their own district council, which Olazábal would head. According to Isabel Flores (another former member of the Assemblies of God), the plan required Olazábal to run the council from his El Paso church while starting a Bible institute and a printing press. Opposition to Olazábal's promotion came from the Euro American members of the Assemblies of God, who, according to Flores, believed that "el pueblo Mexicano no estaba capacitado para dirigir el trabajo" (the Mexican people were not qualified to direct the work).[103]

In December 1923 Guillen interviewed Olazábal at his home in Port Arthur, Texas, and the interview supported Flores's account. Olazábal recalls meeting with Assemblies of God leaders to explain why he raised money for his church. He mentioned Alice Luce's philosophy of autonomous Mexican leadership. The leadership was offended at his reference to Luce and suggested he showed disrespect. When Flower, the Assemblies of God leader, asked who had authorized his fund-raising, Olazábal answered that he had received authority to raise funds at the last Texas Assemblies of God convention (1918) from Flower himself. Olazábal's response to his dismissal was this: "Yo sali de entro los Metodistas y crei que habia entrado mas cristiana, pero ahora veo que un Ruso, un Griego puede se misionaro menos un Mexicano." (I left the Methodists and I thought I had been among Christians, but now I see that a Russian, a Greek, can be a missionary, but not a Mexican).[104] With that, Olazábal set off to found his own church. In 1923 El Concilio Latino Americano de Iglesias Cristianas began.

The Assemblies of God recollection of events differs significantly from Olazábal's. Glenn Gohr, an Assemblies of God historian, believes that Olazábal became "disconcerted" with the predominantly Euro American denomination.[105] Other Assemblies of God recollections of the Olazábal controversy are sparse. Henry Ball commented on the controversy in a 1940 retrospective on his career:

> El hermano Francisco Olazábal se retiró de las Asambleas de Dios el
> dia de 13 de Enero de 1923. Era un gran evangelista y se retiró de nuestro movimiento cause disturbios de caracter serio indudablemente esturiamos mas avanzados.[106]

> [Brother Francisco Olazábal withdrew from the Assemblies of God in
> January 1923. He was a grand evangelist. His retirement from the movement caused a great disturbance in the character (of the movement).
> Unquestionably, we would have been much more advanced].

Ball concluded that the Assemblies of God mission would have been much stronger had Olazábal stayed with the church. Despite his popularity in the Assemblies, Olazábal left and convinced a core group of Assemblies of God ministers, including the future church superintendent Demetrio Bazán, to leave the church to join Olazábal in establishing churches in Texas and California.[107] This episode between Olazábal and another Pentecostal denomination clearly speaks to the tenor of the times in which Olazábal preached and reflects how Euro American leadership viewed him.

After Olazábal left the Assemblies, he continued his healing campaigns. One campaign in East Los Angeles in 1927 attracted the attention of Foursquare founder Aimee Semple McPherson. McPherson and Olazábal were invited to preach in each other's churches, but this cozy relationship did not last long. When McPherson asked Olazábal to merge his new denomination with her's, the Concilio membership defeated the proposal. Undoubtedly, in the aftermath of the Assemblies of God split, Mexican members had had enough of Euro American leadership. McPherson did not take the rejection well and requested the return of her $100 "love offering." When Olazábal refused, McPherson set out to counter Olazábal's work in Los Angeles by starting Foursquare's own Spanish-speaking churches.[108] From its inception, Olazábal's vision of Pentecostal revival and salvation for Mexico in the "last days" powered the Concilio.

In 1923 Olazábal wrote to the Pentecostal minister Richey and asked for support to fund a campaign Olazábal planned for Mexico. He offered two reasons for the campaign: (1) the millennial inspiration of the Second Coming; and (2) the need to "save" Mexico from " 'a avaricia y absolutismo del clero romano, que por cuatro centurias ha esclavizado la consciencia de ese pueblo en el 99 por cento de su populación" (the avarice and absolutism of the Roman clergy, who, for four centuries, has enslaved the conscience of 99 percent of the population).[109] Although Richey did not respond to this request, Olazábal's frequent campaigns across the United States seem to indicate that he soon became a very popular healing evangelist.

Olazábal's campaigns focused on healing and educating converts on the theological nuances of what Pentecostals believed. He writes of a campaign in Texas:

> Muy pocos de los que han sido sanados en mis servicios de sanidad han vuelto la cara atras y casi todos los que had sido salvados por la operación de los milagros y la sanidades ha sido completamente regenerados y llegan hoy una vida ejemplar.[110]

> [Very few of those who have been healed in my healing services have turned back, and almost all those that have been saved through the working of miracles and healings have been completely renewed and today lead exemplary lives.]

Healing changes lives and, in so doing, gives converts the opportunity to lead exemplary lives. Olazábal brought his campaigns to San Fernando, California, El Paso, Cleveland, Tennessee, New York, and Puerto Rico.

Reporting on his crusades, the media noted the great crowds and miraculous healings. The *Cleveland Daily Banner* pointed out the unusual nature of an all-night service, where the "Aztec missionary" Olazábal led the crowd in an all-night prayer meeting. The paper also notes the merger of his church with the Church of God, claiming Olazábal could deliver fifty thousand Mexicans to the denomination.[111] Why Olazábal would leave the predominantely Euro American Assemblies of God for the predominantly Euro American Church of God is unclear. When Olazábal died in a car accident in 1937, the merger had not been completed. Another publication, the *Christian Herald*, wrote of Olazábal's growing ministry and the success the "great Aztec" had in ministering to Mexicans.[112] The Aztec imagery reflects the racial component intoned by many Euro American observers and missionaries when writing about Mexican ministers and converts. The author of an article about Olazábal's New York ministry prefaced the piece by suggesting that the "barbaric" nature of Aztec priests and the "jungle dances" of Harlem bespeak an impossible situation for anything positive to come out of Harlem, where Olazábal's outreach reportedly converted and healed hundreds.[113] What makes Olazábal acceptable? Despite his Aztec ancestry, his Protestantism legitimizes him as civilized and godly—unlike his ancestors.

Commenting on contemporary racial attitudes, Roberto Almaraz, an As-semblies of God minister, says that this patronizing attitude plagues Lati-no/Euro American Pentecostal relations to this day. Says Almaraz: "The problem is that they [Assemblies of God] continue to view us as a mission field, as converts . . . not as equals."[114] The stereotypical language, using Aztec iconography, employed by the writer in the *Christian Herald* contin-ues to this day by Olazábal's admirers themselves, who call him "el Azteca" as a term of affection.[115]

As part of his two-tiered ministry, Olazábal took time out of his healing serv-ices and campaigns to answer questions about Pentecostalism and wrote re-sponses in the church's magazine. During the 1930s the Pentecostal movement was considered "bizarre," and the misinformation about their spiritual prac-tices was widespread. On several occasions the prejudice descended into ver-bal and physical violence.[116] Detractors accused Pentecostals of practicing witchcraft, devil worship, and sexual promiscuity. They threw rocks and garbage, mobbed Pentecostal meetings, slashed meeting tent ropes, and set churches afire.[117] With this history of contention, Olazábal's role as a promot-er of Pentecostalism meant that he had to promote its acceptance as a part of orthodox Christianity. A question came from an unnamed person who wanted to know if Pentecostalism was equivalent to Spiritualism. Olazábal responded:

> No, en ninguna manera si el pueblo conciente que pertenece al dicho movimiento Pentecostal es responsible de lo malo que encontrate en este o en aquel individuo por el hecho de que el dicho individuo ase-guran pertenecer al dicho movimiento . . . el movimiento Pentecostal ensenaque es error todo lo que contradice, el material de doctrina, lo que esta escrito en la Biblia; considera como pecado toda rebelda con-tra la voluntad al Dios y toda disobediencia de su santa ley.[118]

> [No, in no manner is the Pentecostal movement responsible for such bad things. The Pentecostal movement teaches that [Spiritualism] is in error in doctrinal matters, in what is written in the Bible; it is consid-ered a sin and rebellion for such bad things. The Pentecostal movement teaches [that Spiritualism] is in error in doctrinal manners, in what is written in the Bible; it is considered a sin and rebellion against God and totally disobedient of His Holy law].

Olazábal had two concerns: (1) to educate his growing congregation, and (2) to convince his flock of the uncomplimentary practices of Spiritualism. Spiritualists, along with using intermediaries to attempt contact with the deceased, practiced speaking in tongues. This practice for a time made Spiritualism an attractive option for Pentecostals who where "deceived" into attending Spiritualist churches.[119]

Olazábal's crusades and teaching came to an end in 1937, when he died in a car accident on his way back from a campaign in Texas. The denomination he started did not merge with any other Pentecostal denomination and, for the most part, had relied on generational growth to continue to fill its churches. Holland calls the Concilio "the most conservative and introverted of the Pentecostal denominations."[120] This observation is supported by a personal conversation with Latino Pentecostal ministers who have close ties to the Concilio, one of whom, a family friend of the Olazábal family, told me that the church has little interest in working with others, rarely grants interview requests, and, in his estimation, is still suffering the effects of the Olazábal split with the Assemblies of God more than seventy years ago.[121] Despite the church's reluctance to discuss its history or current work, what should be kept in mind is Olazábal's work in the early years of Latino Pentecostalism, and his insistence on autonomy—an insistence that would be bolstered by the writing and work of Alice Luce.

Alice Luce began her "Mexican work" as a missionary to Mexico. Forced to leave on the eve of the Revolution, she became a missionary to Mexicans in California. She wrote an open letter to the Assemblies of God warning them of lost opportunities if they did not support the Mexican work. In order for this mission to work, the Assemblies of God would have to send many more workers to the border.[122] Luce's missionary impulse concentrated on two points: (1) to spread the word about the Pentecostal cause among Mexicans, and (2) to "save" Mexicans from the continuing influence of the Catholic Church. She writes: "We are proving the good old gospel to be the power of God unto salvation for these poor, dark, Mexicans, just as for the white people. The opposition of the priests has been terrible."[123] Luce's sentiments demonstrate some ideas commonly held by Protestants raised in the nineteenth century, (Luce was the daughter of an Anglican bishop) that Catholicism kept people in darkness. But her idea that evangelization efforts succeeded in converting "white" people as well as "poor, dark" Mexicans displays a crucial element she had for her missions: that they be turned over to Mexican control as soon as possible. It should be noted, however, that Luce's partner, Henry Ball, did not have the same idea regarding Mexican control. Ball writes: "We need more American missionaries. I have in the past two years, trained several Mexican workers, but while they are excellent workers, they need American oversight."[124] Creeping paternalism as it worked its way into Protestant missions to Mexicans before Pentecostalism continued despite the gains made by Mexican pastors and Luce's work.

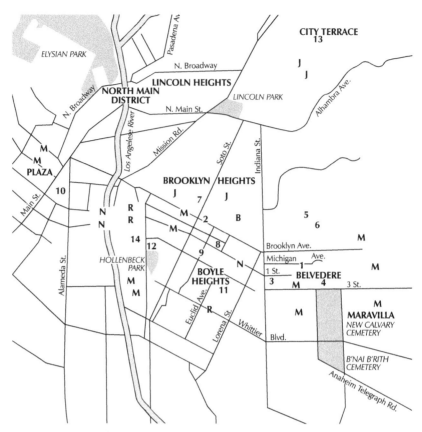

MAP 1 Houses of Worship in East Los Angeles, 1930s

Pentecostal Churches in East Los Angeles, c. 1930s

1. Assemblies of God–El Aposento Alto, Michigan Ave. and Hicks St.; Assemblies of God–El Sendero de la Cruz, not located
2. Assemblies of God–La Puerta Abierta, Michigan Ave.
3. Latin American Council of Christian Churches–Iglesia Evangelica, Indiana St.
4. Church of Foursquare Gospel–Misión Mexicana McPherson, Belvedere area
5. Church of Foursquare Gospel–Iglésia Cuadrangular "Pan American," Brooklyn Ave. and Rowan St.
6. Church of God, Anderson, Indiana, 200 N. Humphreys

Other Denominations in East Los Angeles, c. 1930s

7. Breed Street Shul (Jewish)
8. Konko Church–Independent (Japanese), E. First St.
9. Los Angeles Japanese Baptist Church, E. 2nd St.
10. Union Church of Los Angeles (Japanese), San Pedro St.
11. Molokan Church (Russian), Sabina St.
12. Molokan Church (Russian), North Gless St.
13. Orthodox Jewish Community Synagogue, not located
14. Molokan Church (Russian), Clarence St.

East Los Angeles Ethnic/Racial Communities, 1930s

M= Mexican, approx. 90,000 (total, Los Angeles)
B= Black, approx. 2,000
J= Jewish, approx. 10,000
R= Russian Molokan, approx. 7,000–10,000
N= Japanese, approx. 20,000 (total, Los Angeles)

Source: Richard Romo, East Los Angeles: History of a Barrio (Austin: University of Texas Press, 1983), 3, 61, 63–67.

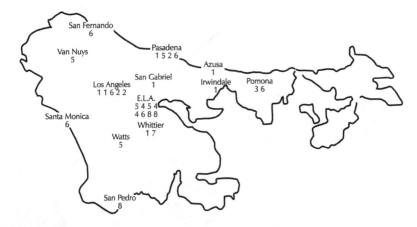

MAP 2 Mainline Protestants, Los Angeles County

1. Presbyterians
Northern Pasadena (1875); Misión Mexicana Whittier (1882); Antonio Diaz Misión Mexicana de los Nietos Los Angeles (1880s); Diaz Misión Mexicana de los Olivos Los Angeles (1888); Primera Iglesia Presbyterian Mexicana Irwindale (1889); El Divino Salvador (1941); San Gabriel (1891); Diaz Iglesia Presbyterian Mexicana S.G. Azusa (1912); Iglesia Presbyterian Mexicana

2. Northern Methodist Episcopal
Fort Street Methodist Church (1879); Los Angeles Diaz Los Angeles (1898); Pasadena (1907); Los Angeles (1910); Sunset Blvd.

3. Congregational Church
Pomona (1897)

4. Northern Baptist
East Los Angeles (ELA) (1905); Calvary Baptist ELA (1905); Misión Mexicana de Calle Rio ELA (1913); Iglesia Bautista de la Calle Garnet ELA (1923); Misión Mexicana de Lorena Heights

5. 7th Day Adventist
ELA (1905); Misión de Boyle Heights ELA (1932); Belvedere Van Nuys (1920s); Pasadena (1920s); Watts (1920s)

6. Church of the Nazarene
Los Angeles (1910); Bunker Hill Pasadena (1920s); N. Lincoln Santa Monica (1930s); San Fernando (1930s); Pomona (1930s); ELA (1930s); Boyle Heights-Breed Street

7. Quakers
Whittier (1915); Misión de Jimtown

8. Free Methodist
Los Angeles (1917); Misión de Calle Sotelo/N. Main San Pedro (1920); Terminal Island ELA (1932); Palo Verde east of Lincoln Heights ELA (1932); Maravilla Park

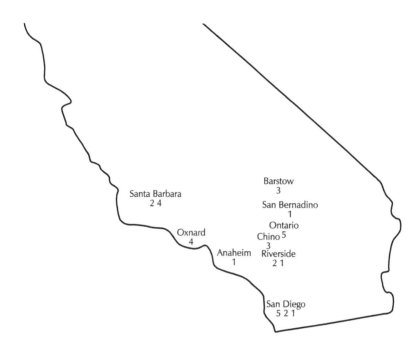

MAP 3 Mainline Protestants Outside Los Angeles County

1. Presbyterians
(1882) Anaheim; (1903) San Bernardino; (1904) San Diego; (1910) Riverside

2. Methodist Episcopal
(1881) Santa Barbara; (1900) Riverside; (1900) San Diego

3. Congregational
(1906) Chino; (1910s) Barstow

4. Northern Baptist
(1901) Santa Barbara; (1903) Oxnard

5. Church of the Nazarene
(1920s) Ontario; (1920s) San Diego

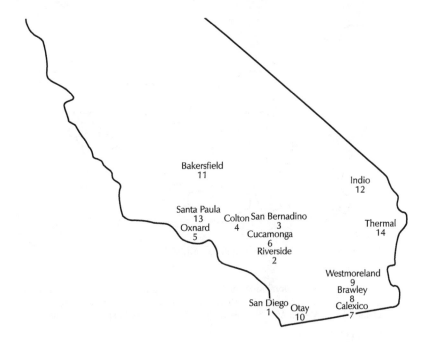

Bakersfield
11

Indio
12

Santa Paula
13   Colton San Bernadino
Oxnard   4   3   Thermal
5   Cucamonga   14
6
Riverside
2

Westmoreland
9
Brawley
San Diego Otay   8
1   10   Calexico
7

MAP 4 Apostolic Assembly Churches Outside Los Angeles County

Apostolic Assembly

1. Misión de la fe Apostólica—San Diego (1912); earliest known Pentecostal church founded by Juan Navarro
2. Misión Apostólica de Riverside (1917); Marcial de la Cruz
3. Iglesia Cristiana de la Apostólica (1918); San Bernardino Marcial de la Cruz
4. Misión Apostólica de Colton (1918); Marcial de la Cruz
5. Misión Apostólica de el Rio-Oxnard (1918)
6. Misión Apostólica de Cucamonga (1922)
7. Misión Apostólica de Calexico (1920s); Antonio C. Nava
8. Misión Apostólica de Brawley (1920s)
9. Misión Apostólica de Westmoreland (1920s)
10. Misión Apostólica de Otay (1920s)
11. Misión Apostólica de Bakersfield (1920s)
12. Misión Apostólica de Indio (1920s)
13. Misión Apostólica de Santa Paula (1920s)
14. Misión Apostólica de Thermal (1920s)

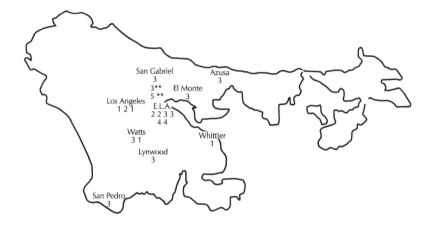

MAP 5 Pentecostal Churches, Los Angeles County

1. Apostolic Assembly
"Spanish Apostolic Faith Mission"(1912) on N. Hill, 627 Alpine, Pastor Genaro Valenzuela; Misión Apostólica (1917), Calles Angeles y Aliso, Francisco Llorente; Misión Apostólica de Watts (1918), Vicente Garcia; Misión Apostólica de Jimtown (1922), Bernardo Hernandez Cruz

2. Assemblies of God
Misión de la Plaza Olvera (1917), El Aposento Alto, Alice Luce; Iglesia El Sendero de la Cruz (1922), ELA, Francisco Nevarez; Iglesia la Puerta Abierta (1934), ELA, Michigan Avenue

3. Latin American Council of Christian Churches
Iglesia de Bethel, Belvedere (1923), Olazábal; Templo Bethel, El Monte (1926); Templo Bethel, Watts (1928), Olazábal; Iglesia Bethel, San Gabriel (1930); Templo Bethel, Belen, Azusa (1933); Iglesia El Salvador (1933), Lynwood; Templo del Refugio, ELA (1935); Iglesia Evangelica de CLADIC, ELA (1939); El Tabernaculo Central (1939), San Pedro

4. Church of the Foursquare Gospel
Misión Mexicana McPherson, ELA (1929); Iglesia Cuadrangular "Pan American," ELA (1930s)

5. Church of God, Anderson, Indiana
Iglesia de Dios de Belvedere, ELA (1931)

Luce founded a Pentecostal mission in the Placita in 1917. El Aposento Alto was located on Los Angeles Street. Like other Protestant missions who set up in the plaza decades earlier, a distinct Pentecostal presence that had begun at the Azusa Street mission continued with Luce's mission and continued to reap the benefits of a large Mexican population of religious seekers. In 1922 Luce took a failed Pentecostal mission in the Belvedere section of Los Angeles and moved her fledgling mission to what the Reverend Samuel Ortegón in 1932 described as the largest, most progressive settlement of Mexicans in East Los Angeles.

A large percentage of the 20,125 East Los Angeles residents were Mexican and Mexican Americans. Ortegón counted eight churches in the area. A Presbyterian church and settlement house, two Pentecostal churches, a Spiritualist church, a Baptist church, and two Catholic churches[125] (see maps 1–5 for specific locations of churches). Belvedere's progressive status did not mean that other areas of East Los Angeles fared as well. Ortegón noted that Maravilla Park, just east of Belvedere, was the poorest section, with people "living in shacks, and eating practically nothing."[126] He mentioned that the two Pentecostal churches, Misión Mexicana McPherson and the Iglesia Pentecostal Bethel, Olazábal's church, had fifty members. The McPherson church was a part of the International Church of the Foursquare Gospel Church in Boyle Heights. Ortegón reports that most of the members came from other Pentecostal churches. The church sat eight hundred and had five hundred members. Ortegón, a Baptist minister, comments on the appeal of Pentecostalism: "The healing services . . . appeal strongly to the Mexican mind." The mission's other appealing features were its women's society, the clothes sale, and the food giveaways, which, during the Depression, fed four hundred every week.[127] In addition to these churches, the Latter-Day Saints rented a hall for services, and the Catholic Church, in addition to its churches, had three settlement houses in Boyle Heights, Los Angeles, and Maravilla Park.[128] The religious choices facing the burgeoning population in East Los Angeles must have made for a competitive and lively contest for the allegiance of the recent immigrant and long-time resident alike. Pentecostals proved to be well equipped for the fight.

Luce relied heavily on Mexican workers to help run El Aposento Alto, placing Francisco and Natividad Nevarez in charge soon after its move. The Nevarezes received the Pentecostal baptism in 1916 at Luce's tent revival in Los Angeles; they had converted from Presbyterianism. They ran the church until the 1950s, when they left to develop other Pentecostal missions to Mexicans in Mexico and Mexicans in East Los Angeles and Watts. According to Victor De Leon (an Assemblies of God minister who wrote the first and one of the only histories of Latino Pentecostals), many Mexicans who received Spirit baptism in these early years came from the Presbyterian, Baptist, and Methodist churches in East Los Angeles.[129] Though he offers little evidence for his assertion, his description matches that of the Nevarezes. Mainline denominations offered a gateway to Pentecostalism for a variety of reasons. For one, Holiness denominations like the Methodists experienced the "come-out" movement and lost many members to Pentecostal groups. For another, Protestants, such as the former Baptist Arnulfo López, had nowhere else to go once they experienced Spirit baptism. For them, the Assemblies of God served as a new home and refuge: "Bro. A.M. Lopez . . . a young Spanish brother of considerable ability . . . received the baptism of the Holy Ghost . . . here in Austin last winter, on account of which church officials rejected him."[130] López went to work for Ball's church in Texas and was instrumental in introducing the future Latino leader Demetrio Bazán to Pentecostalism by praying for him to receive Spirit baptism.[131] Natividad Nevarez also recalls that from 1916 to the 1930s she encountered many Latinos open to proselytism by Pentecostals.[132] This view may be supported by the thirty-four Pentecostal missions, of various denominational persuasions, throughout southern California.[133]

Despite the presence of other Pentecostal groups, the Assemblies of God was still the most predominant. Why? Because it had the most extensive foreign-language ministry among Latinos.[134] Healing and spiritual gifts certainly account for some of the popularity of Pentecostalism among a people not estranged from supernatural religious expression. Pentecostalism became a faith easily communicated through a common language of salvation, often spoken in Spanish. The acceptance of an active supernatural life made the acceptance of Pentecostal spirituality all the more enticing. Simply put, Pentecostalism nullifies the doubt one might have about the existence and efficacy of God through direct personal experience. Olazábal's healing ministry, the mission to Mexicans in their own language and within their own communities, and the Pentecostal baptism offered by all missionaries meant that this faith, far from being "bizarre" to Latinos, became quite natural. No church organized, institutionalized, or laid a better foundation for posterity than the Assemblies of God and the work of Henry Ball and Alice Luce.

Luce constantly sent written reports back to Assemblies headquarters and provided valuable insights on her daily work. She began the mission on Fifteenth and North Los Angeles Streets, where she worked with Florence Murcutt, an Australian immigrant doctor. The two missionaries offered Bible studies and Sunday school, and distributed Pentecostal tracts. Believing in the importance of conversing in the native language of potential converts, they conducted church services and missionary activities in Spanish. The Assemblies of God allocated her the following salary scale for male pastors—$30 a month for a married pastor, $20 if single; $30 if the pastor was white, $20 if Mexican. The dual-wage system, so common to Mexican laborers throughout the Southwest, even extended to the ministry. Historian Paul Barton, writing about the Methodist Episcopal Church and the subordinate/dominant relationship between Latino pastors and their Euro American overseers, noted the wage discrepancies that became cause for further tensions among the groups.[135] Outside ministry work and throughout the Southwest, dual-wage systems kept Mexican laborers from earning equal wages for equal work. Historian Mario García noted that in Texas, among carpenters, smelt workers, and mine workers, Mexican carpenters made $3.50 per day in contrast to Euro Americans who averaged $8.00 a day. Mexican smelt workers were paid $2.00 to $2.50 less than their Euro American counterparts. Mexican mine workers made $2.00 a day whereas Euro Americans averaged $6.00.[136] One should note that through the formative years of Luce and Murcutt's work in California, they were funded at a consistently lower rate than any male missionary.

By 1920 Luce had gathered a congregation of fifty Mexican converts. Her greatest difficulty at the time centered on the inroads made by the Oneness movement. "The new issue error is the greatest difficulty here, they are trying to steal away our flock all the time."[137] In addition to Oneness, Luce's other problem stemmed from her perception that the Mexican population moved around too often to enable her to establish roots: "The Spanish-speaking people of California are a floating population as they move from place to place to get work according to the crops or fruits, or vegetables, making it difficult to establish ministry."[138] There is some evidence to Luce's observation that generally the Mexican population was transient, moving in and around the United States when work was needed. Future Latino leader Josué Sánchez from Texas had to leave the ministry temporarily in the 1950s with his family, so they could pick beets in Saginaw, Michigan.[139] Undoubtedly similar stories exist if Luce's observations were correct. Despite her difficulties, Luce continued her ministry in Los Angeles for the next six years. To promote stability and autonomy among her workers, she continued to promote Mexican control of the churches.[140] She writes:

> There are some on this continent for which we would especially plead. We refer to the Mexican people. The Mexican work has a special claim upon the people of their country; first because of the proximity of Mexico to our borders . . . the need of building up the converts, and the need of prayer for more laborers. Seven years ago, there was no Pentecostal Mexican work . . . the Gospel is the power of God unto salvation

to everyone that believeth, and there is no difference whether they be American or Mexican.[141]

As Luce moved her mission to the Belvedere section of East Los Angeles, other faiths competed for Mexicans. In 1923, along with the Assemblies of God, at least six other Protestant churches, including two other Pentecostal churches, were seeking converts in East Los Angeles. Added to that were the Spiritualist church, which Luce referred to as "spiritist," and the three Catholic churches. With so many religious choices available in East Los Angeles, competition was strong. Mexicans availed themselves of these choices as they did decades before. Of the ten churches operating in East Los Angeles, all of them had established other churches in the plaza or other parts of southern California before 1923. Their move to East Los Angeles signified an important change: Protestantism, in less than fifty years of work in southern California's Mexican communities, had established itself as a viable option to the Catholic Church, and Pentecostalism was on its way to promoting itself as the option to mainline Protestantism. Luce's observation demonstrates the aura of competition:

> They [Mexicans] are so afraid of the priests that they hide their children when we go to invite them to Sunday school. This suburb [Belvedere] is a stronghold of spiritism which is gaining a great hold upon the Mexican and there is a large spiritist church a few blocks from us whose emissaries came into our meetings to entice our Christians. . . . we are in the midst of a large Mexican population, hundreds of them purchasing their lots and erecting little homes, some living out in the open in tents.[142]

The reluctance parents expressed in allowing their children to attend Sunday school became an extension of the overall reluctance potential converts experienced when Pentecostals pitched their tents in the community. Three years earlier, Arnulfo López expressed disappointment with the reluctant community: "The Mexicans do not like to go in a house and I thought I would try [sic] them in a tent. They come and stand around and mock, but there are from thirty to fifty or more of the children who come under the tent."[143] The role of spectator appealed to Mexicans, who saw spiritual safety in remaining outside the Pentecostal sacred space of the tent or hall. Entering a Pentecostal place of worship seemed to signal acceptance of the faith — an acceptance that almost automatically meant their separation from their families and friends. What could Pentecostals do to retain their converts, tempted by what Luce and others saw as the heretical theologies of Spiritism, Oneness, and Catholicism? How were they to promote Mexicans in their new

Pentecostal skin? Luce did what any good Protestant missionary would do: she started a Bible school.

The Berean Bible Institute opened in October 1926 in San Diego. Luce prepared the lessons and taught classes. Running into financial problems within its first few years, the school moved to Los Angeles in 1929 with only a handful of students. Little record remains of the San Diego location or of the early years in Los Angeles. The Texas counterpart, El Instituto Biblico Latino Americano (The Latin American Bible Institute), opened the same year with tuition at $2 per month, including meals, a bed, and study materials.[144]

By May 1928 the Texas institute graduated its first class. All were baptized into the Assemblies of God, but only one received Spirit baptism.[145] Texas proved to be fertile ground for Assemblies of God work. Six years before the institute's founding, an unnamed Assemblies of God missionary wrote of the potential in Texas:

> The Mexicans are an intelligent people, and Pentecost is not without competitors in the Mexican field. . . . A movement is afoot in Texas to establish a Bible training school for the American work. It would be a splendid thing if it might include a Spanish department presided over by a competent superintendent.[146]

It seems fair to speculate that the writer referred to the future Bible institute. Accounts of the lives of these early students are rare, but a few young men did record their reflections in later life for a serial history of Latino Assemblies of God members published in Henry Ball's publication, *La Luz Apostólica* (hereafter, *LA*). Ball began the periodical in order to keep in touch with the Mexican population. He speculated that the Mexican Revolution caused the immigrant population in Texas to scatter to find work. The intent was to keep his new converts adherent to the faith.[147] In this retrospective, converts recalled what compelled them to become Pentecostal. Conversion centered on a crisis. For example, Josué Cruz's first introduction to Pentecostalism began when his mother was cured of a brain infection; a local pastor had prayed for the entire Cruz family, and they converted. Cruz decided to study at the Latin American Bible Institute, and he became a minister upon graduation in 1928. Like Olazábal's campaigns, healing proved integral to the initiation of potential converts into the Pentecostal faith, an initiation practiced today. I shall turn now to the Texas work outside the Latin American Bible Institute, which Ball began in 1915 in Ricardo and Kingsville, Texas.

Ball's first mission in Ricardo was destroyed by a tornado in August 1916. This perceived prophetic event spurred his followers to make their Kingsville mission much more successful than the Ricardo mission. In these early years Ball established a printing press in Pasadena, Texas, where he published the first issues of *LA*.[148] The conditions Ball and his workers faced amid war refugees, hostile priests, and poor residents bordered on being hopeless. Homeless, poverty-stricken war refugees also carried the burden, as Ball saw it, of being lost to "Romanism" far too long.[149] These conditions, printed in the Assemblies of God magazine, *The Weekly Evangel* (hereafter, *WE*), concluded with a plea for the funding of the Mexican work. At the start Ball's mission in Ricardo, Texas, was small with thirty baptized members, five of whom sought to become ministers. The schooling the Assemblies of God provided included Bible study and free "literary" school, presumably to teach students how to read.[150] When a tornado destroyed this mission, the Assemblies of God responded by supporting Ball in his new mission in Kingsville. By the end of 1916, Ball had received $120 for his mission.[151] During the first five years of Ball's Texas mission, he estimated that between eighty-five and one hundred people attended the informal conventions held between 1918 and 1920. No records remain of those conventions, but one may speculate that the planning for the building of new missions from El Paso to Houston took up much of their time. By 1920 Ball's mission grew to five hundred members.[152] Some of the most active of Ball's first converts included Loreto Garza, who left with his family to evangelize in Mexico, and Arnulfo López, who worked with other Texas missionaries from 1917 to 1923 before leaving to join Olazábal's church. Spreading the Pentecostal message by distributing religious literature was of the utmost importance to Ball and to his partner, Luce. Ball received funds to buy a wagon, from which he would distribute thousands of Gospels, tracts, and Bibles. He also hoped to increase the circulation of his magazine, *La Luz Apostólica*.[153] But it should be reiterated that, along with their evangelism, the missionaries worked with a sense of urgency, because as long as Mexicans remained under the influence of Roman Catholicism, they were lost to "romanism."[154] Again, critical to the growth of the Assemblies of God mission among Latinos was the role they played in helping to evangelize their own.

In 1920 Demetrio and Nellie Bazán, two of the most prominent Latino members of the Assemblies of God, received ordination. Demetrio converted under Ball's ministry and, before receiving ordination in the Assemblies, was once offered a chance to go to seminary under the auspices of his boss, a Methodist who owned a hotel where Demetrio did odd jobs. Bazán declined, aware of the theological tension between Methodists and Pentecostals, especially over the issue of spirit Baptism.[155] This awareness of theological tensions bolsters my claim that Latino Pentecostals within the first generation understood themselves to be different. Ordination for women during the formative years of the Assemblies of God did not result in the kind of controversy the question caused in later years. The Assemblies of God reiterated the affirmation of the role of women in ministry as early as 1916:

> If a woman gave birth to our Lord, why not her daughters take part in His great work? Men have hypocritically objected to women making themselves conspicuous in pulpit work, but thank God, this conspicuousness is of God Himself. They did not push themselves to the front, God pulled them there. . . . Today more than one-half of the missionary force is composed of women.[156]

The Bazáns came to the Pentecostal faith like many others, through a healing experience Nellie received. She describes her healing experience: "también me sano de una enfermedad incurable y peligrosa del pulmón. Cuando Dios hace la obra la hace perfecto" [also he healed me of an incurable and dangerous lung illness. When God does the work, he does it perfectly].[157] Just as healing had become a gateway to Pentecostal belief, other, more remarkable phenomena vied for the attention of religious seekers like Nellie. She describes her experience:

> tuve una enfermedad sencilla, pero enganoza, tuve que ir al hospital y fue tanto asi la enfermedad que las doctores que me atendian me declaron muerto despues de varios dias de luchar para salvarme. Fue solamente asi que probi el poder de la resurreción de Cristo. Después de varios horas de muerte le levanto y volvi a la vida.[158]

> [I had a simple illness, but it was misleading, I had to go to the hospital and I was so sick that the doctors that attended to me declared me dead after several days of struggling to save me. It was only then that the power of Christ's resurrection was put to the test. After several hours of being dead I rose and came back to life].

Resurrection accounts date back to the earliest days of the Pentecostal movement. Anderson and Wacker both recount them in their survey of dozens of Pentecostal magazines, "every manner of disease and disability was alleged to have been cured, and the most spectacular miracles were claimed including the growth of new fingers. . . . Numerous persons testified to having seen the dead restored to life."[159] Nellie's story became emblematic for Latino Pentecostals. The story not only was part of the Bazáns' autobiographical work, but this particular story received corroboration in Josué Sánchez's rendering of his life story. Sánchez's version follows. Nellie died and her body was placed in the hospital morgue. The doctor informed Demetrio that she was dead, and Demetrio went home. According to Sánchez, Demetrio pleaded with God not to take his wife and prayed with such fervency that it reminded Sánchez of the biblical story of Jacob wrestling with the angel. God then told him that his wife was alive, and Demetrio went back to the hospital. The head surgeon was called in and, to appease a frantic husband, went to the morgue and had Nellie's body removed. According to the head surgeon, Nellie was alive.[160] Those unfamiliar with Pentecostal doctrine might not understand the spiritual impetus for even claiming such phenomena possible, but, for Pentecostals, the seeking and exercising of spiritual gifts forms a larger part of their faith lives. The biblical reference to spiritual gifts in 1 Corinthians 12 includes the "working of miracles." A miracle such as resurrection, for the Pentecostal, seeks to restore the faith of the Apostles.[161] Contemporaries of Nellie Bazán echo her experience. Roberto Almaraz says that, in his thirty years of ministry in the Assemblies of God and with other ministries, he has "seen numerous healings and resurrections."[162] As stated earlier, one reason why Pentecostals did not develop a systematic theology was because all that was necessary was the Bible and the Holy Spirit. Throughout the literature Pentecostals published about their fantastic spiritual experiences, clear themes emerge. Chiefly New Testament motifs occur repeatedly. Resurrections, healings, and, interestingly, food motifs. Food resources that have run out miraculously become enough to feed families and guests, similar to the loaves and fishes accounts. That these themes are repeated in magazines, books, and orally through churches and families signifies a process of narrative scripting. Scripting repeats certain motifs almost exactly like New Testament accounts, and, with that same sense of authority, there is rarely a need to prove them. These scripts support the faithful, and our analysis of them will continue in succeeding chapters.

In 1932 Demetrio Bazán's rise to the Presbyter of the Conference for east Colorado signified the first time a Latino was elected to a prominent leadership role within the Assemblies of God. Bazán's mission workers established several churches throughout the Rocky Mountain states of Utah, Colorado, and New Mexico, expanding the Pentecostal message to the migrating Latino population. Missionaries who planted the missions used house churches like their Azusa Street and Apostolic Assembly counterparts. The appointment of Bazán and the expansion of the mission did not mean that the hardships and persecution of Pentecostals ceased. Lillian Valdez and Berta García, co-pastors of the Greeley, Colorado, church describes the work and hardships of one unfortunate pastor, Humberto López.

On one occasion a group of men entered the church with chains and began beating members at the altar who were experiencing the Pentecostal baptism. Valdez and García described an attempt on López's life by a passerby with a rifle, but López was unharmed. Other acts of arson and vandalism to church property also occurred.[163] My interviews with Pentecostals confirm that these actions continued into the 1950s. An Apostolic Assembly member, Stella Cantú, recounted an incident where she was attacked with stones while singing gospel songs with her father in Texas during the 1950s.[164] Simón Melendres, past president of the Latin American Bible Institute in La Puente, California, recounted an attempt on the life of future superintendent Jose Girón in the early 1950s.[165] Anderson notes that the violence Pentecostals experienced during the "come-out" era stemmed from theological disagreements between themselves and Holiness advocates who attempted to enforce their idea of orthodoxy by physically attacking Pentecostals.[166] In the case of Latino Pentecostals, it might be safe to assume that other Protestants would be less likely to attack Pentecostals, since they both are minority faiths within the predominantely Catholic world of Latinos in the United States.

Some insight into the motivation of an anti-Pentecostal attack might come from the comments and actions of Miguel Sánchez, a neighbor to the Aposento Alto church in East Los Angeles. He recounts hearing Pentecostal worship service one evening during the mid-1950s with "howling and singing . . . all kinds of noise." He and a friend pelted the church with stones, hoping to silence the congregation. He did not know that they were Pentecostals, only that the unusual nature of the service disturbed him enough that he acted to stop the service he perceived as foreign to his understanding of worship, which meant Catholic worship.[167] It might be appropriate to echo the sentiments of Figueroa Deck's insightful comments. Pentecostalism represents a "profound cultural, social, and familial rupture." The foreign nature of Pentecostals in a community dominated by a Mexican and Mexican American Catholic population remained well into the 1950s, despite the fact that they, too, lived, built homes and churches, and worked in areas like East Los Angeles alongside their Catholic neighbors. This otherness formed the crux of the question Mel Robeck asked about a violation of culture—where do Latino Pentecostals belong? Where is their loyalty? Becoming Pentecostal often proved to be a dangerous vocation.

The solidification of this identity was well in place by the time Ball held more conventions to note the growth of this movement. The 1933 convention counted 17 ordained ministers, 32 licensed ministers, and 10 "exhorters" (evangelists).[168] The 1935 convention in Dallas had 41 ordained ministers, 96 licensed ministers, and 37 "exhorters."[169] Few, if any, contemporary records remain of these conventions. The formative years of a young denomination had little use for the written historical form. Ball was the first superintendent of the Latin American District Council (which did not receive full status in the Assemblies of God until 1973).[170] In 1992 the Latin American District Council encompassed 398 churches, 58,676 adherents, and 595 ministers. The district remains the most successful at church growth throughout all the Assemblies of God. Gregory S. O'Brien studied church growth among the Latin district and concluded that their approach to evangelization and growth was what made them successful. The district begins with a demographic study to determine the area of need. They then search for an established church to "mother" the work. They used their Bible college students to minister to and work in the new churches.[171]

Expansion on the practical methods of evangelization continues in the succeeding chapter on the Latin American Bible Institute. Ball and others established and organized institutional processes of inculcating the Pentecostal faith among the Mexican communities of the Southwest. Like Luce's philosophy of autonomous churches, Ball appears to have made efforts to place Mexicans in charge of their own churches. Bazán headed the Colorado and New Mexico areas by the mid-1930s. Neither Ball nor Bazán's conflict with Olazábal appears to have driven off potential converts who steadily built up the district throughout its first fifteen years of existence and populated its two Bible institutes in California and Texas. In 1940 Ball and Luce wrote a retrospective on their careers. In his piece, Ball writes of Mexicans as possessing two natures, one European and one Indian:

> From these two people, both proud and of great historical and cultural heritages, both artistic, and both possessed of a deeply religious nature, come the Mexicans of today. . . employers of Mexican labor speak of them in the highest terms, preferring them to all other imported laborers. One of these employers, representing a large railroad when speaking in favor of them in a recent debate, gave the following six virtues: love of family, cleanliness, religious nature, love of music, bravery, and sobriety. In addition to the laborers on the fruit ranches, on the railroads, in factories, and in canneries, we find Latin Americans working as doctors, mechanics, lawyers, tailors, theatrical managers, restaurant owners . . . indeed they find occupation in every brand of industry.[172]

Ball noted a religious nature that he gladly tapped into with his new faith. He also noted that the Latinos he knew found work outside the fields, as entrepreneurs and professionals. They, along with the laborers, would continue through the missions Ball and Luce founded to become Pentecostal and to pass that faith on to the postwar generation.

An examination of how the Assemblies of God continued its work and how that work evolved to include social justice missions is the focus of the next several chapters on the Latin American Bible Institute, Victory Outreach, and the Vineyard. It is my hope that by tracing the contours of religious and ethnic identity, answers may be found to the problems that arise from conversion: Is conversion to Pentecostalism in 1906 or 2002 a violation of culture? Or is it a natural process of transmigrating faiths from one culture to another?

2. Workers for the Harvest:
LABI and the Institutionalizing of a Latino Pentecostal Identity

This chapter examines the formation of a Latino Pentecostal identity through the work of the Latin American Bible Institute (LABI). In particular, the formation of that identity began in the first years of LABI and continues to the present day primarily through four processes: (1) reinforcement of Pentecostal orthodoxy through pedagogy; (2) encouragement of spiritual gifts to deepen one's spirituality; (3) reinforcement of moral codes; and (4) development of a sense of mission. Pentecostals concern themselves with the spiritual realm, constantly guarding against ungodly spirits during their practices. Orthodoxy concerns Pentecostals in ethereal and temporal spaces. Thus safeguards for both are required: Pedagogy and spiritual exercises guide them in both areas of their lives. Through LABI's three-year program, students learn biblical principles of evangelism and a chapter-by-chapter study of the Bible, preparing them to follow the Pentecostal way. Like most Pentecostal institutions, LABI encourages students to seek spiritual gifts, namely, speaking in tongues, healing, and prophecy. Since 1926 codes of conduct and dress served at first to enforce conformity, but that has changed over the years, reflecting perhaps a compromise with modernity. Enforcing moral codes builds a Pentecostal identity because these codes provide a correlate between right belief, right conduct, and right living. The development of a sense of mission completes what Pentecostal theologian Cheryl Bridges Johns calls the Pentecostal catechism, a developed characteristic to spread Pentecostal Christianity, especially to other Latinos. LABI ensures that the successive generations of Latinos continue the faith. It should be noted that these four points do not manifest themselves chronologically; in fact, they occur simultaneously in students' lives. By examining each of these points in the context of LABI's history, this chapter demonstrates the pedagogical processes, initiated by Alice Luce, of melding classical Pentecostalism with Latino spirituality. As theologian Eldin Villafañe notes: "Hispanic indigenous Pentecostalism in a formal and substantive way has been influenced theologically by classical Pentecostalism. Albeit filtered through the interpretive nuances of Hispanic culture and history."[1] Just how this new religious mixture occurred can be gleaned from LABI's history, beginning with its founding and leadership under Luce.

From their Holiness and Higher Life–inspired roots in the mode of D. L. Moody's Northfield conferences, Bible institutes were places where students were urged to experience the Spirit's immediate power and presence.[2] Historian Edith Blumhofer writes that Pentecostal Bible institutes created by the Assemblies of God were "similar to that offered in the growing number of fundamentalist Bible institutes; they set out to proclaim a point of view and to locate it where those who differed were in error."[3] Thus, Bible institutes were part of the pedagogy of orthodoxy that LABI began during the Assemblies of God's second decade of existence, when debates about the need for formalized education plagued the Euro American branch, education was viewed as an essential component of creating and maintaining a Latino Pentecostal identity.

Within the first decade of the "Mexican Work" (1915–25), Henry Ball and Alice Luce began to lay the foundation for the establishment of missions for Mexicans and Mexican Americans in the United States and Mexico. Luce proved to be an eloquent advocate for such a cause. She wrote several articles in Pentecostal magazines soliciting funds for her ministry and for her struggling Bible school, which, through its first years, barely had enough funds to keep its doors open. Luce writes of visiting a Mexican Pentecostal family whose lives had been changed by their conversion.

> It seemed they could never get over the wonder and glory of His forgiving love. . . . Suddenly they heard a sound of weeping from the baby. . . . It was not long before the Spirit's power fell upon her and she began to speak in other tongues. . . . The girl of 8 leads the singing in the Sunday school. . . . *Does it pay* to make some sacrifice to give the Gospel to these strangers within our gates?[4]

Luce began her plea by noting how this family was "lost." The parents living "for sin and the world." The four children growing up neglected, "wild and incorrigible."[5] The initial conversion experience brought this family out of their "degradation," but what then? Aside from the loaded language equating being "lost," a not so subtle reference to the family's Catholicism, with a degraded state of living, Luce's evangelistic concerns were often delivered through anti-Catholic language masked in the evangelical lexicon of salvation. What do you do to ensure that new converts stay in the faith? How do you perpetuate a faith to a predominantly Catholic community? The Assemblies of God, primarily through the continued missionary work of Ball and Luce, decided to open Bible institutes with the intent of preparing more ministers, teachers, musicians, and field workers for evangelization of the Mexican population in both the United States and Mexico.

Two LABI schools were founded in 1926. While this chapter focuses on the institute in California, the one in Texas will be mentioned if there is a significant difference in terms of the chapter's general theme. LABI spent its first fourteen years in San Diego as part of the Berean Bible Institute. These difficult times saw sparse attendance with an average of only ten students per year; however, no records exist of the number of students who enrolled through correspondence courses. Spanish was the language of instruction, and Luce wrote many of the lessons herself.[6] From the beginning, Luce elicited support for the school from fellow Pentecostals. In her words:

> Opportunities are opening up for the Spanish-speaking people to receive instruction. . . . We began with six students and the number has increased to nine, not counting those who come to evening classes. . . . I am preparing the course of study and the lesson notes. . . . There are great numbers of our Latin American workers who desire to attend Bible school, but who are unable to do so on account of lack of funds. Please pray the Lord will enable them to get good work during the summer months so that they may be able to support themselves during the eight winter months when school is in session.[7]

Throughout 1926–27 the Assemblies of God did not earmark funds for LABI, though the teaching staff lent individual support as missionaries. Women received an average of twenty-five to thirty-five dollars per month, and men received an average of fifty-five dollars per month.[8] Let us compare these wage differentials to others. For example, in the 1920s skilled male dress operators earned one dollar an hour, and skilled women earned ninety-nine cents an hour. Male dress cutters made earned forty-five dollars per week, and female sample makers earned thirty dollars per week. Wage inequality was evident in both private and public sectors. During the Depression, the Federal Works Progress Administration paid men five dollars a day and women three dollars a day.[9] One idea that seemed to undergird this inequality lay in the notion that women had husbands to support them and that jobs, especially in the Depression era, were for men only. The only legitimate, socially acceptable reason for women to work was if they needed to work.[10] For Luce and her fellow missionaries, mostly women, the issue of need appeared to be superseded by the need to evangelize.

Texas LABI teacher H. May Kelty echoed Luce's concerns regarding faltering finances and the urgent need to evangelize for fear that the Catholic Church would regain the upper hand in the evangelizing of Latino communities. In 1926 she noted that twelve students lived in cramped housing, and the school faced closure in its first year. Kelty wrote: "Think of those precious lives snatched from the darkness of sin and Roman Catholicism and then see the possibility of having to close down this promising school for lack of suitable premises."[11] Concerns about Roman Catholicism play a crucial role in the rationale for the founding of the Bible institutes. Along with engendering a sense of mission to Latino communities, LABI engendered a sense of the orthodox and a sense of dedication among its missionaries:

> Some of the congregations support their own pastors, others are only able to raise part of his support; while in many cases the pastors have to work to maintain their families, especially in new fields where there is much opposition and not enough believers as yet to support the pastors by their tithes. The only foreign missionaries that I know of as receiving regular support from the General Council are along the Mexican border are one married couple in Texas, one in Arizona, one in San Diego, one in Fresno and two single workers. I mention this only to show how the work has spread largely through the converts themselves.[12]

Financial support was crucial to combat the erosion in orthodoxy that Luce found in the burgeoning Oneness movement. By the late 1920s Oneness enveloped at least more than a dozen churches and spread throughout southern California. Luce's partial solution for the loss of converts to Oneness centered on sending more American missionaries to southern California. She writes:

> This will result in keeping them [Mexican Assemblies] from many of the specious errors which are being spread in such a subtle way among the Spanish-speaking people in this day. In many places the New Issue and other false teachers have become strongly entrenched among them in the years gone by because there was no American Assembly to watch over the Spanish one and warn it of its error.[13]

Luce's views on her mission field appear to be contradictory. She believes in autonomy for her converts and continues to write in support of Mexican control. However, her idea that Euro American overseers could prevent defections to Oneness by steering the Mexican Assemblies away from their "error" denotes condescending and patronizing attitudes on her part. The suggestion that Euro American missionaries could watch over converts and prevent conversion to Oneness seems disingenuous, especially when the most competitive Oneness group, the Apostolic Assembly, had competed effectively with the Assemblies of God in the Southwest since the early twentieth century. Does

Luce's dedication to autonomy mitigate her maternalism? Clearly Luce's attitude toward her converts' abilities to distinguish theological differences and choose the correct path displays a lack of confidence in their intellectual and spiritual capacities. However, her statements on autonomy are striking:

> It seems to me that here we have a fundamental principle which we do well to observe, namely that of handing over the oversight of everything that concerns the local church to its own members. . . . The native Christians would make mistakes but they would learn from their failures, as we all do; and if only we could keep humble enough to help and advise them when they ask us to do so and to eliminate ourselves to submit ourselves to them whenever possible, we could teach them to walk alone. . . . Even when there is no apparent discontent, it seems to me that we foreigners ought to urge the native converts to carry on the work themselves and to make them feel that theirs is the responsibility of evangelizing their own country.[14]

Luce believed in autonomy, but, in practice, preached supervision when faced with the competitive market of religious ideas in southern California. Luce refused to risk the loss of orthodoxy and therefore emphasized education in order to imbue converts with that same sense of right belief. Pentecostal minister and historian Victor De Leon speculates that the "small groups that had identified with Alice E. Luce kept good order. [Many] were swept off their feet by this new light of doctrine, but not those associated with Miss Luce."[15] His inference that Luce's converts remained untouched by Oneness indicates that she dedicated a great deal of time to expunging any hint of Oneness among her small but growing community. Pedagogy reinforced orthodoxy and helped mold the spiritual character of LABI students, four of whom, despite LABI's financial difficulties, graduated in the summer of 1928.

All graduates became missionaries. Theodoro Bueno returned twelve years later to become president of LABI.[16] LABI's financial stability improved significantly by 1929, when a sympathetic benefactor, a Mr. Grable, retired the remaining seventeen hundred dollar debt.[17] However, by 1930, Luce made another plea for financial support by noting the great influx of Mexicans who could "work on the fruit ranches and in the cotton fields." From the early 1920s to the early 1930s Mexicans comprised 75 percent of California's cotton workers, with as many as 90 percent on larger ranches. Many of these workers arrived through the Imperial Valley where they eventually made their homes. Historian Devra Weber describes communities like the Imperial Valley as places where workers created their social networks and transmitted them into the fields.[18] Part of maintaining those social networks lay in the resiliency with which Mexicans retained their national identity and language through a variety of methods, including displaying the Mexican flag at public events and continuing to communicate in Spanish.[19] Within this community of workers intent on maintaining their identity and language, Luce preached and distributed Spanish-language materials, thereby making their acceptance more likely. In fact, Luce often pleaded for support to produce more materials to take into the fields. By that time, Luce had produced books on "Divine Healing, Bible study notes, a Sunday School quarterly . . . two song books . . . [and] Bible school courses in all subjects used by our . . . Bible schools."[20] Luce recognized that her students worked in the fields and could be reached in the fields, a notion shared by her fellow LABI teacher, G. H. Thomas, who also wrote a letter to the *PE* pleading for more money to defray the costs of tuition. When school ended, many of the students spent the summer months picking fruit. According to Thomas, the money they earned in the fields they spent on tuition.[21] Both he and Luce asked for money to produce literature to be used in the fields and at LABI — to reorient the converts' religious center away from their previous experiences and turn them into orthodox Pentecostals.

Twenty-three students enrolled in LABI's three-year program in 1930. The curricula for the first year included courses on personal evangelism, Christian doctrine, prophecy, music, the New Testament, and the Old Testament. Classes in the second and third years included the first-year classes and, in addition, Divine healing, Holy Spirit, homiletics, and pastoral theology.[22] LABI's pedagogical direction in the early years mirrors other Pentecostal Bible institutes of the era, as did its financial instability. Many Bible institutes moved from place to place. Local preachers and evangelists comprised the teaching staffs. Evangelistic outreach, not academics, remained the focus of the curriculum. Similarly, high school diplomas were not required, and the institutes rarely applied for or received accreditation. Students paid little or no tuition. Women studied and taught at the institutes.[23] The purpose of such schools "must be viewed as a process of evangelization, teaching, and training through which the trainee experiences the new birth and nurture in the direction of Christian maturity."[24]

By the 1930s LABI sufficiently emerged from its financial crises partially owing to the consistent support of the Assemblies of God, which decided, by 1928, to include LABI on its funding roster. In terms of reporting levels of support, the *PE* did not distinguish between the Texas and California schools. In 1928 the *PE* reported that distributions averaged thirty-eight dollars per month and in 1929 averaged forty-four dollars per month. Reflecting the onset of the Great

Depression, the average distribution dropped by thirty-six dollars per month. The magazine ceased publishing missionary distribution lists after 1930.

In 1936, one of the few years during the 1930s for which statistics exist, Luce reported ten graduates (see figure 1). She also noted that LABI students began ministering to prison inmates and helping at the local rescue mission.[25] The next year LABI students in Texas and California so impressed the Assemblies of God leadership that one writer made this statement in the *PE*:

> The Latin American people make splendid Christians and their willingness to sacrifice personal interests and their devotion to the Lord is inspiring. . . . Graduates of these schools are now making effective ministers of the Gospel not only in the U.S.A., among their own people, but also among the Spanish-speaking people in Mexico, Nicaragua, Cuba, and Spain.[26]

By the late 1930s the school succeeded in persuading its benefactor, Mr. Grable, to retire the rest of their debt in the San Diego school, thereby allowing the school to move to Los Angeles in 1940. Repairs and modifications to the new quarters closed the school for one year. Classes resumed in the fall of 1941 in East Los Angeles on the ground where El Aposento Alto once stood. LABI opened in the new location with ten students and increased enrollment

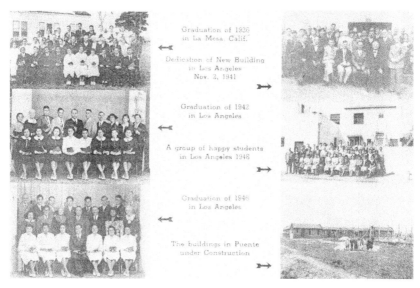

FIGURE 1. Various pictures from the 1948–49 yearbook. Courtesy LABI Archives, 1948–49 yearbook.

to seventeen, but attendance dwindled back to ten when the United States entered World War Two. The 1941 staff of eight included five women (see figures 2–3). This appears typical of Bible institutes, as Hong Yeun-Cheng Yang's study of other Bible institutes notes that women were crucial to the founding of the Rochester Bible Institute. And, more important, it was a woman at the Bethel Bible Institute in Topeka, Kansas, Agnes Ozman, who reportedly received one of the most prominent experiences of the Pentecostal baptism in 1900 under the ministry of American Pentecostal pioneer Charles Parham.[27]

LABI's school year ran thirty weeks. Students who could afford it paid three dollars a week for tuition. For those who could not afford tuition, Luce exhorted readers of the *PE* to sponsor these students who were rich in spirit but poor in financial resources. Luce notes that seventy students graduated during the fifteen years LABI was in San Diego and that about two hundred students at a time participated in her correspondence courses.[28] In 1943 Ball reported that twenty students were enrolled at LABI in Los Angeles.[29] The growth of LABI cannot be gauged precisely, but the need for larger quarters suggests that LABI's enrollment grew by the end of the decade. The district superintendent Bazán raised money for the construction of new schools in California and Texas.[30]

LABI began keeping records once the school moved to La Puente under the administration of Theodoro Bueno, a former Latin American missionary converted at Aimee Semple McPherson's crusade in Denver, Colorado.[31] By examining the remaining records in the LABI archives, much more can be said about the student body, curricula, teachers, and the tenor of the times that forced LABI to change from its insulated training for missionaries to a school with a mission to ease the ills of society. Preceding LABI's change in focus, Luce's influence molded the pedagogy of LABI until her death in 1955.

Luce's *Probad los Espiritus, Si Son de Dios* (Test the spirits to see if they are of God) provides lessons for budding Pentecostals. Since Pentecostals are greatly concerned with the spiritual realm, they must always be on guard for the appearance of demons.

> La prevalencia de estas doctrinas falsas se debe una fundación de demonios como fue profetización en *Apocalipses* 16:13–14. "Y vi salir de la boca del dragon y de la boca de la bestia y de la boda de falso profeta, tres espiritus mundos, como ranas, porque son espiritus de demonios que era prodigios, los cuales salen a los reyes del todo mundo habitao, a juntarlos para la Guerra del gran dia de Dios todopoderoso."[32]

> [The prevalence of these false doctrines is founded in demons and is prophesied in *Revelation* 16:13–14. "And I saw out of the mouth of the

FIGURE 2. LABI staff from the 1930s to the 1940s. Courtesy LABI Archives, Box 1.

1. Alice E. Luce, secretary treasurer
2. Berta E. Thomas, Veterans Affairs, assistant secretary and treasurer, New Testament Apologetics
3. Jose Girón, secretary treasurer of the Latin American District
4. Jovita Bonilla, women's counselor, Grammar, Doctrine Christian Evidence
5. Simón R. Franco, superintendent, Old Testament, Homiletics, Parlimentary Rules, Pastoral Theology
6. Francisco Medina, Hermeneutics, Bible Geography, Introduction to Bible History, Sunday School, Poetical Books
7. Violet Mardock, chorus director, Homiletics, Music, Old Testament
8. Luisa Guerrero, New Testament, Visual Aids

FIGURE 3. LABI teacher Esteban Camarillo in uniform during World War II. This picture was part of a spread that honored returning GIs. Courtesy LABI Archives, c. 1955.

dragon, and of the beast, and of the false prophet, three world spirits like frogs, because they are prodigious spiritual demons, the ones that come to the kings of the earth and inhabit the earth, to gather them for the war of the great day of the Almighty God."]

Luce's statement illuminates several points that are important not only for Pentecostal orthodoxy but also for Pentecostal spirituality. Luce equates competing religious faiths to demons released in the world on the precipice of Armageddon. Therefore, in keeping with the premillennial outlook of Pentecostalism, the appearance of other faiths, Roman Catholicism among others, are all spiritually suspect and signal impending doom.[33] Wacker observed that Roman Catholicism served as "largely symbolic foes" for Pentecostals. Pentecostals challenged Roman Catholics, new religious movements, and theological liberals but at a level that failed to take their theological contributions seriously.[34] Pentecostals usually did what Luce did, set the boundaries between Pentecostals and others as a battle between heaven and hell. By equating different faiths with evil forces, Luce sought to demonize these faiths and at the same time target their members as subjects of evangelization. In order to explain Luce's spiritual foundations regarding premillennialism, prophecy, and pedagogy, it may be useful briefly to note the work of Pentecostal theologian Stephen J. Land, who argues that Pentecostal spirituality emanates from premillennialism inherited from its Holiness roots. Pentecostals interpret biblical passages like Joel 2:28 as signaling the last days, and, in effect, they view the entirety of the movement and its place in history as fulfilling prophecy.[35] Pentecostal spirituality integrates the beliefs of orthodoxy (right praise), orthopathy (right affections), and orthopraxy (right praxis). What makes Pentecostal spiritual formation different from other Protestant processes of education lies in the emphasis of the Holy Spirit in the daily lives of believers. Some scholars posit the idea that Pentecostalism's unique doctrines qualify it as a countercultural movement because of its worldview that revelation continues to the present day and can be accessed by anyone open to the inspiration of the Holy Spirit. The construction of this worldview requires knowledge—of God—derived from personal devotions and Bible study. Pentecostal historian Jackie D. Johns describes the role of the Bible in Pentecostal theology: "The Bible is a living book in which the Holy Spirit is always active. 1. primary reference point for communion with God. 2. The Bible serves as a template for reading the world. 3. Link to God's people and God's presence in the world throughout the ages."[36] The educational process produces knowledge, but it also serves as the proverbial "spark of the soul." Luce's work encourages students to test the spirits, to begin their education not with academic but with spiritual learning, thus establishing their Pentecostal spiritual formation.

Luce's work divides doctrinally suspect groups into various sections and discusses why they are wrong and what students can to do counter their arguments. Luce's concern included doctrinal orthodoxy and reinforcing moral codes, suggesting that those who advocate unconventional marriage and *"el amor libre"* are emissaries of Satan.[37] However, reinforcing moral codes are not the central argument of her work. Some of her most interesting and important points concern evangelizing Catholics.

"Romanists" should be guided to read the Bible, writes Luce. Despite her pejorative tone toward Catholics, Luce asks her evangelists to approach them with respect and in a nonconfrontational manner. They should point out to them that the sacramental and intercessory ways of Catholicism are no longer necessary because all one needs is a personal relationship with Jesus.[38]

Luce's second important work, *El Mensajero y Su Mensaje: Manual para Obreros Cristianos* (The messenger and his message: A manual for Christian workers) takes the student step-by-step through the processes of becoming an effective preacher: what to say, how to say it, what topics to pick, how to pick a topic, how to be led by the Spirit. For Luce, being an effective preacher depends on the virtue in one's private life.

> La eficacia de la predicación depende de la vida íntima del predicador. Si la conducta del mensajero no está en cosonancia con su mensaje, sus palabras serán solo motivo de escándolo y opprobio para la causa de Cristo.[39]

> [The efficacy of the preaching depends on the private life of the preacher. If the conduct of the messenger is not in consonance with the message, his words are solely motivated by scandal and are opprobrium for the cause of Christ.]

In preparing a student to preach, emphasis was placed on enriching personal prayer. Private prayer, wrote Luce, remained the most effective way to anoint oneself for preaching. She placed her preachers in the same historical lineage as famous Protestant evangelists David Brainerd and Adoniram Judson.[40] Part of that private prayer included speaking in tongues. Occasionally, the communion with God might even place a Bible verse directly in the preacher's mouth: "Que solo necesitarás abrir la boca, pues el Espíritu te proporcionará la facultad de expresar tus pensamientos [All you need is to open your mouth and the Holy Spirit will give you the faculties to express your thoughts].[41] As the Spirit leads, it leads preachers to parse the Bible for complementary verses. Luce warned her students that the Bible required interpretation. The Bible's language might be literal or figurative—metaphors required identification—but always the Bible was used to promote orthodoxy. Luce writes:

> Las ventajas de la lectura biblica son de sumo importancia, en primer lugar para el predicador. (a) Es un método más fácil que los demás, y un bueno para el obrero nuevo o joven. (b) Lo satura de versiculos biblicos y de las enseñazas de Cristo. (c) Lo protégé de los errors doctrinales y le proporciona un conocimiento biblico equilibrado.[42]

> [The advantages of the Bible lecture are of the highest importance in the first place for a preacher. It is the fastest method of the others and a good method for the new or younger worker. Saturate yourself in the Bible verses and teachings of Christ. You protect against doctrinal errors and proportion an equal knowledge of the Bible].

Luce's work prepares preachers to learn the Bible, trust the Spirit, and guard against doctrinal errors and, in doing so, lead exemplary lives for others to emulate. LABI became a training ground for Latino ministers because Luce, the missionary and teacher, helped lead the first generation to their new reality, not as Catholic converts but as Pentecostals. Pedagogy done the Pentecostal way sacralized knowledge to the extent that the need for academic training of any kind did not occur to LABI's instructors until recent years.[43]

In 1949 LABI enrolled nineteen students (see figure 4). The 1949 LABI catalogue stated the school's goals and restated its commitment to training both women and men who had been admitted and taught at LABI since its inception. LABI aimed to educate "those Spanish-speaking young people of both sexes who feel the call of God upon their lives and wish to consecrate themselves to His service for the salvation of other souls so that they might have a place where they could prepare for this higher calling."[44] Part of the preparation for this higher calling included not only training in orthodox Pentecostalism, and encouraging spiritual gifts, but disciplining students to become transformed people. Part of consecrating oneself to service evidently included the adherence to a moral code implemented by the school. "Discipline" included the following codes:

> 1) Every student must maintain constant communion with God, respect for his teachers, and courteous fellowship with his fellow students.

There shall be absolutely no distinction of race or color among us. 2) No relations between the sexes other than the usual amenities of Christian society will be allowed. 3) The use of cosmetics, permanent wave, bobbed or hair hanging loosely will not be allowed.[45]

Let us consider point number 1. For Pentecostals, being in constant communion with God meant not only a vigorous and continual exercise of spiritual manifestations but prayer and intercession for daily living. Proper relationships also entailed respect for teachers and fellowship with other students. That no distinction between race or color was permitted at LABI demonstrates that the school appeared dedicated to imbuing its students with non-racist attitudes—a moral obligation not usually stressed in the early years of the Pentecostal movement.[46] Although much was and continues to be said about Pentecostalism's egalitarian beginnings at Azusa Street, racial reconciliation has never been one of the movement's calling cards. Although flashes of racial awareness are certainly apparent in the pages of Pentecostal maga-

STUDENT-BODY AND FACULTY OF 1947

FIGURE 4.   Student body and staff at the Los Angeles location. Courtesy LABI Archives, 1948-49 yearbook.

zines, Jonathan Perkins, a white Methodist who converted at an African American revival in Kansas in 1923, describes how he found it most distasteful to be in a room with so many of "them" but that his Pentecostal experience allowed God to shake him from his racist ways: "God surely broke me over the wheel of my prejudice."[47] Who actually wrote the statement and why it appeared in this 1949 catalogue is unclear. Considering that Euro American, African American, Asian, and Asian American students did not attend LABI in 1949, it seems curious that the administration felt strongly enough about making this third point clear and part of a Pentecostal's proper relationship with others. One might speculate that the incipient civil rights movement fostered sympathy among LABI staff. It was, after all, the decade after the mass deportations of approximately one million Mexican and Mexican Americans during the 1930s, the era of restrictive housing covenants in Los Angeles, and an overt segregation of Mexicans and Mexican Americans in restaurants, theaters, public swimming pools, and businesses.[48] It may have been this sense of racial equality that helped to open LABI to a sense of mission beyond training missionaries.

It is my contention that LABI took another turn in the 1950s and 1960s, a turn outward toward the pathologies of drug abuse and gang violence. A group of students brought the stark realities of urban life for some Latino youth to LABI. Two individuals, Nicky Cruz of Teen Challenge and Cruz "Sonny" Arguinzoni of Victory Outreach, established a pipeline for future ministers to receive their education in much the same way as first-generation converts had—with little formal education but with a passion to evangelize Latinos. Before detailing the history of this new mission, it is useful to place this mission in the context of Latino Pentecostalism and Pentecostal pedagogy.

Villafañe believes that Latino Pentecostals experience a heightened sense of mission: "One cannot fathom the growth and the depth of Hispanic Pentecostalism and its spirituality without coming to terms with the quest for community."[49] Latino Pentecostals' search for community correlates to how they create their religious identity and how that identity resonates throughout their lives. Villafañe cites the story of a Puerto Rican preacher named Leoncia Rosado, affectionately known as "Mama Leo." Rosado began preaching in New York in 1935 with the remnant of Francisco Olazábal's church, *Iglesia Cristiana Damascus*. Her desire to work with drug addicts brought forth the Damascus Youth Crusade in the 1950s.[50] Rosado's quest for community necessitated that she reach out to the marginalized of her community. Villafañe believes that this type of work signifies a "Hispanic Pentecostal social ethic." The quest for community became essential because, as he writes, "the cities, especially New York City in this case, received the Puerto Rican migration in the 1930s, and the postwar years of the 1940s–1950s did present a cold and alienating context."[51] Part of this cold and alienating context stemmed from feelings of homesickness that many Puerto Rican immigrants felt and the discrimination they faced on their arrival.

Historian Virginia Sánchez Korrol notes that immigrants established political organizations to fight against discrimination, retained their modes of expression using popular culture, and resisted assimilation by clinging to their national identity. Creating a circuitous pattern of migration, Puerto Rican immigrants went back to Puerto Rico and returned to New York in attempts to retain a sense of attachment to their homeland.[52] Pentecostalism became another avenue for immigrants to counteract this alienation. Villafañe says that Latino Pentecostalism must "serve as a means of communication between the rich, overaffluent and misdeveloped world of the North, and the poor . . . [and] continue to be bilingual and bicultural. . . . [It] must reaffirm and see itself as a locus where the poor and oppressed can find liberation."[53] His last points seem particularly important because they define the Hispanic Pentecostal social ethic. Pentecostalism serves as a place of cultural survival. It is a social safety net, and the Pentecostal community becomes a formative part of retaining religious identity. The work of Nicole Rodriguez Toulis complements Villafañe's on these points. Her work with African Caribbean Pentecostal women found that their faith created "a powerful forum for the construction of new identities which are used to negotiate the dominant and often injurious representations made about African Caribbean people by others in British society."[54] Villafañe's admonitions to Latino Pentecostals to remain engaged and, as a community, serve as a nexus between affluent North America and poor immigrants and to retain signifiers of ethnic identity, namely, language and culture, is a call to remain Latino as one becomes Pentecostal. The creation of a modified type of Pentecostal liberation theology is Villafañe's message. That Latino Pentecostals are willing to be that "locus of liberation" occurs in large measure through their pedagogical orientation. Engendering a sense of external mission at LABI began that process decades before Villafañe's work.

LABI provided one of the very few pathways to higher education for those without a formal education. Sánchez argues that by the 1930s the school was one of the three institutions, along with the family and the workplace, that framed the experiences of Mexican American adolescents and young adults in Los Angeles.[55] Undoubtedly some of those were young Pentecostals zealous for affordable religious education. Sánchez writes that the importance of education was seen in the growth of one institution in particular, the Mexican American Movement (MAM), which emerged from the Young Men's Christian Association (YMCA).

MAM members put forth three arguments as to why Mexican youth should continue in school. First, educated Mexicans were less likely to be targets of discrimination and prejudice. A college degree, therefore, held out the possibility of acceptance by the larger society despite one's race. Second, MAM members saw education as key to understanding the world, and thereby transcending the limited confines of the barrio. Finally, they understood education to be a way of advancing socioeconomic mobility.[56]

Such desires rarely found fulfillment in the segregated schools of southern California. In the early 1930s, 53.7 percent of Mexican girls and 43.7 percent of Mexican boys dropped out of school between the ages of fourteen and sixteen. Immediate financial problems at home were identified as the primary reason for leaving school, while about 13 percent of students reported that they quit school because they were simply not encouraged to stay.[57] Sánchez writes that as early as 1926 Mexican Americans realized that segregation and inequality constituted significant barriers to education in California's schools. Out of this environment came the graduates and dropouts who felt called to LABI's California and Texas campuses. Dropouts, like Jesse Miranda and Simón Melendres, who attended LABI Texas in the late 1950s, both recalled how the Bible institute afforded them the higher education they could not have received otherwise.[58] The postwar years gave rise to the beginnings of Victory Outreach and the establishment of a social mission born out of a desire to ease social and spiritual ills. Throughout the 1950s LABI graduated at least 226 students and probably close to 249 students. The majority were from California, and they split nearly evenly between men (115) and women (101).[59] The school succeeded so well that by 1959 the board of supervisors, headed by the superintendent Bazán, decided to recruit more teachers. One teacher was a twenty-one-year-old minister who had graduated a year earlier from the Texas LABI school. Jesse Miranda, a high school dropout from Albuquerque, exemplifies the 1950s Bible institute and teacher.

During Miranda's first stint at LABI as an instructor, from 1959 to 1973, he found that the school served a distinct purpose. For many working-class Latinos with little formal education, LABI became one of their only options for college. Miranda cites his own life as a high school dropout, as someone who had never heard of the possibility of college. "My father never thought beyond the lumber mill where he worked. My mother was a housemaid."[60] LABI's Texas school became Miranda's chance to go to college. For others, like Miranda and past president Simón Melendres, LABI's policy of not requiring a high school diploma was the difference between their ability to fulfill their calling to the ministry and their not being able to fulfill that call.[61] This policy proved instrumental in fostering a new brand of student to LABI in the late

1950s and early 1960s. Among those students who began attending LABI were Cruz and Arguinzoni.

A fledgling ministry, begun by Assemblies of God minister David Wilkerson, converted Cruz, a former gang leader from Brooklyn. Moved by newspaper accounts of New York's crime problems, Wilkerson relocated from Pennsylvania to New York to begin his rehabilitation program. Cruz was one of his first converts.[62] Cruz, in turn, became an effective witness and attracted others like Arguinzoni, who became Cruz's first convert. A heroin addict from Brooklyn, Arguinzoni followed Cruz's lead after conversion, attending LABI in the early 1960s. The two worked in Teen Challenge for a time after Arguinzoni's graduation, until Arguinzoni formed Victory Outreach Ex-Addict's Church in 1967, and Cruz went on to become an independent evangelist. Miranda views the entrance of people like Cruz, Arguinzoni, and others not as a problem for the school but as a challenge. "[They] made us more aware of a society that was changing."[63] Miranda taught these students and found them passionate about their mission to drug addicts and gang members. He recalls Arguinzoni, the future Victory Outreach founder, heading to Los Angeles every Saturday to evangelize among gang members. He also notes that this new breed of student received a dose of discipline at LABI.

Miranda relates how, throughout the decade of the early 1960s to the early 1970s, very little changed at LABI (see figure 5). The teaching staff remained the same; it was like a family, according to Miranda, a family that even lived on campus. All the teachers, like the students, were required to perform *tareas* (tasks). For students, *tareas* were and remain a means to pay tuition; for teachers, *tareas* were a service to the school. According to Miranda, the living conditions resembled those of a commune, where students and teachers all knew one another and together participated in the maintenance of the school.[64] This sense of community echoes past attempts to remake society by bringing together like-minded people with a common goal who separate themselves physically or spiritually from the surrounding society often in the hope of creating a utopia on earth.[65] In the case of LABI, the attempt was not to create utopia as much as it was to create a community of believers willing to promote the faith and act as the support network for the maintenance of the institute. Miranda notes that this communal feeling lasted more than ten years (from 1959 to 1971) when the staff of LABI remained virtually unchanged and most staff lived on campus or nearby.

Arguinzoni and others became students at LABI at the behest of the Teen Challenge program in New York. Wilkerson's letter vouching for Arguinzoni's character, ability to preach, and dedication to the case proved important, since

FIGURE 5. LABI staff at La Puente circa 1960s. Top row, left to right: Jovita Bonilla, Vicente Sordo, Pres. Teodoro Bueno, Choir Dir. Barbara Sheldon. Front row, left to right: Esteban Camarillo, Joel Torres, Jorge Esquivel and Jesse Miranda. Courtesy LABI Archives, 1992 yearbook.

Arguinzoni had neither a high school diploma nor was he fluent in Spanish.[66] Cruz, Arguinzoni, and their fellow student David Torres of the Los Angeles Teen Challenge program inaugurated a new era at LABI. LABI grew, as more than 160 students graduated during the decade of the 1960s. The largest entering class was in 1963 when 80 students began their studies, many of whom came from Teen Challenge centers in New York and Los Angeles. For example, the graduation rate for both men and women approached 50 percent in 1969; nearly 31 percent were natives of California, and 6 percent were from New York. The smallest percentage throughout the decade came from Latin America, where students comprised less than 1 percent of the graduates.[67]

Unfortunately little written record exists of the students themselves. However, a rare personal statement found in the 1960 yearbook chronicles the beginning of the mission to drug addicts. The future Teen Challenge leader Torres wrote:

Fui criado en un ambiete de calle y de pandillas. A causa de ese ambiente fui introducido a las drogas a la edad de doce años y para el tiempo que y habia cumpliado 17 años de edad, empeze a usa heroina y habia cumplido tres años en differentes escuelas reformatories. Por la misericordia de Dios fue salvo y El cambio mi vida el dia 19 de Marzo de 1960.[68]

[I was bred in an environment of the streets and gangs. Part of this environment was the introduction of drugs, and by the time I was twelve years old until I was seventeen I began using heroin and spent three years in different reform schools. By the mercy of God I was saved, and He changed my life on 19 March 1960].

Torres's story resonates with those of others who used the education they received at LABI to enter the mission fields previously untouched by many LABI students—drug addicts and gang members. As Miranda notes, the desire to turn the Pentecostal mission inside out to the world of the streets became something the students themselves initiated. Miranda's survey, conducted in the mid-1960s, found that LABI students believed that Latinos not only needed to be reached through spiritual resources but that their social concerns had to be met.[69] The pipeline to LABI among Victory Outreach has continued until recently where concerns over the institute's lack of accreditation has lead to an exodus of Victory Outreach students to other accredited institutes. It is a problem that plagued the school for decades as the history of the school moved into the 1970s.

Social and economic factors forced LABI to change during the 1970s. Limited sources on the decade nevertheless provide evidence of this change. As an academic institution, LABI needed to raise its standards. The accomplishment of this goal presumably required an infusion of money. Success for LABI, like many colleges, meant tuition hikes. The 1975 catalogue lists tuition at $985.00, a figure that rose to $1,775.00 by the end of the decade.[70] Part of the explanation for this increase lies in the growth of the student body. Graduation figures suggest a range from 195 to as many as 219 students graduated throughout the decade. Half the graduates were men (113), many from California (95).[71] Sometime during the 1970s a requirement for admission to LABI included the possession of a high school diploma. Though the requirement for a high school diploma may be waived in certain cases, this requirement remains significant because it demonstrates that LABI administrators knew they needed to raise academic standards, because LABI students failed to qualify for pastorships.[72] The intellectual shift also meant that provisions needed to be made for those without formal education but who had received a calling to the ministry. The 1970s can be considered another significant decade of graduating missionaries, evangelists, pastors, and teachers.

The 1980s appeared to be a pivotal decade for LABI. The necessary changes to its curricula that LABI began in the 1970s began costing the institute in terms of attendance. This was partially owing to the dramatic rise in tuition and LABI's failed attempt to become a college. Graduation figures seemed smaller than usual. During the 1980s only 99 students graduated. If figures are averaged for 1983–87, the years for which yearbooks were produced, as many as 194 students may have graduated. Tuition rose briefly from $1,775 in 1980 to $2,500 in 1982 before it again declined to $1,170 by the middle of the decade. Tuition was lowered because LABI abandoned its attempt to become a full-fledged college in late 1982. In addition, during the 1980s a very small group of Asians, Africans, and Europeans (5–10) began attending LABI in 1989–91, presumably to become missionaries.[73]

Unquestionably one of the most contentious and difficult periods in LABI's history occurred between 1980 and 1982. According to Miranda, the Latin American Pacific District asked him to become president and implement changes to turn LABI into LABC—the Latin American Bible College. In a short-lived LABC newsletter, Miranda explained the change from LABI to LABC. He noted that a fourth year of study meant that the college would grant bachelor of arts degress as well as Bible certificates.[74] The LABC experiment failed within two years of its inception in 1980.

Miranda believes that district officials could not commit the resources necessary to establish a college. His faculty also was unwilling to commit to committee work and increased work hours, and many refused to continue their *tareas*. Miranda expressed frustration that the district's inadequate planning doomed the plan from the beginning. District officials did not realize the extent of the financial drain that funding a college would have on the already poor district. To pay for college faculty adequately, LABC needed to raise tuition on students already stretched to their financial limits. With the experiment failing, Miranda offered a compromise to district officials in an effort to save LABC and to ensure that LABI's sorely needed academic credentials would be acquired through partnerships with other colleges. He suggested that LABC become a satellite campus of the larger, more prosperous Southern California College (now Vanguard University), in Costa Mesa, California. District officials rejected the plan, unwilling to place LABC under the shadow of the college (an Assemblies of God liberal arts college) and, in doing so, subsume LABC's ethnic identity. When Miranda confronted the district members who voted against his plan, they told him they feared that LABC would cease to be the same institution that had served Latinos well for fifty-five years. Because some of those very same district members had attended predominantly Euro American Fuller Theological Seminary (a nondenominational evangelical seminary), Miranda did not understand their opposition. He argued that Southern California College had a heritage of educating Latino ministers, including himself, and that a merger would presumably only strengthen that heritage. Miranda believes that he failed to communicate his plans adequately to district officials, whom he characterized as conservatives unwilling to take risks. He did discover another way to implement his plan when he founded the Latin American Theological Seminary as a part of LABI. He also arranged for Southern California College and Azusa Pacific University to accept LABI credits for admission to their liberal arts programs.[75]

LABI's partnerships with other Christian liberal arts colleges demonstrate that LABI recognized its students' demands for education—a competitive education by making partnerships with accredited, degree-granting colleges crucial to LABI's future. The first-generation Pentecostal and LABI past president Melendres believes that the changes LABI underwent to improve its academic standards became essential because, unlike those in his generation, his students' futures required a broader education.[76] In addition to preparing ministers, in recent years LABI determined that this generation of students demands more and expects more than past generations—they expect and want to fulfill their educational goals before assuming any leadership mantle in the Pentecostal world. The disadvantages of LABI's Bible study curriculum appear evident.

LABI rebounded throughout the 1990s. With lower tuition and an updated curriculum, at least 138 and possibly as many as 166 students graduated in the period from 1991 to 1997. More than 65 percent of the graduates were men (90).[77] Tuition began at $1,170 in 1991 and rose by $780 to $1,950 in 1997.[78]

Aside from the consistency of the curriculum, today's LABI scarcely resembles the LABI of the past. A book located in the LABI archives, which appears to have been handmade, entitled Berean Bible School (LABI's first location), lists the following lessons: Dispensations, Prophecy, Christian Doctrine, and Personal Work (Evangelism). It is a book of lessons presumably used at the school during its early years from 1926 to 1941.[79] By the time LABI moved to La Puente, its curriculum was fundamentally the same; additional classes included Old Testament and New Testament Surveys, Spanish Grammar, Bible Geography, Music, Homiletics, Poetry (Psalms, Proverbs), Christian Evidence, Apologetics, and a host of classes intended to prepare LABI students to teach their own Sunday school and Bible study classes.[80] Important changes in the curricula from San Diego to La Puente include preparing future Assemblies of God teachers in the substance and method of teaching. The addition of an Apologetics course demonstrates the desire of LABI instructors to impart to their students lessons on "heresies and false doctrines, and how to avoid being deceived by them."[81] Apologetics also becomes a key requirement to creating and buttressing a Pentecostal identity because it teaches believers to defend their faith. Curriculum changes appeared minimal throughout the 1950s and 1960s.[82] Throughout the 1970s the only significant changes to the curriculum appear to be the addition, in 1976, of a General Psychology course and a Family Life course.[83] The former course, one could speculate, would signal the need for LABI to face the growing reliance on psychology evident in evangelical Christianity during the 1960s and 1970s.[84]

The greatest changes in LABI's curriculum appear evident throughout the 1980s and 1990s. Some of these changes can be credited to the attempt to become a college in the early 1980s. The yearbook for 1980 includes Humanities, Greek, Public Speaking, Social Science, Sociology, and Language. The curriculum remained the same in 1981, and by 1982 LABC began to confer Baccalaureate degrees.[85] The next yearbook produced by the school in 1988 noted only one different class, Christian communications, presumably to train students in the use of different media.[86] By 1993–94 LABI expanded its curriculum to include eleven Bible courses; nineteen general education classes, including classes in Cultural Anthropology, and Comparative Religions; sixteen education classes, including classes in Church Growth, Church Administration, and Church Planting; and five courses in Theology including Pentecostal Foundations.[87]

The obvious patterns of growth and expansion evident in the inclusion of topics outside the traditional Bible institute purview provide another avenue for examining the creation of a Latino Pentecostal identity. Curriculum changes support my contention that pedagogy done the Pentecostal way imprints a religious identity on a predominantly Latino student body that benefits from the encouragement of seeking Spirit baptism on a consistent basis and learning how to pass their faith onto others. The addition of courses like Cultural Anthropology and especially Comparative Religions denotes recognition that LABI's curriculum had to encompass traditional Humanities courses in an attempt to broaden the student's education. I would argue that the inclusion of these classes signaled an evolution in the pedagogical life of LABI's students, who learn about other cultures and religions in the hopes of understanding them and gleaning insights into how to evangelize to other people groups. When I completed fieldwork at LABI in the summer of 1997, I arrived on a fieldtrip day for the Comparative Religions class that included visiting Hsi Lai Buddhist Temple in Hacienda Heights, California. My surprise at this trip was compounded by the statement of an LABI staff member who noted that the trip was an educational one, not an evangelistic one.[88] LABI administrators throughout their curricular changes tried to remedy the lack of academic depth and, in doing so, have broadened the lives of LABI students to include stronger biblical foundations for their lives as ministers and stronger Humanities courses for their intellectual lives. With an updated curriculum in place, today's LABI students share some similarities and many more differences with their predecessors.

When one becomes Pentecostal, and when that process is reinforced by education, a Pentecostal identity develops as a possible alternative to any previous identity. Toulis's study of African British Caribbean Pentecostal women helps to explain the process. Toulis writes:

> Religious behavior provides members of the church with the means to construct and maintain an alternative identity as "Christian." This identity, which begins and ends with the person—thus giving deeper meaning to the idea of identity based on self-ascription—mediates questions of suffering and status because it can be used to negotiate social experience and to structure personal relations with others in society.[89]

LABI students, past and present, correspond to Toulis's description in several ways. The dedication with which first-generation Latino Pentecostal ministered to one another and sought one another's company demonstrates the need many had to share in evangelizing their own community. LABI continues to play a significant role in that process. Their self-ascription as "Christians" says much about this separate identity they have created.

Recent LABI students, when asked to describe their past religious affiliations, described their families history as Catholic but now refer to themselves as "Christians." Students referred to themselves as "brothers" and "sisters," signifying that their similar religious affiliations now makes them part of a community. Their identity as "Christians" is one that they claim for themselves; their self-ascription defines who they are primarily not as an ethnic group but as a religious one in fellowship with the larger world of evangelical Christianity. Toulis explains: "By explicitly drawing the boundaries of identity around that which is religious rather than that which is ethnic, members assert their right to self-representation."[90] The creation of a Latino Pentecostal identity is predicated primarily on becoming Pentecostal, with residual signifiers of ethnic identity lingering, and often depending on social location, and left for others to ascertain the ethnic identities' relative strength or weakness.

Pentecostalism helps generations of Mexicans deal with a new life in a new land by creating community as well as an alternative healing system and an alternative way through the Southwest's often unsympathetic educational landscape. The Pentecostalism that Mexican Americans practice does, in some fashion, integrate them into the larger work of evangelical Christianity. Indeed, Toulis even suggests that Pentecostalism invalidates the "logic of racism" by labeling all followers "Christian" and no respecters of race.[91] Based on my interviews, I contend that Latino Pentecostals subsume their ethnic identity to their religious identity because of perceived biblical mandates which suggest that race and ethnicity are no longer important. This assimilation is part of becoming grafted onto the larger, overwhelmingly Euro American subculture of evangelical Christianity. That race and ethnicity are not problematized is fodder for future chapters; for now, the following is what my LABI interviewees told me repeatedly when I asked about the subject. They quoted Galatians 3:28, which states that there is "neither Jew nor Greek, slave nor free, male or female, for you are all one in Christ Jesus." This nonattention to race and ethnicity was often explained by this verse alone, a fairly typical response from many of my informants, who, being well versed in the Bible, look to it as a guidebook for living and use it to explain all aspects of their faith lives.

I have found little evidence of what the first generation of Pentecostal students thought about such matters as ethnicity and religious identity. Therefore, to begin to grasp how LABI students define themselves, it is appropriate to examine eight students whom I interviewed at the La Puente campus for clues as to how they view themselves as Latino Pentecostals.

The eight students I interviewed all described themselves as becoming "Christians." All but two were raised as second- and third-generation Pentecostals. Four openly distinguished themselves as "Christians" rather than Catholics. Only two wished to stay in predominately Latino communities and minister in them. This sample illustrates certain aspects of LABI life today. It also shows how a group of Mexican American students identify themselves as Christian first and also as Latino Pentecostals imbued with a sense of external mission.

Clementina Chacón is a third-generation Assemblies of God member. She distinguishes between being Catholic and Christian and views Latino Catholics as potential objects of conversion, demonstrating this by explaining how her stepfather converted to "Christianity," leaving the Catholic "religion" upon his marriage to Clementina's mother. Because she is a child of divorce, she wishes to use the skills she develops at LABI to counsel couples. Her desire to attend LABI began when she felt called to enter the ministry after finishing continuation high school two years ago. In addition to the education she receives at LABI, she also hopes to find a husband at LABI and become a pastor's wife.[92]

Leonard Andrade is a former homeless drug addict in his late thirties. Andrade grew up in a home with no religious faith. After years of drug abuse and homelessness, Andrade tried several times to commit suicide before experiencing the Pentecostal baptism at a multicultural Easter Pentecostal service in Los Angeles. Unable to pay tuition to attend LABI, Andrade works through a barter system, doing contracting work and construction for the school in lieu of tuition. He wants to open a rehabilitation home and pastor a church "geared to reaching suburbs . . . Asians, blacks, Latinos, [and] Anglos. [To] reach out, bring them in, let Jesus perform miracles of love and unity."[93]

Xuileth Santibenez's parents were "hard-core" Catholics. His mother converted to Protestantism first and then succeeded in converting the rest of her family. After a few years of heavy drinking, Santibenez became depressed and lost touch with his church. He rededicated himself to his faith at a retreat and decided to attend LABI shortly thereafter. Santibenez, unlike most students at LABI, has no desire to go into the ministry, but he wishes to transfer to a four-year Christian liberal arts college and become involved in local politics. Southern California's Latino political scene impresses Santibenez sufficiently that he wishes to follow the lead of local role models and one day run for office himself. Santibenez wishes to help the Latino community in a very different way than many of the students at LABI.[94]

David S. Galindo grew up in an Assemblies of God missionary household. His father served as a missionary to Alaska's native American population. He has no desire to follow his father's path. Instead, Galindo wishes to work in an administrative and organizational capacity for the Assemblies of God, producing dramas and musical acts for various church functions back home in Stockton, California. Galindo, like all these students, decided to attend LABI after a series of personal crises. Galindo escaped serious prison time as the wheel man in a drive-by shooting. He explains that the court, namely, a church-sympathetic judge who was also a Christian, ordered him to attend LABI. The former gang member believes that he can have a positive effect on youth by producing dramas and musical performances.[95]

Adrian Muñoz, like Andrade, wants to run a men's home in order to help his homeboys overcome their substance abuse back home in Indio, California. Muñoz, a third-generation Pentecostal, returned to the church after several years adrift in gangs and drugs. At a past youth retreat, a minister prophesied over Muñoz that he would be a pastor in the church. He believes he is fulfilling this prophetic word by attending LABI.[96] Muñoz differs from the other students in that he wishes to work with Victory Outreach because their evangelistic orientation attracts him. He contends that the Assemblies of God does not evangelize with the same intensity or frequency that he has found with Victory Outreach.

A third-generation Pentecostal, KC (a pseudonym) is the only student interested in continuing the family lineage as an Assemblies of God pastor. He hopes to assume the role of senior pastor at the church his grandmother pastors. Like all these students, KC chose to attend LABI after a crisis. He sought refuge at LABI after being arrested for driving under the influence, and he faced possible jail time for the offense. Locked in jail, KC asked God for a miracle and, when the time came for the authorities to administer a breath test for alcohol, the test came back negative. KC escaped with a suspended driver's license. He believes that he has to serve God because God spared his life in jail.[97]

James (a pseudonym) is a second-generation Pentecostal from Calexico, California. Having just started attending LABI three weeks before our interview, he seemed unsure of his educational goals and did not articulate his opinions about LABI, its programs, or his reasons for attending the school. The most interesting point to be gleaned from James's story is the power of the recent revival occurring in a few churches across the United States and Canada. James's father traveled with his son and nephew to the Brownsville Assembly of God, which was in revival at the time. James recalls "people falling down . . . my cousin was just crying . . . he couldn't stop and I couldn't stop laughing."[98] Deeply influenced by the revival, James enrolled at LABI after several years of lax churchgoing.

Gabriel Martínez shares perhaps the most focused vision of service to Latinos through his ministry as a future youth leader. From a working-class family in Modesto, California, Martínez wants to return home with a LABI certificate in order to help the church retain Latinos in its Latin American Pacific District and stem defections to the Euro American districts. When I asked why retaining Latinos was important to him, he replied that "Latinos should help themselves. . . . Catholics only go to church on Easter . . . [in the Assemblies of God] you're going all the time,"[99] Evangelizing Catholics, says Martínez "is not easy . . . they're stubborn." "The Lord brought us out of the fields," Martínez says proudly, crediting his family's conversion to Pentecostalism as a sign of upward mobility. His grandfather worked in the fields with his children, but all the children moved out of the fields and went to college. One of his children, Gabriel's mom, earned her master's degree; Martínez believes that Catholicism does not offer the same opportunity because of his knowledge of fieldworkers back home. According to Martínez, those workers who convert to Pentecostalism become imbued with the discipline to change their lives, whereas Catholics do not receive the same desire to change. Though not overtly stated, Martínez implies that the individualism that Pentecostalism supports contributes to the social mobility evident in his family's successes.[100] Crediting Pentecostalism for such mobility has historical precedents. A missionary to the Mojave Indians in

California attributed the Indian's economic degradation to their "superstitious" religion. Only a conversion to the full gospel would help them to rise out of their degraded state.[101]

All these students attended LABI to promote the Assemblies of God in some fashion and, more broadly, to support the conversion of others to Pentecostalism. Although not all articulate a vision of external mission, those who do support my contention that, since the late 1950s and early 1960s, LABI has undergone a dual transformation. Seeing the apparent futility of fighting against the tide of popular culture's influences in the evangelical world, LABI administrators acquiesced to its use for evangelistic purposes and thereby acknowledged its power to overwhelm the ascetic tendencies of the faith. At the same time that LABI turned away from the insistence that inward purity could only be achieved by insulating students from a myriad of external influences, its external sense of mission, which always existed, became sharpened to focus on the social pathologies plaguing some Latinos.

Many of my interviewees believe that a merciful God, whom they now serve, spared their lives from drugs, drinking, and behavior they characterized as "partying." Muñoz describes this behavior as including "[involvement with] gangs, drugs, drinking, disobeying parents . . . not going to church." Andrade said that he was "really disgusted with myself" after years of drug abuse and drug dealing. At one point, he dealt drugs for money to buy school clothes. Andrade became so enamored with the lifestyle that he believed "that's how Latinos lived." As both men see it, they were saved from a life of partying, and that rescue played a significant role in their decision to attend LABI.[102] Because of drinking and drug abuse, they began to fail in school and became entangled with the law. Some grew depressed and suicidal. Of the eight, Andrade, Muñoz, and Galindo are former gang members, familiar with the violence of that subculture. James, Andrade, and Galindo all dropped out of school, and Chacón fell so far behind that she completed high school in continuation school. Andrade's drug abuse and Santibenez's drinking precipitated the former's descent into schizophrenia and the latter's suicidal depression. All believe that they attended LABI at the behest of God, who sent prophetic words to them through different vessels. Chacón reports that a prophetic dream helped her see that God was calling her to the ministry. Santibenez and Muñoz were attending respective youth retreats when preachers prophesied that they would attend Bible college and enter the ministry. It was Martínez's grandmother, whom he refers to as a "prophet," who prophesied that he was headed for some church role. Andrade reports being told by the Holy Spirit that he would attend LABI. Galindo says that he, too, was influenced by the prophesy of a preacher at a youth retreat, but, unlike other prophesies, Galindo reports that the preacher foretold Galindo's death if he did not turn his life around.[103]

Since these students all seemed intimately familiar with the gift of prophecy that Pentecostals practice with regularity, what they needed to turn their lives around consisted of continued spiritual formation and a structured environment where they would be initiated into the ritual life of Pentecostalism. Pentecostal students at LABI are ritualized into a life that centers on routine, spiritual discipline, and work:

> First, at the level of a person, the moral efficacy of ritual continuously engenders and affirms belief. Secondly, it is through rituals that saints make manifest their internal state to others and thus demonstrate that they are members of the same moral community. Finally, rituals address a collective whose boundaries are not clearly demarcated.[104]

The ritual life consists of prayer, worship, testimony, song, and witness. Today the students' day begins, as it did in the past, with communal breakfast at 6:00 A.M. and morning devotions at 7:00 A.M. Classes commence at 8:00 A.M. and run until 11:00 A.M. Chapel begins at 11:00 A.M. and continues until communal lunch. Afternoon classes, study periods, or *tareas* last until 5:30 P.M., when communal dinner begins. Nighttime activities include church functions, choir, study, or personal time. Students may leave campus to work but must be back in their dorm for the evening. Students must ask permission to leave the campus on weekends.[105] This regimen enforces discipline and creates a sense of community among a very young group of people (most of my formal and informal interviewees were between nineteen and twenty-three years of age). Specific times are set aside during the day when students can familiarize themselves with Pentecostal spirituality.

The course of study these students are required to take at LABI may not in and of itself contribute to their attitudes, but the training they receive at LABI certainly adds to to their sense of mission to Latinos. The present curriculum at LABI includes many of the same classes offered in 1926. The only new courses appear to be Effective Evangelism, Urban Missions, Church Management, Psychology, and Comparative Religions.[106]

The work of Pentecostal theologian Cheryl Bridges Johns illustrates how religious education sparks a sense of mission. Johns attempts to articulate a philosophy of Christian education which she calls a "pedagogy among the oppressed" based on the educational philosophy of Paolo Friere. She believes that Friere views education as never being neutral; rather, it fosters either humanization or oppression.[107] Johns argues: "Conscientization in the context of a Pentecostal environment is initiated and maintained by the Holy Spirit who unveils reality in a manner which incorporates but supersedes human praxis. Pentecostal conscientization is thus an ongoing dialectic of humanity and deity."[108] Her argument depends on the location of the historical roots of conscientization that she finds in the African American roots of Pentecostalism, for within these roots lies the idea that there can be no division between the social self and the spiritual self in Pentecostalism. "The active presence of the Holy Spirit called for a radical equalizing of blacks and whites, males and females, the rich and the poor."[109] The melding of the social self and the spiritual self displayed itself in the early years of LABI, and it received further confirmation when LABI became a refuge for the marginalization in the late 1950s and 1960s.

Johns's argument of pedagogy as an agent conscientization remains appealing despite the limitations of her theoretical model and her co-opting of Friere's ideas birthed in secular humanism and grafted onto Pentecostalism by Johns. Like many scholars of Pentecostalism, Johns falls into the bi-racial model of black/white Pentecostalism, excluding Latinos from analysis. Johns's work becomes relevant to a historical model of Pentecostal pedagogy at LABI as it developed a sense of internal and external mission.

Johns uses the term *Pentecostal catechesis* to describe the process of faith building. The goal of catechesis involves "promoting a lived Christian faith that is actualized in both the life of the community of faith and the world at large." She adds: "The church is to live as an alternative community, announcing God's gifts for wholeness for the world and renouncing oppressive structures which do not see people as God sees them."[110] The LABI regimen of devotion, school, chapel, chores, and study proposes to bring order to the students' lives, making LABI an alternative community where students find solace from the world. The student takes an active role in Pentecostal formation because the catechesis communicates through both written and oral forms in stories, testimonies, and songs that ensure the ongoing melding of the world and experience. Devotion and chapel reinforces the testimonies, stories, and songs that students use to formulate their spiritual experience. Johns describes several settings for learning that helps the process of conscientization: water baptism, communion, foot washing, testimony, healing, spirit baptism, songs, and dances.[111] Testimonies, healing, spirit baptism, songs, and dances all may occur at LABI during chapel and worship services. The precept of conscientization becomes realized in LABI's history of building racial tolerance, demonstrated in the 1948 catalogue which demands that no student be treated differently because of race. Another sign of this precept can be seen in the work of the students in missions at jails and rescue missions as they minister to drug addicts, gang members, the homeless, and other marginalized people.

In examining Toulis's notion of self-ascription as generating agency among ethnic Pentecostals and Johns's notion of conscientization and the role it plays in Pentecostal pedagogy, I see these two notions as working together. Privileging religious identity over ethnic identity does not prevent Latino Pentecostals from seeking to establish various social missions. Indeed, they have figured out a way to diminish the boundaries between the social self and the sacred self. The empathic response to help others who experienced the kinds of crises these students have experienced emanates from a deep sense that their own lives have been spared for a reason. What drives Latino Pentecostals in their lives of social mission is the spiritual experiences which they believe strengthen them to face a secular world. Since their ethnic identity has little or no influence on experiencing manifestations of Holy Spirit, their ethnic identity ceased to be an empowering force in their sacred self. Any correlation between ethnic and religious identity resided in their social selves where the command to love one another as you love yourself takes on various forms of social mission activity. This idea that all the complex parts of one's self must be tempered and placed under control of the sacred self can best be seen in the active reinforcement of traditional gender roles that characterized LABI's history.

Throughout LABI's history women have always attended the institute in equal numbers to men, and for most of its seventy-six-year history have also graduated in equal numbers to men.[112] Since it is usually men who become pastors, women appear to have served auxiliary roles for much of LABI's history, without much fanfare (see figures 6 and 7). Women made no statements of faith in any of the yearbooks I examined. Influential women, such as LABI founder Alice Luce, deferred to men when it came to serve as LABI presidents, none of whom were women. Notable women graduates, like Julie Rivera, who would marry Sonny Arguinzoni and help to found Victory Outreach, do not have their folders preserved in the LABI archives, as those of their husbands are. LABI, like other Pentecostal Bible institutes and colleges, became a way for women to meet like-minded, "saved" men and to find a suitable marriage partner.

Sociologist Margaret Poloma and historian Felipe Agredano Lozano have analyzed this phenomenon. Poloma researched the Assemblies of God, and Lozano researched the Apostolic Assembly. Poloma notes: "[A] woman desiring a pastoral role would best be advised to marry a minister. As one male respondent quipped 'young women who hear the call of God to the ministry should head down to the Central Bible College [referring to the denominations' Central Bible College] in search of a husband who is called to the min-

FIGURE 6. A woman preaching during
chapel services in 1955. Courtesy LABI
Archives, 1955 yearbook.

FIGURE 7. A woman preaching during ministry
class in 1955. Courtesy LABI Archives. 1955 yearbook.

istry.' "[113] Poloma supports this anecdote with figures indicating that out of 3,430 female ordained ministers, only 581 are single.[114] Lozano's study of Apostolic women supports Poloma's findings. Lozano found that women's opportunities to minister are curtailed toward reinforcing patriarchal roles. The Apostolic Assembly does not permit women in ministry, and therefore their roles are severely curtailed from the start. Oneness Pentecostal colleges, like the United Pentecostal Church's Bible college, Christian Life College, have been nicknamed "Christian Wife College."[115]

Figures for the number of women who married men they met at LABI are nearly impossible to determine. If this small group of students is any barometer of its past, LABI also fits the pattern of other Pentecostal institutes. Both past presidents, Melendres and Miranda, met their wives at LABI.[116] The previously noted case of the Arguinzonis also supports this idea. Chacón, who admits wanting to find a husband at LABI, also adds this interesting comment that may explain women's motivations in certain cases. When I asked if her goals were to get married and co-pastor a church, she replied no, emphatically stating that she did not want to co-pastor, she wanted to "just be a pastor's wife."[117] This attitude, like most others, is firmly rooted in the understanding many Pentecostals have regarding what the Bible says about the role of women: "Now I want you to realize that the head of every man is Christ and the head of the women is man." (I Cor 11:3). Verses such as this one, which some Pentecostals interpret to mean that women be submissive, support inferences like Chacón's, that somehow to co-pastor means to share authority. Sharing authority is incompatible with the biblical injunction that "[a] woman should learn in quietness and full submission. I do not permit a woman to teach or to have authority over a man, she must be silent"(I Tim 2:11–12). A melding of traditional renderings of this passage and the idea of republican motherhood creates the presumption that women are the bearers of virtue and have a duty to educate their children to be moral and virtuous. A woman's private sphere where she was to be silent and a child bearer, notes historian Sara Evans, changed throughout U.S. history. Volunteerism became the bridge that allowed women to attain public roles previously considered unthinkable.[118] Pentecostalism, like other voluntaristic evangelical faiths, allows women to transgress the private/public sphere.

The reinforcement and, one could argue, one of the foundations of Western notions of traditional gender roles begins with the reiteration of passages like those listed above through Pentecostal institutions entrusted with shaping successive generations' notions of gender, as well as notions of God. The catechesis involved in reinforcing traditional gender roles at LABI, as Johns noted, is to promote faith in the community life and the world. By implicitly

FIGURE 8.   Chapel service 1961. Men and women sat separately. Courtesy LABI Archives, 1961 yearbook.

making the expectation of marriage part of the educational experience at LABI, and thereby making that expectation one of the few ways women ascend to the pastoral centers of power, LABI's pedagogy extends beyond the creation of a Pentecostal, that is, a religious identity that seeks to perpetuate socially constructed gender roles to the larger segments of society.

To return to the points of LABI's 1948 catalogue, those that specifically dealt with women's attire and a dress code, apparently these points were intended to regulate women's behavior in order to preserve purity and enhance piety. Separate dorms for men and women and a chaperoned traveling choir are some overt attempts to prevent sexual relations outside marriage and therefore reinforce the LABI code of conduct (see figure 8). Women were expected to abide by restrictions on certain types of clothing, cosmetics, and hairstyles as certain fashions or appearances presumably posed risks to their purity. With regard to LABI's chaperone system, it differed from other forms of traditional manifestations of "familial oligarchy" described by Ruiz. In both cases, chaperonage was dictated by elders—familial in the case of Ruiz's examples and by religious elders at LABI, who exerted other pressure on students, whose lax morals would diminish familial honor and, more important for Pentecostals, endanger their spiritual lives should they succumb to temptation. While chaperonage may have disappeared for many Mexican Americans by the 1940s, the LABI choir, as it has in the past, continues to travel with chaperones.[119] The regulations against cosmetics, permanent wave (bobbed hair), and loosely hanging hair not only were attempts to de-sexualize young

Pentecostal women, and thereby secure their purity, but it also appears to have served another purpose. By forbidding these rather popular accoutrements, LABI staff attempted to stave off the influences of popular culture.[120] Implementation of a dress code served the same purpose, not only with LABI students but with several Pentecostal denominations including the Oneness Apostolic Assembly and the United Pentecostal Church, both of which place dress restrictions on their members.[121] They forbid "immodest" dress for gym class, meaning that shorts are not to be worn by girls and women. The Apostolic Assembly forbids both men and women from wearing gold jewelry. Additionally, women cannot cut their hair or wear pants.[122] At LABI, however, the restrictions on denim jeans excludes their wear for work time, and presumably only men can wear them. Dress codes for men intended to make men look more formal, requiring that they wear dress slacks and a shirt to school. Dress codes for women intended that they present themselves as virtuous Christian ladies. The prohibition against cosmetics and hairstyles remained intact until sometime during the late 1960s to early 1970s, as the catalogues of 1975 and 1976 no longer listed such prohibitions.[123] Yearbooks from those years depict women with long hair and wearing pants, and men with long hair and sideburns. In the 1980s and 1990s more concessions were made to modernity (see figures 9–13).

Abandoning the dress code signaled a concession to popular culture. On campus today the popular urban dress of baggy pants, tennis shoes, and shaved heads marks many young men. Jeans are the favorite garments for both men and women. Women wear pants, makeup, and dress themselves in the latest fashions and hairstyles. Young men dye their hair and wear earrings — attire undoubtedly unheard of in the early years of the school. The lax dress code and the acceptance of virtually all the trappings of youth culture, including Christian rock and rap, demonstrate that the administration, without approving the attire and music, acknowledges that, in order to reach the youth, more is required than sincere evangelism, namely, some measures of accommodation.

Through their implicit acceptance of popular cultural forms, LABI administrators also seem to understand that they are incapable of stemming the intrusion of contemporary fashion, music, and culture into their community. Instead of attempting to regulate behavior by means of codes, administrators, as have many others in leadership roles in the Pentecostal world, have learned that one way to defeat the influences of secular popular culture is to co-opt portions of it for evangelistic purposes.

Using rap music and dramas reflecting the realities of drug use, gang membership, and the foibles of the party life meld together with Pentecostal spiri-

FIGURE 9. Classroom circa 1960s. Women's hairstyles had changed from the conservative style of previous decades to beehives like the one pictured. Courtesy LABI Archives, 1992 yearbook.

FIGURE 10. Women enjoying recreational time during gym class. Courtesy LABI Archives, 1992 yearbook.

tuality to create evangelistic techniques that often meet with resistance from the older, traditional churches. Traditional churches frown on including such influences, preferring to reach the "lost" with traditional hymns and old-fashioned revivals. LABI students who evangelize and hold revivals among their peers—they know traditional methods do not work—believe that rap and dramas remain the most effective tools for furthering their cause. Evident in this explicit use of popular culture is the confluence of several strands of evangelicalism that coincidentally have their roots in the Jesus movement of the late 1960s and early 1970s.

Appropriating the tools of the secular world—popular music and dress to evangelize their generation—the largely Euro American Jesus movement attempted to retrieve lost souls from the counterculture scene of the late 1960s. Within the larger context of charismatic and evangelical Christianity that exploded in the late 1970s and early 1980s, there arose a need within other churches to reach their own youth. However, rather than make use of the music prominent in Euro American contexts like Maranatha, Hosanna Integrity, or Vineyard, LABI students like Martínez, Galindo, and Muñoz use the urban sounds of rap to bring their message to their peers. The use of rap represents a tributary through which the popularization and restructuring of American Protestantism passed through, transporting Latino Pentecostals, who, as they became away of their own needs, found representative modes of expression for their own messages distinct from the Euro American Jesus movement and charismatic movement of the 1970s and 1980s.

Three LABI students, Martínez, Muñoz, and Galindo, offered their perspectives on the controversial use of rap and dramas as evangelistic tools. Martínez related how he felt unappreciated when he attempted to introduce rap to traditional Mexican Pentecostal churches. He was disappointed in the lack of response he received when he performed, having grown accustomed to receiving just the opposite reception when rapping before younger audiences. However, he understands the lack of response among traditionalists and the hostility they often exhibit toward his music, recognizing that the "worldly" aspect of rap makes them uncomfortable. Muñoz, who also raps at LABI, raps as well back home in Indio, where he entertains homeboys from his former gang, hoping to wean them away from gangs to Jesus. He, too, feels the lack of acceptance among traditionalists but notes that rap "is the only thing that works."[124]

Martínez, Muñoz, and Galindo are also involved in producing, writing, and acting in dramas. Galindo organizes, writes, and produces performances for various churches and events. His perspective on these evangelistic tools reflects a different attitude from that of Martínez and Muñoz. Galindo believes that

FIGURE 11. LABI classroom circa 1970s. Hairstyle changes include longer hair, sideburns, and beards. Courtesy LABI Archives, 1992 yearbook.

FIGURE 12. LABI choir circa 1970s. Courtesy LABI Archives, 1992 yearbook.

many performers allow their moment of fame to cloud their reason for performing, namely, to save souls. He is frustrated at the extent to which ego overtakes the message. Nevertheless, he believes that his future with the Assemblies of God, upon graduating from LABI, will include organizing events and managing performers. The dramas often deal with difficult subjects, such as drug and alcohol abuse, and gang violence and death, and they are presented with a simplicity that teenagers and young adults appreciate. Martínez related the plot of one drama in which he had a starring role, portraying a character much like himself. The character arrives at a party and is tempted by drugs, alcohol, and sex. His character is encouraged to smoke marijuana, and he enjoys himself until God "convicts" him of his error, just as he begins to follow a siren/teenage girl to a sure spiritual death. He then recognizes her as a demon. They wrestle, and he kills the demon with the Bible.[125] This scene, and indeed the message of the drama, reinforces not only traditional literalist interpretations of the Adam and Eve narrative but, on a deeper level, reinforces the notions that women are not to be trusted and are historically gateways to sin. That little is made of the young man's sin in the drama demonstrates the continuity of the argument that women tempt and deceive, and men follow blindly.

Despite the problematic nature of such stereotypes and unexamined notions of such depictions, these dramas are produced because they are effective

FIGURE 13. Students at worship. Use of electronic keyboards (drums and guitar not pictured). Courtesy LABI Archives, 1996 yearbook.

witness tools. Martínez claims that many young teens react to that message by answering the altar call and converting. Martínez, Muñoz, and Galindo all agree that nothing reaches youth like rap and dramas. Muñoz declares that the "suit and ties don't work," meaning that the traditional evangelistic techniques of properly dressed missionaries distributing tracts did not reach him or his peers.

Muñoz, the grandson of an Assemblies of God pastor, is attracted to the efforts of Victory Outreach, a church that effectively uses dramas and rap to attract youth. The young men seem convinced, at least at this stage of their young careers, that reaching youth is the future of the church. Galindo and Muñoz both lost close friends to gang violence, and Martínez's brief estrangement from his family occurred because of his drug and alcohol abuse. All three are second- and third-generation Pentecostals, who, in their late teens and early twenties, decided that the prophetic utterances of their relatives and a series of near-tragic events brought them to LABI. The upbringing these students received in Pentecostal homes did not inoculate them against the secular world. Indeed, while completing my fieldwork at LABI several years ago, I was told that students would not be available that day because a LABI student had committed suicide. A student informed me that she knew the student in question and knew that something was wrong. It appears there is little sanctuary a young person can find from the rigors of life when even the secure confines of a Bible college provide little comfort.

The institutionalization of a Latino Pentecostal identity began and continues at LABI through a process that ultimately relies on what Wacker calls the character of Pentecostalism: "[the] supernatural wedded to the pragmatic."[126] LABI recognized that its success in attracting students depended on its steadfast reliance on the Holy Spirit. However, LABI allowed itself to change by modifying dress codes and drawing on evangelistic uses of popular culture. Most important, the staff has realized that the institute simply does not offer students a sufficiently broad education to satisfy current students' desires to ensure their future success. LABI students became Pentecostals through a melding of praxis and practicality. Orthodoxy served to create the template of faith needed for such praxis. Moral codes tie Pentecostalism to its Holiness roots with the intent of molding character, regulating behavior, and creating conformity with traditional values. The sense of mission, a perpetual staple of LABI's vision, began with Latinos and now has widened its reach to include global missions as the quest for community continues. The following chapters on Victory Outreach and the Vineyard demonstrate how this quest for community solidifies and changes the character of a Latino Pentecostal identity.

3. "Normal Church Can't Take Us": Victory Outreach and the Re-Creation of a Latino Pentecostal Identity"

In 1967 Cruz "Sonny" Arguinzoni, a former drug addict turned Pentecostal minister, purchased a house in the Boyle Heights section of Los Angeles. Through his first vision, "East L.A. for Jesus," Arguinzoni sought to carve out a familial, cultural, and religious space for addicts, gang members, ex-convicts, the homeless, and others. Before Arguinzoni began reshaping the Pentecostalism he had learned at LABI, Assemblies of God minister David Wilkerson pioneered the need for a Pentecostal social mission to drug addicts. Wilkerson's ministry, Teen Challenge, attempted to build relationships between the church and teenagers, who, in today's parlance, would be called "at-risk youth." Teen Challenge served as a template for Victory Outreach.

Victory Outreach opened the Pentecostal world to those outside the confines of mainstream society while focusing on youth as a viable market for Pentecostalism's continued growth among Latinos. I shall return to the work of Victory Outreach with youth in the next chapter, but first, in order to understand and sift through the diffuse history of the church, it is necessary to examine here the work of Teen Challenge and its influence on Victory Outreach, and the social location and milieu that gave rise to the need for an affordable faith-based drug rehabilitation ministry. From there I shall examine the sociological dynamics within Victory Outreach and its methods for re-creating a Pentecostal identity among its members. I focus on the ways that rehabilitation homes, conferences, and pedagogy reinforce orthodoxy and the unique vision of the church. I then discuss the consequences of a re-created, ritualized life that, more often than not, begins and continues a process of the inculcation of conservative social values. This process begins by returning to the roots of the Pentecostal social mission to drug abusers on the streets of New York.

In 1958 David Wilkerson began visiting New York after reading about the ongoing youth gang problems there. He reported receiving a prophetic word from God about these youth: "They could begin life all over again, with fresh and innocent personalities of newborn children . . . they could be surrounded by love instead of hate and fear."[1] The program called for the removal of the abuser from their environment. A church group affiliated with Wilkerson and Teen Age Evangelism was formed in 1960, the same year Wilkerson purchased a house in Brooklyn that became Teen Challenge's first residential center. The center then became affiliated with the Assemblies of God. In 1961 a training center that provided long-term rehabilitation was established in rural Pennsylvania.[2] One of its first converts was Nicky Cruz, a native of Puerto Rico and an active gang member. Wilkerson began organizing his ministry to at-risk youth at the Teen Challenge Center.

> It would be headquarters for a dozen or more full-time workers who share my hopes for the young people around us, who saw their wonderful potential and their tragic waste. Each worker would be a specialist: One would work with boys from the gangs, another with boys that were addicted to drugs; another to work with parents. . . . There would be women workers; some would specialize in girl gang members, others with addiction. . . . They would live in an atmosphere of discipline and affection. They would participate in our worship and our study. They would watch Christians living together, working together, and they would be put to work themselves. It would be an induction center where they were prepared for a life of the Spirit.[3]

Wilkerson's mission statement may be taken as a blueprint for the future mission of Victory Outreach. Recovering addicts and gang members, among others, were separated by gender in the rehabilitation homes and ministered to by people who had experienced the same addictions and legal entanglements. Unlike those associated with Teen Challenge, the evangelists in Victory Outreach were generally from the same background as their flock. In addition, Victory Outreach began to organize its evangelism teams around the rehabilitation/reentry homes and around special groups like "Barrios for Christ," a team that targets high-profile gang areas. Teen Challenge provided Victory Outreach with a method for scheduling its activities and organizing time at the homes.[4] As discussed below, Victory Outreach homes operate on much the same premise: Their aim is to inculcate the Pentecostal faith with constant prayer and worship and to ensure that recovering addicts, gang members, and others are kept busy with activities that both reinvent their faith lives and reintegrate them back into societal norms of work and rest cycles. Routinization helps the person in recovery to reestablish patterns of behavior to which they were accustomed before being in prison, that is, their behavioral patterns at work, at school, and with their family.

This separation from society also served another function, according to anthropologist Luther Gerlach, who writes on Pentecostal organizations: "It cuts [the convert] off from past patterns of behavior and often from past associations. It involves him with movement participants, and provides high motivation for changed behavior and for striving to accomplish group and movement objectives."[5] How does this home structure, borrowed from Teen Challenge, reorient Victory Outreach members? It does so in the same way that Teen Challenge does. Pentecostalism's ritual life reorients converts first to the possibility that a divine force "saved" them from their previous lives to the certainty that such salvation is only possible through a life-changing relationship with Jesus and that recidivist behavior can be tempered by an active seeking of the Spirit. Anthropologist Thomas Csordas describes this as a transformation of time, where "routines involving the organization of time include periodic events such as weekly prayer meetings, periodic seminars and courses, retreats, workshops, 'days of renewal,' and annual regional or national conferences."[6]

Wilkerson believed that the Holy Spirit restored people to life, healing their addictions without using medication. Pentecostals believe that to be baptized in the Holy Spirit prepares one for a sanctified life and heals the most intransigent of afflictions. Wilkerson catalogs the successes:

> Harvey . . . has been deeply addicted to heroin for three years, but after the baptism, he said the temptation itself went away. Johnny had been on heroin for years, and pulled away successfully after his baptism. Lefty has used the needle two years, and after his baptism he not only stopped using drugs, he decided to go into ministry. Vincent used heroin two years, until his baptism, he stopped instantaneously.[7]

Heroin became one of the drugs of choice among African American and Latino youth of New York. Drugs were prevalent in the communities where Teen Challenge ministered—with heroin and cocaine making a path from Brooklyn to east Harlem as early as the mid-1950s.[8] Teen Challenge's program for drug rehabilitation used no medication, allowed no smoking, and relied on prayer to help cure the addict. Wilkerson wrote: "Narcotic addiction is a moral, spiritual problem that demands church action."[9] Another important component, part of inculcating self-respect and discipline, was that the Teen Challenge center required residents to work. Victory Outreach went so far as to imitate Teen Challenge's daily regimen of communal breakfast, morning prayer and study, work, and afternoon street evangelism or outreach.[10] Wilkerson describes his system:

> Teams of two or three workers would start walking over a prescribed route, keeping an eye out for signs of trouble. They would be trained to

spot the symptoms of narcotic addiction, they would be on the lookout for the teen-age alcoholic, or for the girl prostitute. They would talk to gang members . . . and they would not go with an eye to gaining converts but with an eye to meeting a need. The conversions would take care of themselves.[11]

Victory Outreach replicated these ideas, adding a crucial component which insisted that the addicts minister to themselves. Arguinzoni took it a step further and made sure that the future leaders of the church came up from the ranks of the converted and thereby became a self-perpetuating entity.

A combination of gang affiliation and peer pressure appears to have consumed Arguinzoni. He described a happy home life and religious foundation. He lived with his parents and sister in a three-bedroom apartment in Brooklyn. They were a churchgoing family, and Arguinzoni's father served as an elder in the Assemblies of God. At the age of twelve, Arguinzoni ran away from home to Texas, where he ran into his first conflict with law enforcement. Developing a reputation as a tough guy back home, he became involved in gangs. He describes his gang life: "In between rumbles, we partied in our clubhouse—we'd rent a run-down apartment. There we loaded up on wine and pills, smoked marijuana, and danced all night."[12] He began using heroin shortly after that and took to stealing to support an addiction that led to jail time and rehabilitation programs. One of his stints was at the federal hospital for addicts in Lexington, Kentucky.

Through a mutual friend, Arguinzoni met Teen Challenge evangelist Nicky Cruz. Cruz witnessed to Arguinzoni, telling him that if God could cure him, a gang leader, God could free Arguinzoni of his addiction, and Cruz asked God to send the Holy Spirit to change Arguinzoni's life. After that prayer, Cruz and Arguinzoni were locked in a room and, as Arguinzoni describes it:

> I threw myself on the floor in front of the altar and cried and cried. . . .
> I was on my knees at the altar, and before you knew it, I'd raised my hands and was saying "Thank You Lord, Thank You Jesus." I kept saying it over and over again, and from deep down in my belly, something started to rise and it rose up till I thought I couldn't contain it anymore, and suddenly I was singing and shouting, and it wasn't in English, but in some strange language that kept flowing off my tongue.[13]

Csordas categorizes speaking in tongues in two forms: prophetic utterance and individualistic prayer. In Arguinzoni's case, the act signified an individual prayer, since no one who witnessed the manifestation interpreted the language.[14] This experience led Arguinzoni to give up his past life as a drug addict and gang member. He began working with Cruz at Teen Challenge in 1962. From that time on, Arguinzoni and other converts describe their lives as being under the control of God; they see events in terms of what God does to lead them through the most mundane and sacred of activities. In Arguinzoni's case, his pending burglary charge was dismissed; when a Teen Challenge member spoke of his newfound faith, the judge offered him an alternative to prison. The desire to see events in miraculous terms continues through the narratives described in the following pages.

Sometime in the mid-1960s, Wilkerson recommended that Arguinzoni follow Cruz's footsteps and attend LABI in La Puente, California. Arguinzoni hesitated but accepted the offer despite his insecurity about relating to Los Angeles, and his less than fluent grasp of Spanish. Arguinzoni's first months at LABI proved difficult. Academic studies, chapel, and Bible studies were all in Spanish. A few of Arguinzoni's grade reports remain in LABI's files and reflect his relatively unsuccessful academic start at LABI. Probably in part because of his language difficulty, he received "C's" in most courses. Further, the files reveal that Arguinzoni listed his profession before attending LABI as a truck driver who attended school only until the eighth grade.[15]

If Arguinzoni did not excel at academics, he did impress his teachers with his determination to minister in the barrios of nearby East Los Angeles. Former teacher Jesse Miranda recalls how Arguinzoni, nearly every weekend, went to the Maravilla housing projects to evangelize to gang members and drug addicts.[16] Arguinzoni gathered a team of evangelists at LABI, including Teen Challenge Los Angeles leader Dave Torres, Gary Rivera, and Julie Rivera (Gary's sister), all of whom ministered in the projects.[17]

During a summer crusade in the Maravilla projects, a young gang member and heroin addict, Roberto Almaraz, and some of his homeboys tried to convince Arguinzoni's team that the corner of Mednick and Brooklyn Avenues was not the best corner to hold church, that the gang, Kern Maravilla, could not protect them if they continued their crusade in a prime spot for drug sales. Before leaving the projects, Arguinzoni's team succeeded in giving Almaraz a card advertising Teen Challenge's services (a facsimile of which he carries to this day).[18]

After another stint in jail, Almaraz, at his mother's request, began attending a Teen Challenge meeting. After attending several of these meetings, Almaraz reports being supernaturally delivered from the desire for heroin. He became Arguinzoni's first convert and later became a worker for Teen Challenge Los Angeles.[19]

Almaraz became the link to the Kern Maravilla gang and soon brought in more converts, his brother, Cal, for one, who also began working with Arguinzoni. Arguinzoni was promoted to field evangelist by Teen Challenge Los Angeles because of his success in bringing in gang members and drug addicts. Along with the promotion came a small apartment at the Teen Challenge Center and a steady salary.[20] In 1966 Arguinzoni began to oversee a new organization within the Teen Challenge structure called Challenge Temple in East Los Angeles.[21] He writes of how this new organization and his evangelist position still did not fulfill him.

Arguinzoni resigned from Teen Challenge in 1967 and joined Cruz as a traveling evangelist, but that, too, left him wanting more. He told his wife, the former Julie Rivera, that he needed to go to the Rivera's family home in San Diego to fast and to pray for five days. He left on the fifth day, convinced that God had placed a prophetic word in his heart to build an addicts' church. Arguinzoni reported that God spoke to him: "I want you to open up the church and I am going to fill it up with drug addicts and their families, and it's going to be a lighthouse and a testimony that's going to glorify my name around the world."[22] The prophecy Arguinzoni received appears to be an encouragement to him and his small group of followers that Victory Outreach was intended to move beyond its modest beginnings in East Los Angeles.[23]

From the beginning Arguinzoni's motivations, aside from the deeply spiritual influence of conversion, has been guided by his own self-consciousness at being a former drug abuser, the shame of that stigma propelled him to begin Victory Outreach. He describes an incident that shaped his ideas about his ministry.

> I went to my mother's church (after converting) and when they saw the son of Sister Arguinzoni, her drug addict son, all the women got hold of their pocketbooks and moved their daughters away from me. . . . That offended me. I wasn't a thief or a drug addict anymore! Jesus Christ had changed my life! People need a church where the pastors came from their same background. People need a congregation where they don't have to be so sophisticated, but instead can come in and feel at home. People need a church where they could just be themselves and worship the Lord in Spirit and in truth.[24]

Probably no statement in this chapter better defines Victory Outreach than this sentiment. That this ministry stands alone with the dispossessed is its imprimatur and signals the creation of a unique Latino Pentecostal identity—

one in which social location is of prime importance under the rubric of evangelical Christianity.

According to both Cruz and Arguinzoni, Teen Challenge greatly influenced Victory Outreach. Cruz notes that it was at the Brooklyn Teen Challenge Center where Arguinzoni first learned the need for effective disciplining: how to train a convert to live a Christian life and how to effectively win more converts. Winning converts depended on empathizing with street kids. Cruz and Arguinzoni both agree that they would be more effective than "some squeaky-clean Bible school student from the farmlands of Iowa."[25] Arguinzoni acknowledged the crucial role of families in the success or failure of an addict's recovery, and Challenge Temple began services specifically for family members. However, more was needed. Arguinzoni wanted a separate church for addicts—pastored addicts with familial participation.[26]

Almaraz recalls how Teen Challenge's system differed. Teen Challenge leaders took Almaraz and other converts to visit different churches as a way of demonstrating the program's successes. These visits strained the already fragile familial ties established at the Teen Challenge Center.[27] In New York Teen Challenge concentrated its efforts on young addicts, people in their late teens to early thirties, many married, often to women who were addicts themselves, and with children. In couple's where the children were older, the children, too, were involved in drugs and crime.[28] Arguinzoni's view that lack of familial encouragement places an additional strain on addicts supports Almaraz's contention that programs that divided families hindered an addict's recovery. "As long as a convert remained at the Center, the family night provided a link with the wives and children."[29] Arguinzoni began another organization under the auspices of Teen Challenge, called Teen Chapel, with the goal of ending the practice of having addicts give testimonials and, instead, establishing a place where families could support their recovering addicts.[30] Though not explicitly stated, the cultural importance of families in the Latino communities must have played a role in Arguinzoni's reasoning and in his conviction that addicts recovered faster in the presence of a familial support system.

A flyer for "Victory Temple Ex-Addict Church" describes its services as the Victory Home for Girls, prison outreach, narcotic prevention, rehab, evangelism, Bible training, and fellowship.[31] This newly named church represents Arguinzoni's first foray into ministry beyond his Teen Challenge beginnings. The early years of the ministry were difficult and nonproductive. Arguinzoni received little support outside the small group that followed him from Teen Challenge. In these years Arguinzoni held services and lived with a small group of addicts in the Aliso Village housing projects in Boyle

Heights. Contributions to the ministry in the form of tithing were almost non-existent. Unable to support his family, he received encouragement from Cruz to return to Teen Challenge and travel as an evangelist. Arguinzoni considered quitting his ministry, but, because of his faith in prophecy, he believed he could not possibly fail. He persevered and gained converts by using people like Almaraz as a core group that could establish a pipeline between gangs such as El Hoyo Maravilla and Victory Outreach.[32] This core group focused on developing Bible studies and visiting converts. Arguinzoni organized the congregation into teams, each responsible for visiting converts at least once a week and sometimes immediately if the convert missed a service. "Although our people were being drawn together into a fellowship, they were often completely oblivious to one another's needs. As addicts, they had lived in isolation for so long that fellowship was difficult and at times impossible for them."[33]

For the program of rehabilitation and church to work, Arguinzoni had to devise a plan to reorient the addict away from the routinized pathology of "lying around the house shooting up drugs for kicks."[34] Spiritually Victory Outreach sacralized time: Instead of time being characterized as something to be wasted, it was viewed as something of great value. Both personal time and organizational time had to be reoriented toward the sacred. The Pentecostal experience which Victory Outreach used as a healing mechanism for addiction became only one of many ways in which the rehabilitative process became Pentecostal and, in so doing, created a religious identity. For recovering addicts who sought help at Arguinzoni's fledgling ministry, Pentecostalism served at least two purposes: First, it became the healing mechanism that might cure their addiction; and, second, it became the regulating force of their social lives. In Arguinzoni's words: "It [conversion] meant establishing new and orderly patterns for living with your family. . . . As a Christian, the former addict suddenly recognized his responsibility of being a husband and father and a conscientious employee."[35] Themes of miraculous healing abound in Victory Outreach testimonials that place the church squarely in the evangelical ethos of recovery. For example, two members of Arguinzoni's core group, Almaraz and Gilbert Garavito, both experienced healing. Almaraz reported being cured of heroin addiction, and Garavito's epileptic son was reportedly healed after being baptized in the Holy Spirit.[36]

Victory Outreach's Pentecostalism became a road to the therapeutic. Equating evangelical religion and recovery, historian R. Marie Griffith's study of the "Women's Aglow" organization provides insight into this process. Griffith says that themes of recovery are prevalent in evangelical religion, because both stress the surrender of one's life.[37] The extent to which a supernatural event receives credit for curing addiction, repairing relationships, and healing abused people demonstrates that one way in which one becomes a "new creation" in Victory Outreach requires that one become sensitive to the leading of the Spirit, in effect, that one become Pentecostal before one can solve one's problems. Victory Outreach thrives on ministering to the margins, probably because of the life experience of the founder and the tenor of the times that nurtured the need for such a Pentecostal social mission.

The world in which Victory Outreach was born in the late 1960s had for at least twenty years witnessed the scourge of substance abuse. Before exploring how Victory Outreach established its rehabilitation ministry and how it establishes a ritual life, it is first necessary to place Chicano gangs—their social organization, relations to law enforcement, and descent into substance abuse—into a socio-historical context.

Sociologist Martin Sánchez Jankowski's work examining social organization and Chicano gangs helps to illuminate their origins and motivations. Sánchez Jankowski's examination of thirty-seven gangs from three urban centers over a ten-year period from 1978 to 1988 suggests that gangs are not a result of social disorganization but are, in fact, organizations in their own right. Gangs "oriented around an intense competition for, and conflict over, the scarce resources that exist in these areas [inner cities]. These comprise and alternative social order."[38] Historically Chicano gangs in Los Angeles arose not primarily as economic organizations, as was often the case on the East Coast, but rather as part of an effort to resist Euro American prejudice. Sánchez Jankowski notes that Chicano gangs sought to maintain a separate culture and physical space in order to protect their neighborhoods.[39] In fact, Sánchez Jankowski's research found that Chicano gangs, more so than other gangs, emphasized identification with, and loyalty to, one's family and community; as a result, they generally were not interested in accumulating money as much as they were serving as a protective barrier for their families and community.[40] While Sánchez Jankowski's depiction may tend to portray gang members as romantic protectors of *la familia*, he cannot escape the fact that Chicano gangs had no prohibitions against certain drugs, especially heroin, as other gangs had, and therefore the use and sale of drugs became part of the staple of barrio gangs. Presumably the drug trade significantly damaged the idealized notion that Chicano gangs were more interested in protecting families than in selling drugs—if that were the case, one might also presume that Victory Outreach would not have had such a huge field in which to plant its churches. The fact is that drug use devastated families, and its trafficking created a market economy among gangs. It is within this realm that Victory Outreach carved its niche.

Historian Edward Escobar's depiction of the Los Angeles Police Department (LAPD) versus Zoot Suiters is of particular interest in continuing to paint Victory Outreach's historical landscape. The descendants of the *pachucos/as* became the youth gangs of the 1950s and, in some way, became the Victory Outreach members of today. The criminalization of Chicano youth began decades before the Zoot Suit era of the 1940s, but certainly the cultural and legal war against them exacerbated a preexisting problem. Congregating around a store or a neighbor's yard became a suspicious activity during the war years in Los Angeles. The arrests of Chicano youth had both social and personal consequences. Youth were arrested if they were in the vicinity of a crime and were usually charged with vagrancy or curfew violations. Chicano youth began compiling extensive arrest records that affected their employability and often strained their families' finances. The inflation of the arrest statistics for Chicano youth added to the already presumed fact that they were a criminal class and in need of police surveillance. According to Escobar, "the myth of Mexican American criminality became a self-fulfilling prophecy."[41] When many of these same youth began wearing what the larger society considered outlandish clothing, sporting distinctive hairstyles, speaking in their own language (Caló), and dripping with attitude, law enforcement redoubled their efforts to rid the streets of this emerging predatory class.[42]

Reacting to complaints from business owners and community leaders, the LAPD stepped up its presence, increasing surveillance, conducting more field interrogations, and making more arrests in Mexican American neighborhoods. By the time of the Zoot Suit riots in June 1943, local law enforcement had concluded their decades-long attempt to link race and criminality. Not only were Mexican American youth viewed as being biologically inclined toward criminal behavior, they were seen as violent predators against whom police needed to take harsh measures in order to control them.[43] Indeed, Escobar and sociologist Joan Moore concur that the aftermath of the Zoot Suit riots saw the rise of gang-related criminal activity, particularly youth gangs prevalent in the barrios, characterized by violence and the heavy use of hard drugs. The post–Zoot Suit era gave rise to gangs like White Fence in Boyle Heights and El Hoyo Maravilla in East Los Angeles. White Fence became known as being exceptionally violent in its bid for territorial control. Both gangs also began experimenting with heroin for the first time.[44]

Moore notes that by the late 1970s there were seventy thousand Chicano addicts in the Southwest.[45] The drug of choice was heroin but barbiturates were also common. The pill trade, especially barbiturates, appeared on the streets in the early 1950s. Barbiturate use became popular because it was used in tandem with alcohol at parties. Moore believes that heroin transcended local neighborhoods and generated its own special subculture.[46] The narratives of several Victory Outreach members provide testaments to Moore's notion of the power that heroin had on users and sellers. In the mid-1950s, the state of California increased prison terms for drug offenses. The sentence for serious drug crimes grew from five years to life. During the 1950s the first mass federal arrests took place in Maravilla; many of the men incarcerated in the mid-1950s began to leave federal prison in the 1960s. However, the growth of the trade meant more incarcerations in a new facility similar to the Lexington, Kentucky, and Ft. Worth, Texas, correctional facilities that catered to drug abusers, namely, the California Rehabilitation Center, which was established in 1963. Some prisoners founded self-help organizations that grafted themselves onto the burgeoning Chicano movement.[47]

The *pinto* movement sought to reform prisons through the work of a loose network of jailhouse lawyers that arose out of the Chicano movement of the 1960s. The first group, called EMPLEO, was formed in San Quentin in 1966. It successfully began bilingual education classes, and these classes grew rapidly until all but a handful of the Chicano prisoners in San Quentin joined.[48] San Quentin EMPLEO served as a bridge for newly released *pintos* to gain the support of the San Francisco Latino community in 1968. Another organization, LUCHA (League of United Citizens to Help Addicts) was founded in Los Angeles and was staffed by *pinto* volunteers. There is evidence that Victory Outreach was also a presence in the prisons at that time. Unfortunately anthropologist James Diego Vigil takes the story no further than to mention their existence. He does note, however, that "their work is clearly important as a religious counterpart of the *pinto* self-help movement."[49] There is anecdotal evidence that one other Pentecostal group worked with prisoners around the time of the *pinto* movement. The Oneness denomination, the Apostolic Assembly, was active in Northern California, according to historian and church member Daniel Ramírez, who remarks that his uncle began a ministry to prisoners in the 1960s and worked closely with the *pintos*.[50]

At least one of the *pinto* groups came to a notorious end after being tied to the prison gang known as the Mexican Mafia. LUCHA had little financial backing, and its financial struggles led to speculation that the members of the Mexican Mafia infiltrated certain social service agencies in the Latino community, including LUCHA. Ironically alleged Mafia infiltration has also surfaced with Victory Outreach, as former Mafia members began converting in the 1970s. According to Arguinzoni, the church came under surveillance during the early 1980s when the Los Angeles County Sheriff's Department began to track people's comings and goings at a rehabilitation home in the

San Gabriel Valley, investigating whether Mafia members used the facility as a safe house for drug sales.[51]

The once enthusiastic endorsement of Victory Outreach by state prison officials and several Los Angeles law enforcement agencies soured, when, more than six years ago, an original member of the Mexican Mafia, Ernest "Kilroy" Roybal, left the Mafia and joined the church. Only a handful of ex-Mafia members are in the church, but they continue to garner suspicion, as evidenced by the fact that Art Blajos, a church evangelist, cannot distribute his book, *Blood In, Blood Out*, in California prisons, and Tehachapi Prison refuses entry to evangelists with a criminal record. Nor is suspicion limited to law enforcement. The Mexican Mafia, having been abandoned by high-profile members, has added Bible reading to its list of capital offenses.[52] Thus Victory Outreach members, as is shown below in an examination of the churches' conferences, have been marked by a constructed notion of what defines a predatory class, and this so often has meant adolescent and young adults who are either Latino or black. This position in the social strata then creates an oppositional culture, echoing what Arguinzoni uttered at his mother's church when he said, "they don't care." Thus even religious conversion cannot blot out the social stain of criminality, and so only those marked with that stain can minister to church members' needs. Only when this key principle is understood can the hierarchical and autocratic nature of the church become understandable to outsiders, and we can proceed to examine the inner workings of the lives of church members.

Victory Outreach began to expand from its core group of converts by the second year of its existence. In 1969 Roberto Almaraz asked to be released from Arguinzoni's ministry to become a missionary in Mexico. Almaraz worked, until the mid-1970s, with an evangelical church not affiliated with Victory Outreach. His brother, Cal, succeeded the first pastor of Victory Outreach's first church plant in Pico Rivera, California, and also founded the San Bernardino church and rehabilitation home in the mid-1970s.[53]

Arguinzoni's Aliso Village apartment was the first rehabilitation center. One of the more prominent graduates of the home was a recovering heroin addict, Philip LaCrue. At his mother's urging, LaCrue began to attend the church in Boyle Heights and lived at the rehab home. At the time the director of the rehab home was Arguinzoni's father-in-law, Abel Rivera. LaCrue came under the tutelage of Arguinzoni and fellow rehab resident Cal Almaraz; as a result, LaCrue became the church's first evangelist.[54]

During these formative years and up to today, the dominant personality is Arguinzoni. Eliciting remarkable loyalty, but little financial support, Arguinzoni's ministry survived on the sacrifices he and his family made and because of the work of this small group of converts. Julie Arguinzoni offers another perspective of the difficulty getting by during those early years. Julie, once an aspiring missionary to Mexico, married Arguinzoni when they both attended LABI. Eliciting the same loyalty as her husband did, she has proven an inspiring and emotional speaker at many women's conferences: "All my youth . . . went into establishing this ministry. It hasn't been easy."[55] In describing her fourteen years living with drug addicts and prostitutes, she tells her captive audience that she feels uncomfortable at events when she is not seated beside an addict or prostitute. She calls them her people. Despite the lack of material resources, the Arguinzoni's persevered: "I had nothing . . . secondhand clothes for the kids . . . no stove, just a hot plate for five kids."[56] Julie represents more than simply a role model to the women who have found shelter at the churches. Women in the church believe that Julie has a prophetic role to play as "Sister Julie," a subject I shall return to later when examining the individual stories of church members.

To return to the history of the church, the need for organization arose as the church continued to grow during the 1970s. During these years increased drug use and addiction assured ministries like Victory Outreach of a continued role in the inner cities. The drug problems in the barrios of southern California escalated. According to Joan Moore, the market appeared to be drying up but drug problems, especially heroin addiction, which haunted many Vietnam veterans, was making a strong comeback, particularly in depressed racial/ethnic communities.[57]

One of these heroin-addicted Vietnam veterans was Ed Morales, who, through Victory Outreach, overcame his addiction and eventually became a church elder.[58] Morales decided that Victory Outreach's rehab homes represented a better alternative to methadone clinics. Victory Outreach churches never open in an area without including a rehabilitation system—either in a separate home or in the home of the pastor. As the church grew from its Boyle Heights location to Pico Rivera and beyond, organizing different ministries became crucial.

In the mid-1970s the church began services at an auditorium at Montebello High School. This move served several purposes: larger quarters, space for dramas, and greater visibility of the church. Within a few years the church outgrew the high school auditorium and moved to a local banquet hall, where, according to Philip LaCrue, dramas were held regularly and the church experienced a major growth, going from a few dozen members to a few hundred. LaCrue says that Arguinzoni's appearances on the Trinity Broadcasting Network provided the church with visibility in the late 1970s and that these appearances helped the church to grow.[59] Today Arguinzoni's relationship with Trinity is limited to a business relationship, in which he owns a Trinity subsidiary called the "All-American" television network.[60] Arguinzoni rarely appears on Trinity's flagship program, "Praise the Lord," but because of the visibility the church received from the program, it was able to branch out, planting churches in northern and southern California. Today Victory Outreach has churches located around the world and has recently celebrated its thirty-fifth-year anniversary. Its growth to more than 250 churches is testimony to the need in the Latino community for affordable drug rehabilitation, alternatives to prison, and the confluence of these practical needs with what church members vow is the transcendent power of Pentecostal spirituality.

Building a history from the spiritual life stories of church members, securing an almost mythological place for its founder and his family, and sacralizing the notion of loyalty—all these aspects help to construct the history of the church. The fact that everyone who desires to minister in church must take a course on the history and vision of the church, where the story of the Arguinzonis' conversion, taught by means of videotape, strengthens the idea that the church's history is indelibly linked to the life of the founder and his vision for the church. Thus orthodoxy in the church must correspond not only to evangelical Christianity but also to loyalty to the Arguinzoni family and their spiritual life story.

Negotiating life through the dichotomous prism that Pentecostalism offers is made easier by defining parameters: What is good/evil, godly/ungodly, and acceptable/unacceptable behavior? Often these parameters are defined and redefined by the church members themselves. One rehab resident, John (a pseudonym), offers some insight into why the spiritual support he receives from the church is crucial to his recovery.

John says that he cannot leave the rehab home, he cannot leave the church, because the "enemy" is always ready to take his life. John fears backsliding into drugs, alcohol, and a life of crime. He feels he can function only through the structured environment of the rehab home. What John has recreated is a religious identity wedded to a larger narrative of this particular ministry—that this ministry, its homes, and its leadership are essential to keeping one's sobriety and possibly is one's salvation.

What I chronicled in my fieldwork and interviews with Victory Outreach fits into a category that folklorist Elaine Lawless found in her work with Oneness Pentecostal women in the Midwest. Lawless notes: "Spiritual life stories enable us to assume that these very specific life stories . . . are, in fact, not perfected entities, but rather each is a collection, a pastiche of stories; many of them based on both personal experience and traditional expectations at the same time."[61] Essential to understanding spiritual life stories is that they are compilations—testimonials that convey the sincerity of personal conversion experience and are often replete with supernatural events. Because orality plays such a critical role in Pentecostalism—as history and as worship—orality is the chief source by which the faith is transmitted. Lawless comments on testimony and describes its crucial nature:

> Pentecostals tell and re-tell their personal encounter stories, constantly reaffirming that a spiritual encounter did, in fact, take place. Within the context of the Pentecostal religion, the group members in the religious service create . . . in a very collective, perhaps even communal way, an appropriate story of a spiritual encounter, molding and recreating the story, telling and re-telling in only cautiously by adding or subtracting elements, until not only is an "appropriate" conversion story created for all to draw upon for their own personal "testimony" but a story that, in fact, actually prescribes the conversion experience of future initiates.[62]

Analyzing Lawless's work and adding the work of oral historian Roxanne Rimstead, I wish to describe what I believe these narratives are and how mediating their transmission to text, ordering their reception, and being a participant/observer in many of the rituals served to build what Rimstead calls a "social coalition." In the time they spent with me, these narrators divulged mediated performances of spiritual life stories, which, in a sense, I have collected and transmitted to a larger audience. Rimstead describes the process: "They speak through mediated forms that restage an original performance during which a writer/listener recorded, transcribed, prompted, collected, edited, ordered, or maybe even inspirited the utterances of 'ordinary people.' "[63] These "ordinary" people have begun to build on their private sacred memories and, through the process of oral tradition, testimonial writing, and a pseudo-hagiographic approach to their church's founding, have brought their history into the realm of public memory that all church members can share. It is to their stories we now turn.

No two stories carry as much spiritual power in the church as that of the founders. Julie Arguinzoni's story is emblematic of how Victory Outreach has created its own sacred history. As mentioned above, women in the church believe that Julie has a prophetic role to play as "Sister Julie." She is a mother figure, someone who represents sacrifice. "There is no one else who has influenced my life like Sister Julie."[64] At Sunday services, when the Arguinzoni's attend, crowds surround Julie and women call her "Mom." Stronger sentiments emanate from other women, like Jeanne Alanis, wife of church elder Rick Alanis. She believes that "God has called Sister Julie to be a mother of all nations."[65] Julie earns respect because of her story of sacrifice for the ministry. Her narrative of suffering makes it easier for other women to speak of similar hardships and to call on women in the church to make similar sacrifices for the church. Testimonies intend to garner sacrifices for the ministry and to retain loyalty to the church hierarchy. In addition to the Arguinzonis reiterating these narratives of suffering at conventions, rehab residents and Bible school students alike either meet the Arguinzonis personally or get to know them through taped videos of their stories.

Church members equating Julie with a suffering mother of nations recalls the strikingly similar notion of the Virgin Mary in Catholicism. Although church members never make that association, it is an interesting one to consider. Theologian Jeannette Rodriguez has identified five characteristics represented in the Mexican manifestation of Mary, La Virgen de Guadalupe. La Virgen manifests God as a mother who consoles, nurtures, and comforts. She also represents divine power and recreative energy to overcome spiritual deadness.[66] Elevating Julie to such heights is not what church members intend when they describe her, yet she seems to embody some of these traits. Church members consider Julie to be a mother to all nations because she heads the church's mission effort overseas, and, since her days at LABI, she has wanted to be a missionary. Church members speak often about how Julie has talked to them in the rehab homes, visited them in jail, and sacrificed her life for the ministry. By serving as the archetypal servant, Julie teaches other women how to be loyal church members, thereby ensuring more disciples through personal ministry and at conference appearances.

Arguinzoni begins her speech by exhorting the women to be loyal and faithful to the "things you've been taught." Disloyalty to the ministry represents the work of the "enemy." There must be loyalty to the leadership and the pastors of the church. "Remember when you came in you didn't know how to pray . . . you didn't know the word of God. You didn't know anything. You couldn't even walk. Some of you had never worn high heels in your life . . . didn't even know how to dress."[67] Members, like rehab director Miriam (a pseudonym), corroborates such statements. Miriam remarks that when she arrived at rehab in the early 1990s, she dressed like a man, wore boxers, and never acted feminine in her life. Sister Julie helped her to become more "like a lady."[68] In reinforcing traditional gender roles, evangelical women, according to Griffith, "creatively balance compliance with strength as they transform themselves into ideal Christian women. At the same time, submission works as a valuable tool for containing husbands and thereby regulating the home, and may subtly be modified or subverted, so that women retain a kind of mediated agency through their reliance on the omnipotent God."[69] Among many of the church leaders, securing loyalty to the ministry appears to be more important than regulating the home.

At a women's retreat in 1996 Mary Ann Lavayen uttered similar refrains about loyalty and sacrifice. She had harsh words for women who were unwilling to sacrifice all for the ministry. Women who "can't put their kids through that" come in for a particularly difficult critique. She describes her life as a pioneering pastor's wife. Only nineteen years old, Lavayen moved with her husband to Detroit to found a church. Pregnant, she moved into an apartment with twelve men in rehab, and, once the baby arrived, she found herself without adequate supplies for her newborn. Humiliation, however, was tempered by gifts of clothing, diapers, and other items. She exhorts the audience: "He didn't save you so you can sit there and you can look pretty."[70] The purpose of this exhortation is to imbue the audience with the same sense of urgency to the ministry because of a shared sense that Victory Outreach is a prophetic ministry. "This vision thing is happening, I know we got the goods. . . . God has given us the anointing . . . start doing the work for God, for our pastor Sonny."[71]

The vision women speak of is a prophecy Arguinzoni had called "Vision 2000"—helping the church to grow from its 240-plus churches to 1,000 by the year 2000. The vision drove almost every aspect of the church. The number of churches currently is between 250 and 300 churches. The mild success at planting roughly two dozen churches is viewed as a crucial win against the "enemy." Faith Martínez, wife of church pioneer David, captures this sense of urgency: "Go and sell all your furniture, start unloading the house, everybody goes out with nothing. . . . Vision 2000 is a mighty plan of God . . . not the Assemblies of God, not the Methodist church, not the Presbyterians . . . this vision is God's vision."[72] One reason for separating Victory Outreach from these other denominations is to pinpoint the idea that Victory Outreach has a special call placed on it, one that no other Protestant denomination can lay claim to, namely, that Victory Outreach must build more churches and send out more pastors to pioneer these churches. Not to accomplish this goal means relinquishing Arguinzoni's vision to the "enemy." The success of Victory Outreach depends on the financial stability of the new churches, and the proper training of enough pastors to staff its homes, missions, and churches. To build up this leadership, Victory Outreach needs to inculcate this message to its entire organizational structure.

Loyalty and authority remain essential to understanding how religious identity operates within the confines of the church. What appears to occur at

Victory Outreach is the re-establishing of a ritual life that sacralizes lives in disorder. More than providing order and belief, the organization and leadership of Victory Outreach ritualizes people so as to reintegrate them back into mainstream society.

Gerlach's study of Pentecostal organizations can be applied to Victory Outreach: The church is reticulate in nature; it is a network of cell groups tied into loose and informal networks—home groups and Bible studies. This type of organization provides effective communication and logistical financial support. Ideologically the group provides vision and overarching themes of a future presented in symbolic, easily communicated terms. Arguinzoni is the provider and keeper of this vision but also believes that this vision can change.[73] Curiously the vision, narrowly defined as a mission to reach inner cities, can change, but it must cross those boundaries set by Arguinzoni to keep the church committed to inner-city ministry. As Arguinzoni explains:

> Sometimes we have people who never catch the vision—or else show up with a different vision. You know, we really do not encourage people to transfer their membership to our churches. . . . They probably need to stay in their churches and let the Lord use them there. . . . When church people show up at Victory Outreach all excited about what they have heard (about Victory Outreach), we generally counsel them to go back to their home church. . . . They may want you to change your philosophy of ministry to fit their ideas. Well we can't do that."[74]

Arguinzoni's vision and his organizational models guide church leadership. He calls himself a shepherd. "The shepherd has a God-given authority and an obligation to lead the people and instruct them in the things of the Lord. The Kingdom of God is not a democracy."[75] As egalitarian as Pentecostal worship is in inviting all to partake of the spiritual gifts, the structure of Victory Outreach polity does not necessarily follow that example. There are many specific reasons for the authoritarian organization of Victory Outreach. First, the belief within the leadership mandates that strict discipleship of new converts who enter the rehab homes is essential, because they will not respond to unfocused, undisciplined programs. Second, a hierarchy based on loyalty protects the vision of the church. "individual vision must always be submitted to the leadership of your church. Whatever vision you have, it had better be in harmony with the vision God has given your leaders. If it is not in accordance with the vision of the pastor, and the vision of the church, it is not a God-sent vision."[76] Third, the church is organized on two levels: churches and rehab/reentry homes. Within these two organizations exist a myriad of ministries aimed at specific marginalized groups: rehab homes for addicts trying to rid themselves of life-controlling habits, and the "love circle," an informal network the church has with law enforcement to refer parolees or potential parolees to the rehab homes, as well as a host of other programs to be discussed later.

Gerlach believes that Pentecostal ideology sets up an oppositional idea that makes a participant unite against an opposition—for example, a dissenting church member must oppose temptations from the "enemy." Gerlach notes that opposition offers a basis for a commitment process and a force against which to unite. In effect, converts have gone through the physical process of conversion by attending Bible studies and church, and, by partaking in ministerial roles, they have become imbued with the single-minded notion of their mission.[77]

Pentecostalism offers a spiritual template on which to ease life's physical ills. Its emphasis on healing provides access to those without means to traditional health care. Physical healing within Victory Outreach not only means the healing of chronic illnesses, diseases, drug addiction, and other ailments, but there are dozens of reports of spiritual "deliverance" from behaviors that the church views as "ungodly," such as drug use, drinking, and illicit sexual behavior.

Health in the context of broader social goals does not appear to be one of Victory Outreach's prescriptions for spiritual health. The inability to meet basic human needs emanates not from a foundation of political or social disempowerment, but from a personal failure on the part of the addict or from the "enemy's" constant interference in one's life through gangs, abuse, and families. Victory Outreach's Pentecostalism empowers believers to heal their social lives and relationships as well as provide a method of recapturing lost familial relationships. The first building block the church uses to recapture family and to reintegrate people into church life and society are the rehab homes.

The rehabilitation home serves as an entry-level initiation to the church and to a grass-roots Pentecostalism that is used to proclaim a fervent Christian message to troubled people. The homes are usually located in inner-city neighborhoods and, depending on the stage of the church's development, either serve as a rehabilitation/church/parsonage or a rehabilitation/church or strictly as a rehab/reentry home. The difference between a rehab and a reentry home is that reentry represents an advanced stage of recovery where the person is able to work and make further progress in order to reenter society. In the United States there are between 250 and 265 rehabilitation homes, either attached or separate from their churches, and 25 reentry homes.[78] All are operated by the church, use no medication to treat addiction, and rely on prayer and an intensive regimen of chores, activities, and

Bible studies intended to rid addicts of their addictions and to convert and nurture them.

In writing about how to plant a church, Arguinzoni, in *Internalize the Vision*, rages against the obstacles the "world" has placed in the way of the church's efforts toward planting more homes and churches. According to Arguinzoni, churches have fled the inner cities for the calmer, more financially secure suburbs.[79] The difficulties of establishing inner-city ministries are compounded by problems the homes have when city officials, neighbors, and others do not take kindly to having a Victory Outreach home in their neighborhood.

Arguinzoni related several examples of opposition to the churches and homes of Victory Outreach. Church supporters like Nicky Cruz view such opposition as more than citizen complaints and bureaucratic red tape. In keeping with the spiritual focus of the ministry, Cruz believes that such incidents are attacks from the "enemy."[80] Opposition unites believers because, as converts, they know that the "enemy" follows them; it follows, therefore, that when opposition occurs in any form, legitimate or not, it is viewed as a supernatural attack.

> Once established, the rehab home is organized similarly regardless of its relationships to the home church. The supervising pastor relies on the home director to run the daily activities of the home; often the director will empower a reliable resident to be the assistant. How one becomes an assistant or a director remains a highly subjective decision based on the guiding philosophy of the founder: Don't make the same mistake I almost made.
>
> Don't wait for the right one who is already polished or who has already been trained. If you do, you will bypass the ones that Jesus has selected—because you are put off by their raw character and style. They may look raw. Their style may seem a bit rough. So we may pass them by and don't take notice that God has laid His hand on their lives.[81]

The educational levels of the directors does not matter—in keeping with the philosophy of the church, they seek to find "treasures out of darkness." The home director, like any staff at the home, is a volunteer. Titles are given to engender a sense of pride among the residents. The only compensation the director and residents receive are free board and meals. In smaller congregations, pastors live at the home and sometimes serve as directors.

Once someone has decided to enter the home, their time needs to be occupied. Cruz gives a brief rundown of what occurs on entrance to a home;

with little difference, all my informants describe similar experiences in the rehab home.

> All illegal drugs and alcohol are taken away. The staff retains any mon-
> ey and their drivers' licenses for a month. For the first couple of weeks,
> all contact with the outside is handled through the program director's
> office. . . . The first three months concentrate on spiritual and physical
> healing. No medications are used. . . . They are taught responsibility,
> discipline and submission to authority. Then, as a participant progress-
> es into society, graduating rehab residents are expected to get and keep
> jobs. Often graduates are hearing a call from the Lord [to go] into full-
> time ministry.[82]

The rehab program usually lasts from between nine months to one year.
Within the home organization, residents receive counseling, prayer, and
moral support. Residents make an implicit contract with the church that they
will participate in the activities of the home as part of their rehabilitation: raising money, attending church functions, and engaging in street evangelism.

The structure of the church rehab home serves a crucial role in preparing
certain select residents to enter the ministry. At least one veteran minister believes that, although it is not specifically part of the overall program, Victory
Outreach provides a unique ladder of opportunity to enable someone to come
out of the prison system, through the home, and "see the world. . . . Victory
Outreach lets you do more than type the church bulletin."[83] Moving up the
ladder is the way many potential pastors (95 percent, according to church
leaders), attain pastor status. Despite the attempts by the church to shed its
image as a Chicano church, the pastorships and locations contradict the
church's own claims that they are no longer a "Chicano" church.[84] Of the 165
U.S. churches, between 18 and 23 have non-Latino pastors. As many as 115
churches are located in the Southwest, with 93 in California alone.

In the United States, Victory Outreach has both Spanish-speaking and
English-speaking churches. Twenty-six churches are Spanish-speaking, all led
by Latinos; of these 26 churches, 23 are in the Southwest, and, of those, 18 are
in southern California. The church is present in eighteen different countries.
Fifty-seven churches are in Latin America, all led by Spanish and Portuguese
surnamed pastors. When examining the homes, few differences arise. Latinos
dominate both pastoral and home leadership positions.[85]

These numbers support my contention that despite the church's desire to
shed its image as a Latino-dominated church, the leadership is overwhelmingly Latino, and, furthermore, the churches are located in traditional Latino

strongholds: the largest number of churches are in California (93) and the Southwest (22). Close to 80 percent of the rehab homes are also in the Southwest. Focusing on Victory Outreach churches and homes might help make sense out of the numbers and add to the overall theme that Victory Outreach serves as a self-perpetuating center of social mobility for marginalized peoples, namely, Latinos who believe that this church offers them opportunities they would not have outside the church. Examining the internal organization of the churches did little to change my conclusion that Latinos dominate the church, especially Mexican Americans from Southern California. The next section focuses not so much on the demographic dominance but rather on the dominance of a certain social class which comprises much of the church leadership.

I surveyed fifty of the ninety-three English/Spanish churches in California, including mega churches, represented by the La Puente church (3,000 members), as well as small church plants in desert communities in southern California (30 members). Factoring in the La Puente church, the average church has 233 members, and if La Puente is excluded, the figure falls to 172. My survey places total church membership at approximately 11,000, although one senior pastor offers a larger estimate of 40,000 to 45,000.[86]

Pastors have been in the church for an average of fourteen years. David Martínez of the San Fernando church has served with the church since its Teen Challenge years, pastoring for more than thirty years. Most have been pastors for six years; several have pastored for more than twenty years. An average of nine years is required to become a pastor. The East Los Angeles and Pico Rivera churches are the oldest, founded more than thirty-five and thirty years ago, respectively.

Incorporating data from smaller surveys done on select churches in other states results in the following delineation of how a Victory Outreach convert becomes a pastor. Of the fifty pastors surveyed, thirty-three came to the ministry through rehab. Twenty-nine went on to direct rehab homes. The others held various positions within the church, usually as helpers or youth leaders. Fourteen of the pastors are Victory Outreach converts who have chosen to work in church ministry. Two are the second-generation children of preachers. Nine were "saved" at the church when they began attending. Ways in which they worked their way up the ladder included becoming a Bible study leader, a youth minister, an outreach evangelist—only one pastor transferred his membership from another church to make his original church a part of Victory Outreach.

Jerry (a pseudonym), a public relations figure at the church, provided the following cursory figures. He estimates that 20–25 percent of rehab referrals are court referrals and that the remaining 75 percent are church referrals. According to his internal study, a rehab home requires an outlay of $10,000 per month. In contrast, reentry homes are usually self-sustaining because residents hold jobs. Of first-year residents who required a full-term stay of six months to one year to complete the program, internal studies suggest that 35 percent completed the program successfully. Jerry characterized this figure as a completion rate because the church claims that a much larger percentage go through the program in less than a year successfully. However, Jerry provided only anecdotal evidence for that claim. He speculated that 20 percent of rehab residents are on public assistance of some kind. The rest of the money to operate the home is raised through car washes, handiwork, yard work, warehouse work, and donations from supporting churches.[87]

Cruz Arguinzoni places the figures for success at a much higher level. "Out of every 100 men who come to our rehab homes, a third or more stay and graduate. Of those who do, about 95% make it."[88] Quoting an unnamed administrative director, Cruz gives these figures: "Of the 73% who complete the program nationwide, 43% of the residents remain drug-free."[89] The inconsistency in how many rehab residents stay and complete the program has many roots; the most obvious is that the informal nature of the ministry does not lend itself to accurate recordkeeping. Using these figures as a composite, it appears that thirty-three out of one hundred people who enter rehab stay in the program, and, of these, from eleven to thirteen people remain drug-free. More shall be said later regarding those who complete the program.

Once the resident decides to stay, the process begins. For it is in the home where the Pentecostal ritual life is grafted onto drug rehabilitation and where the people, who were previously Catholic, nominally Catholic, mainline Protestant, or secular, become Pentecostal. During the first crucial two weeks in a rehab house, residents are searched for drugs and are restricted from using the telephone and accepting visitors. Concurrently the reparative work of the ritual life is slowly put into motion. The first two weeks, according to Miriam, can be brutal. As a woman enters the home, the staff prays over her as she undergoes the difficult process of withdrawal. Encouraged to pray, she is introduced to the Pentecostal practice of the laying on of hands. Sometimes, Miriam says, a person is "kicking" heroin or alcohol, cold turkey. During this time she is permitted no contact with outsiders so that she cannot attempt to contact drug dealers, gang friends, or family who may try to get her out of the home.[90] While she remains at the home, she must abide by the strict house rules: no television, no working outside the home, three to five hours of prayer/Bible study daily, required attendance at church functions, and a daily set of chores. Disruptive behavior leads to probation, and severely disruptive behavior leads to the person being expelled.[91]

Strong discipline remains vital. As Arguinzoni explains: "That sort of discipleship is appropriate in the rehab home. There, we exert a strong hand. Strong discipleship is important because the men and women there need it. They come in with life-controlling problems, under the bondage of Satan. You can't let them do whatever they want. They don't have any self-control. You've got to put rules in place."[92]

Rules may be said to be the beginnings of ritualizing and organizing the life of the convert, though it should be noted that many leave during this crucial first two-week period. Out of ten, seven may leave, for a whole host of factors, but usually because of their unwillingness to acquiesce to the program's regimen of prayer, study, and chores.[93]

Next, she joins with others in the home to engage in street evangelism and begins testifying at church meetings. It is assumed, and is probably a certainty, that by this time she has converted. The first two weeks also introduces her to the idea that Pentecostal spirituality has the powerful effect of changing lives and should be a faith she would be comfortable with and comfortable sharing back in her neighborhood with her homeboys, homegirls, and family. The new converts continue to pray with fellow residents, commence Bible studies, and are introduced to Pentecostalism through the laying on of hands, healing, and praying for deliverance, and, occasionally, residents receive Spirit baptism.[94] Sometimes the introduction to Pentecostal spirituality is experiential (the person receives spiritual gifts). At other times, residents pray with the hope that they may receive these experiences or can facilitate them to others via prayer.

With the initial stage complete, the teachings may change to include working on the person's character. The values these teachings aim to imbue include self-respect, dignity, and holiness, as well as committing to the vision of the church. The second stage, the preparatory stage, prepares residents to enter the life of the church—as members, lay leaders, and pastors. For those who need further assistance, the reentry program is in place. Before examining the reentry program, certain characteristics of the first two stages of the rehab home bear close inspection under the guise of the creation of a ritual life. For this, we turn to Sherry's (a pseudonym) narrative and the indispensable work of Pentecostal theologian Dan Albrecht.

Sherry came to the rehab home after years of drug abuse, spousal abuse, satanic worship, and several stints in juvenile and adult institutions. She reports having no religious background except nominal Catholicism. She says that she learned about Satan through her grandmother, who taught her how to read Tarot cards. She also used Ouija boards and prayed against her abusive husband. "[I] began . . . worshiping Satan and it seemed like things started getting better. And I would literally pray against my ex-husband. I would sit down and draw the star and with the chants."[95] Despite her attempts to rid herself of her problems, her husband continued to beat her and she continued to descend into drugs, prostitution, and eventually prison.

Sherry benefited from Victory Outreach's cooperative agreements with the court system that allows convicts to serve sentences for minor drug offenses at rehab homes. Before being ordered by the court to attend Victory Outreach's rehabilitation home, Sherry observed a few church meetings, not intent on staying; in fact, she attended several church meetings high on drugs. After the court order, she was arrested again and served an additional year and a half, returning back home only to begin to lose her sanity: "Everything was getting really, really bad, I mean, after awhile I didn't know what was real anymore. . . . I slept days at a time."[96] She began to attend church meetings again but said nothing, and she did not join in worship. One time she became frightened when the congregation began speaking in tongues, and she ran out of the church. Throughout these meetings, people told Sherry that they were praying for her. Sherry was aware of the loyalty and devotion the church members displayed and noticed that they appeared quite comfortable in church. Impressed by their sincerity, Sherry noted that, despite their lack of material goods, they contributed to the offering.

A turning point came when her husband beat her again, and she began to have a nervous breakdown. She drove away from her house, hoping to drive recklessly enough to be taken to jail. She drove to church and met a woman who prayed for her and tried to lay hands on her, but Sherry resisted and returned home. After several other episodes of violence and drug overdoses, Sherry says that she had a personal experience that convinced her to seek spiritual help. She said that she was saved from the grip of a supernatural attack in her house, where an entity came toward her; as she stood underneath a picture of Jesus, the entity left the house. A Victory Outreach pastor helped Sherry make the decision to enter the home shortly thereafter. She calls the home a "sanctuary" from the vicious beatings she received from her husband. However, Sherry was not ready for the discipline of the home. "God deals with your character," she said. "I didn't like black people because I got brutally hurt by a couple of black people one time." Sherry did not want to live with African Americans. She was afraid to face her own prejudice. "I had to let go of a lot of things, you know. I had to make changes in my life I didn't know how to do . . . going into a Victory Outreach home is hard, it's very, very hard because of the way God deals with you and brings you to the point where you totally surrender all things unto Him and you believe."

Sherry reorganized her life in various ways. Her life had consisted of searching for drugs, hiding from her husband, and engaging in occult practices for solace to her mounting difficulties. The home's regimented schedule all served to ritualize time. From an existence with little regard to structure, Sherry was placed in a system that sacralized certain times of the day to be set aside for prayer and worship.

The specter of a church member arriving intoxicated and leaving the service to inject more drugs in the bathroom seems sufficient to have most people banished from church, but because Victory Outreach specializes in what sociologist Tex Sample calls "hard-living" people, church members embraced Sherry. Sample continues: "To know one's life is out of control . . . to find life so rut-filled and violence-prone that one cannot stay put even when one has no place to go: These are the things of which hard-living is made."[97] Pentecostal worship fulfills certain needs: its orality, music, intercessory prayer, testimony, informality, and relaxing of class signifiers such as dress and occupation. There is an invitation in Pentecostal churches to imbibe in the ritual life of Christianity available to the marginalized and the outsider that many do not find in mainstream Protestant churches. That is Pentecostalism's transcendent value: an offering of a ritual life to groups who do not feel welcome in other surroundings.

Prayer to a benevolent deity rather than a deity Sherry described as "evil" served as a crucial restoration of ritual in Sherry's life. Instead of praying to Satan for protection, Sherry witnessed people praying for one another and with her. She came to the realization that Satan could not solve her problems but that he was responsible for her troubles. Albrecht states it well: "[The] priesthood of all believers [is] more practical in Pentecostal/charismatic spirituality. . . . Believers, not clergy only, are expected to be involved in healing rites."[98] Sherry explains that she was surprised to see people pray for her, a sign of concern and caring she had rarely seen in her life.

Because of her unfamiliarity with the Pentecostal practice of speaking in tongues, Sherry ran out of the service as the practice frightened her. Such rites of passage, according to Albrecht, require exposure in a ritualized setting (worship) before they are accepted. Albrecht also notes that Spirit baptism represents a crucial rite of passage in Pentecostal churches, second only to conversion.[99] Sherry needed further exposure to worship, prayer, and finally the sanctuary of the rehab home before she could negotiate the passage from liminality to the communitas of the home. To some extent, home residents like Sherry are still neophytes. Wellness, conversion, baptism, Spirit baptism, and evangelism are all steps that residents are reintroduced to on their way to the communitas of the church, where the motto, "treasures out of darkness," are crystallized, where ex-gang members, former drug addicts, former prostitutes, and ex-convicts worship side by side with the rest of the community and join in the larger world of evangelical Christianity.[100]

To grasp what this state of mind means, one needs to see it from the viewpoint of stepping from a liminal state to a communitas state as described by Victor Turner. Keeping rules, regulations, worship, and fasting are all physical acts. Before physical acts can be sacralized, one's inner life needs to be reoriented toward a sacred sense because that is what constitutes true conversion. Sherry needed to undergo a series of actions that separated her from her past.

Entering the home was a crucial step, having people pray for her was another—but her acknowledgment of her prejudicial feelings toward African Americans, among other inner conflicts, represent transformative events that Pentecostals use to divide people's lives into pre- and postconversion periods. "Conversion radically reshapes life; one is truly a Christian when one is saved. One truly walks with the Lord when one surrenders their life and becomes so vulnerable that they can be touched in an almost supernatural way by God."[101] Before God "dealt" with Sherry, she remained on the outside. Before speaking in tongues, Sherry lived across the social boundaries of the larger society, but when she awoke one day and reported speaking in a language she did not understand, the women of the rehab home laughed and rejoiced with her that she had "gotten the Spirit." Surrounded by like-minded women, praying with similar resolve, and experiencing Spirit baptism, Sherry crossed those boundaries. "You know what, I don't wanna buck heads no more, I surrender, and at that point that's when God started giving me the peace, giving me the joy . . . I'd wake up in the middle of the night speaking in tongues . . . that's when God started really making himself real in my life." The order of events is important because not only does it demonstrate Sherry's acceptance of the practice of Spirit baptism, a crucial step in becoming what Albrecht describes as becoming a Pentecostal ritualist, but it also reinforces orthodoxy and builds on the emergence of a Pentecostal identity. Again, Albrecht notes: "The Pentecostal practices, the enactment of the rites, specifically, helps to raise the sense of community, a community that believes that its community is as indelible with the Spirit as it is with the sisters and brothers."[102] The home, its structure of time, its insistence on prayer and fasting for character development, becomes the community at one with the Spirit, and these individuals carry that sense of loyalty to their neighborhoods, families, and churches.

Sherry experienced other manifestations that contributed to her growing religious identity and helped her in a practical way. Sherry reports being illiterate on her entrance to the home. She felt ashamed and embarrassed to admit her illiteracy to the other women because she could not participate in

Bible study. Until one day: "Finally, one day I [sic] opening up, the words just came out and they [the women] started teaching me and dealing with me and praying with me that God would restore my mind. . . and sure enough . . . I could remember, I could recite." She credits God with giving her sufficient mental acumen to perform rites critical to integrating herself into society. The restoration of her learning abilities not only made her participation in Bible study possible, but she believes it made her future life working for the church possible. After more than a year and a half in rehab and reentry, Sherry found work for the first time in her life and continues to hold that job. In addition, she sings in the choir and is involved with several church ministries, including the music, gang, and prison ministries.

Pentecostals often reenter the world after worship "accompanied by their altered understanding of reality and with the experience of the ritual in order to affect their world. A kind of 'spillover,' a transcending of the ritual space must take place."[103] What makes Victory Outreach unique is its singular vision to take a newly ritualized life back to the neighborhoods, prisons, and gangs; to take part in church building and reaffirming what Latino Pentecostal theologians like Villafañe say is a social ethic built on recognition of ethnic identity, and social location, rather than subsuming such factors to an amorphous American evangelical identity.

To use the theory of Portes and Rumbaut of segmented assimilation with regard to what occurs at Victory Outreach, one needs to incorporate the role of the church into the social capital equation. One main factor that Portes and Rumbaut suggest is responsible for dissonant assimilation is that there are no alternative answers for the inner-city subcultures that pervade many Latino neighborhoods. Coupled with racial discrimination and a limited labor market, the signs point to downward assimilation. Factors that change this outcome are family support, resources, guidance, aspiration, and an alternative to inner-city subcultures. Victory Outreach fills these various vacuums by becoming family and another inner-city subculture. The church provides guidance by invigorating an often moribund religious spirit; it offers support by providing a community of like-minded believers; and, finally, it provides resources for residents who need a place to stay, and becomes a source of employment for those seeking to minister or staff the various churches. Victory Outreach, as an inner-city church, provides the perfect counter to inner-city subcultures such as drugs, gangs, underemployment, and disintegrating families. When these factors are plugged in, acculturation results in upward assimilation.[104] Church members themselves must become participants in their own religious rehabilitation by engaging the ritual life of Pentecostalism.

Victory Outreach members accomplish this ritualized life in much the same way as most Pentecostals do, with a few exceptions. On graduating from the rehab home, residents may leave and continue their lives outside the church, but a significant portion of graduates choose to stay and become active participants in church ministries. Rather than reentering life outside the church, converts like Sherry continue the ritualized life as church employers. They choose to counteract the ills of society by building up the ministry rather than working in society. In effect, they choose not to join the mainstream because they believe it to be hopelessly corrupt. Joe (a pseudonym) represents one Victory Outreach member on a mission.

A maintenance man at a local business, Joe has held that job for more than a year. He was converted by another ministry more than eight years ago, but, as Joe describes it: "I started going to an Assemblies of God church, but, it was like . . . it was an all-white church with . . . elderly . . . I was going for like around eight months, but I wasn't able to stay, I ended up falling away. . . . [I got] back involved in the same stuff."[105] His drug use and other illegal activity sent him back to jail for a year. During that stay, he heard about a noted gang leader who had been converted through the ministry of Victory Outreach.

Because Victory Outreach is largely comprised of recovering addicts, former gang members, and others like Joe, himself a former gang member and recovering addict, Joe had found a church that reflected his life experience and provided him with the community of the home. Thus Joe was able to transfer his Pentecostal faith and identity over to a church that fortified his ethnic identity and life experience.

Joe needed a support system within a community of believers. Reentry homes facilitate the need for community and character development, and they prepare people like Joe for a life in church ministry. Inculcating value into work, ethical living, and traditional family structures occurs with consistent exposure to Bible studies and discipleship led by home directors and overseers. By accepting these values and acting on them as the "proper" way to live, Joe became convinced that conversion equaled social mobility and resulted in inward and outward healing. "Man, once Christ came into my life, I am able to hold a job. . . . I came in, you know, stuttering and now God's doing that, healing . . . I have hope now, I have a future, and its in ministry where I just want to reach my potential."[106]

Coming from a life spent in jails and addicted to PCP, Joe appears genuinely grateful to the ministry, and, through the urging of overseers (church leaders who supervise the homes), he has enrolled in the church's Bible school (the Victory Outreach School of Ministry) in the hope of becoming a pastor. In the meantime, Joe wants to start his own support group for abused men. He believes that he can reach hurting men and that his ministry will prove crucial to fixing broken homes. "The reason why men is because the importance of the father in the home. That's why, because the father in the home is the priest of the home. . . . the leader, that is the way God made the home. If you are going to be the man. If the man is not there, there is a breakdown and the woman doesn't take the role . . . God's called the man to lead the home."[107]

Traditional gender roles that place the stability of the family on men are reinforced through the religious education in the home. Women cannot adopt this role because the traditional reading of certain biblical verses (Eph 5:22, I Cor 14:34, Col 3:18, I Tim 2:12) that explicitly mention the roles of men and women privilege the submission of women to men regarding familial concern. Though there are probably practical and financial reasons for a lack of women's reentry homes (there are only two), it seems fair to speculate that the religious attitudes about women's place in family life prefer that women stay at home while men work. Since the reentry home requires residents to find jobs, there appears to be no need for women to engage in such training. Reentry also appears to be a step more available to men because it is seen as a pathway to full-time ministry. Because few pastoral roles for women exist in the church, and because jobs are viewed as a means of sustenance rather than as careers for women, the lack of reentry homes for women is not an aberration but rather is part of the process of inculcating a religious identity that insists on "responsibility, discipline, and submission to authority."[108]

Rehab and reentry life reorients ritual space and time, personal mores and ethics, and implants ideological musings that help construct social identities and occasionally leads to overt political action. Cruz includes the following rare episode of direct political involvement in his book:

> Rehab residents found themselves involved politically in an important school board election [in New York City]. At stake were hundreds of Christian parents who had decided to run for office to help turn the tide in the city's notorious schools—and to get rid of the noxious Rainbow Curriculum, designed to teach small children that homosexuality is an acceptable option, not a sinful lifestyle. Going door-to-door, handing out a brochure for Christian candidates, Coney Island rehab women were happy to help their pastor . . . by passing out . . . literature.[109]

It may be speculative to say that rehab homes also shape political ideology, because little is known of the residents' preconversion politics or when they began to find their political voices in the church. We shall revisit this idea with a brief discussion of Victory Outreach's potential for reshaping the political values of its converts. For now, let us examine the role of women beyond rehab to their roles in the church. I contend that what occurs in the rehab homes parallels the social and political values that shape one brand of Latino Pentecostal identity; on one plane, through the reinforcement of traditional gender roles, the church supports the age-old role of women in most Latino cultures, and, on another plane, the church supports standard evangelical readings of women's roles. Thus to become Pentecostal, in effect, means to experience a transformative spiritual event that instills a larger worldview but also allows one to retain the male-dominated Latino culture.

The roles most women play in Victory Outreach, acting as stewards of the auxiliary ministries and organizing fund-raisers, differs little from other Pentecostal churches. Most Pentecostal organizations, which historically have made room for women as pastors, preachers, and evangelists, have tended to relegate women outside the centralized authority of the church. Recovering women in Victory Outreach find themselves entering a community of like-minded women who often have come from similar situations. Though Joan Moore's work with women in gangs does not deal specifically with Victory Outreach, it provides a portrait of Latina gang members and their marginalization within the larger Latino society.

Moore studied fifty-one Latina gang members in Los Angeles; of these, 41 percent used heroin at one time or another compared to 70 percent of men in these gangs. Moore notes: "Gang women who became involved with heroin had been largely confined to a street-oriented world throughout their lives."[110] Around 10 percent grew up in homes active in the drug trade. Latina heroin addicts who were active a generation ago tended to take one of three routes. More than one-third became "street people" immersed in the heroin lifestyle. The rest were less intensely involved with the street lifestyle. They tended to alternate between dependence on a man—for their heroin supply and for protection, as well as for daily sustenance—or on their gang homeboys or homegirls. All these women, Moore writes, are outside the traditional boundaries of Mexican American family life. These girls were "bad" because of gang affiliation, and most certainly sank lower in the eyes of their families because of their drug use and even further if they became prostitutes.[111] If Moore asked any questions about religious affiliation, she did not include them in her otherwise helpful study. She demonstrates how Latina gang members are ostracized from traditional Latino families, seek acceptance in gangs and on the streets, and often find themselves in ministries like Victory Outreach. Ironically, that very few of these women came from traditional families does not deter Victory Outreach from reorienting these women to traditional, often idealized versions of family and home life.

Women in Victory Outreach create a spiritual community within the homes and churches, and they become reinvigorated by annual meetings meant to accomplish several things: to encourage new spiritual practices and create social space for them in ministry and to encourage and reinforce the idea that they are special. By being chosen to perform tasks central to the mission of the church, they represent the mothers of the new church and are charged with mission work and with keeping the vision of the church pure.

Such ideas hearken back to well-worn notions of the idealization of feminine piety and an assurance that alleged female spiritual superiority nurtures female moral authority. We should briefly pause here to examine the historic ties evangelicals have to these ideas and how they operated in the context of a very different organization, the nineteenth-century home mission.

Evangelicals, according to Randall Balmer, more than any other group, have perpetuated the notion that women are protectors of the home through their superior lives, which has often kept women frozen in time in the nineteenth century as virtuous homemakers and mothers.[112] The nineteenth-century female home missions agent sought to create similar social and spiritual spaces as did Sister Julie, and claimed that right because of spiritual superiority. In her examination of home missions women, historian Peggy Pascoe found that not only did women take advantage of the honorific title of the ideal Christian woman, they used their moral authority to break out of the tightly prescribed boundaries American society set for them. To draw a parallel between Pascoe's home mission women and Victory Outreach women, one need look no further than the following observation: "Women's depictions of ideal Christian homes were accompanied by a bold critique of male behavior in the family. . . . They found fault with husbands who offered inadequate financial support . . . or who did not restrain their sexual desires or their taste for alcohol, opium, or gambling."[113] Although the critique of men's behavior may not be overt, Victory Outreach's emphasis on rehabilitation and reentry programs, along with its "Mighty Men of Valor" organization, which resembles "Promise Keepers," suggests that critiques of men's overindulgent behavior is implied in the very structure of the church's mission. That the church rarely, if ever, sends out a single male to found a church and rehab home says much about the importance with which they view the traditional family. Sister Julie provides the role model for the ideal Christian life and is the keeper of the church's vision.

Sister Julie's captivating preaching skills would make her one of the more explosive evangelists of the Latino evangelical world if more people knew of her. However, in keeping with the ideal of a role model, she has intentionally kept to her supporting role: dutiful wife and mother. When addressing a women's meeting, "United Women in Ministry," Sister Julie speaks with authority. She begins her remarks with the story of Lot's wife in order to comment on what she views as America's moral decline. She lashes out at the preeminence of gays and lesbians on television, Jerry Springer, former president Bill Clinton, and secular rock 'n roll music.

The title of Arguinzoni's speech is taken from Luke 17:32, where Jesus describes how to know that the Kingdom of God is near. Because Lot's wife looked back on a destroyed Sodom and Gomorrah, she was turned into a pillar of salt (Gn 19: 23–26). She received this punishment because the angels who visited Lot had warned him about the impending destruction of the cities and had granted Lot's request that he and his family be allowed to flee. Her disobedience costs her her life. Jesus' words in Luke suggest that, because Lot's wife tried to preserve her life, she lost it. There are those who will miss the Kingdom because they are disobedient.

Arguinzoni exhorts the women to make a difference. She preaches: "[We are] snatching the twilight treasures (prostitutes) right off the streets. Taking the needles right out of the arms of these girls and they're becoming women of God."[114] There is a spiritual price to pay for their ministry, and so women must remain steadfast and prepare for sacrifice. Women, Arguinzoni says, need to be "faithful to the things you've been taught." Victory Outreach women have been refashioned into godly women ready to fulfill their traditional roles by acting like ladies, which means walking in high heels and dressing modestly.[115] Such a transformation prepares them to disciple other women and also makes them better wives. Interviews and dozens of personal conversations support the idea that Sister Julie embodies the archetypical Victory Outreach woman. Despite her powerful position that would most certainly enable her to guide the church by the sheer power of her persona, she does not. She defers to her husband. "It's easy to follow him. He's my leader, he's been my example, he's the one that fires us all up. He's the one that's been the forerunner in our family and I value that and I look at him as God's man . . . and yes he's not perfect . . . he's the closest that I know of on this earth to God."[116] Arguinzoni positions herself in the place where all Victory Outreach women should be—following their leaders personified in the guise of husbands, pastors, and church leadership. Her near-deification of her husband solidifies the overarching supremacy of loyalty to the ministry as the standard by which women and men are judged.

Examining other speeches by women adds to the idea that such meetings as this one play a crucial role not only in the practice aspects of church growth by demonstrating Julie's influence, but, more important, these speeches reinforce the idea that women are different, that they are called on to be different because they can find acceptance. This church accepts you as you are; Sister

Julie will help you as she has helped dozens of other women. Stacey Lewis, church evangelist, exclaims: "Normal church can't take us. . . . We don't care nothing about how you look."[117] For recovering addicts and prostitutes (as Lewis describes herself), this sanctuary becomes community.

Josey Pineda's speech discusses how the women now have a chance, as new creations, to break generational curses and leave a legacy of faith to their children. She acknowledges that many of the women are from dysfunctional families, that they are not "Ozzie and Harriet." The inference is that, simply because they have not known such idealized domestic existence, that should not hesitate in trying to capture that idealized domestic tranquility. All one need do is look at Sister Julie, and at Pineda herself, for examples of how to keep the church's vision and build families in accordance with biblical principles, rarefied through a newly acquired Pentecostal worldview.[118]

Griffith's work analyzing evangelical women and the power of submission makes an intriguing, yet controversial argument that such submission serves as an empowering tool for women in movements like Victory Outreach. I would like to meld her arguments and those the anthropologist Elizabeth Brusco, who examined the reformation of machismo in Colombia, to make the case that Pentecostalism, when pursued as a reformative faith, becomes powerfully enabling. Examining "Women's Aglow Fellowship," a largely Euro American group in the Northeast, Griffith's insights into Pentecostal women are critical to understanding the power women find in faith. Women's spiritual empowerment emanates from their ability to heal themselves and their families. At Victory Outreach, if women do not already know their need to submit to men, they learn of such matters through the homes or churches.

For Griffith, submission is grounded in recovery discourse—the subtext of evangelical faith that makes religion another form of therapy. Confessional and cathartic, conversion or rededication to God relies on one's ability to throw off one's former self. Griffith says that this discourse is "grounded in notions of surrendering control over one's life, learning to be vulnerable with others and with God in order to cultivate relationships of deeper intimacy."[119] This process begins for women as they enter the rehab home or church and encounter people who insist that they pursue God and that their lives can be changed. The first step to that goal for Victory Outreach women lies in surrounding themselves with people who validate the idea and serve as examples that one's life can indeed change. One story, in particular, encapsulates the refashioning of traditional womanhood and the resultant immersion in evangelical Christianity that initiates women into a social and political value system.

Born in Los Angeles in 1962, Miriam spent half her forty years in and out of prisons. Before kicking her heroin habit three years ago, Miriam had used it for eleven years. For two years, she has been in the women's home; she credits the ministry for saving her from more prison time. She needed the discipline of the program because of her rebelliousness, and she needed "lessons on becoming more ladylike"—an effort, she believes, to reorient her from homosexuality.

A hard-looking woman, with tattoos covering her arms, Miriam continues to fashion herself in the style of a Latina gang member. With a clear voice, heavily made-up face, and pressed pleated pants, Miriam discusses how living in the home and receiving religious instruction convinced her that there were "real Christians" and that her struggles with drugs and her sexual orientation could be changed. The beginning of such corrective instruction begins with the implementation of strict rules and a chain of command meant to instill a sense of order. "You got to discipline yourself, self-control, learning how to pray, learning how to receive correction and orders which are hard . . . [I] don't like to be told what to do."[120] Miriam seems to view her pre-conversion life as one of chaos—she received no religious instruction from her family, even though her mother attended a Jehovah Witness church. Early in her teens, Miriam began using drugs and running with a local gang in San Gabriel Valley. She began spending time in prison for a variety of offenses. Although she had met Victory Outreach ministers during her various stints in prison, she ignored them. But when facing fifteen years in prison for assault, she became convinced that God was really trying to help her when the corrections board at a local women's prison granted her parole to Victory Outreach and placed her on probation.

Her initial rehab stay was difficult. Miriam rebelled, She said they could have kicked her out many times, but they did not. When she first arrived, she wore a buzz cut and boxers underneath her pants. "I didn't know nothing about bein' female. I didn't know nothing about wearing girl's clothes. And in the home, they taught me, step-by-step, daily, how to let my hair grow. I never wore makeup in my life. I came in just totally looking the opposite of what I've become."[121] Miriam credits Sister Julie for teaching her about clothing, makeup, and prayer, and believes that these aspects resulted in her changing her sexual orientation.

Miriam's life in rehab changed two years ago, when she no longer needed to remain there but decided to stay and became a helper at the home doing intakes, praying with women, laying hands on them, and leading Bible studies. Of her own accord, Miriam co-founded the first support group for "ex-gays and lesbians" in Victory Outreach. The suspicious gazes they had to endure made this endeavor extremely difficult. According to Miriam, fellow church members spoke about group members behind their backs and attempted to uncover the identity of members in this confidential group. Such intrusions did not bother Miriam. She was very open about her homosexual "past" and believed that the church was in denial about the homosexuality that existed in the church. In her view, the small group she led (who met in a private residence) barely scratched the surface. Beginning such a group might end whatever chance a resident has in choosing to minister in the church, but this was not the case for Miriam, who has since moved East to run her own home. Taken together, Griffith's idea, Miriam's story, and Brusco's ideas on reforming machismo illuminate the role evangelical Christianity plays in transforming women's lives and helps to explain why, despite a lack of pastoral power, women are able to find spiritual power in the church.

Brusco's groundbreaking work examining evangelical women's lives in Colombia stated that "Colombian evangelicalism reforms gender roles in a way that enhances female status."[122] According to Brusco, the truth of her statement is evident in the "ideology of evangelicalism" against aggression, violence, pride, and self-indulgence and in her description of how conversion rearranges gender roles in the family. Men begin to take an active role in the family; they refrain from being violent, they stop drinking, and they stop frequenting prostitutes. In short, "conversion entails the replacement of individualistic orientation in the public sphere with the collective orientation and identity in the home."[123] Brusco believes that the benefits of ascetic living clearly benefit women. However, what happens when Victory Outreach women become Pentecostal and live their lives as evangelicals, with all the attendant conservative social baggage?

Victory Outreach women, like Sherry or a host of others who take an active role in the building of the ministry, view their self-improvement and social mobility wholly in spiritual terms. They see it as being tied inexorably to their conversion. Rehabilitation is a sacred experience that not only has "cleaned" them up but is also largely a spiritual matter. Careers are important as long as they support a lifestyle in concert with building the ministry and supporting a family. Women, who go beyond such roles, are singled out for being less than fully committed to the ministry. Another example, in addition to Sherry's narrative, demonstrates that, along with the therapeutic benefits of rehabilitation, the ability of Victory Outreach to be a self-perpetuating entity provides its members with opportunities for social mobility; these include having jobs as church workers, traveling as missionaries, and helping to run churches as married women.

Ruth (a pseudonym) did not become a Victory Outreach member via the rehabilitation home; she followed her husband into the church after he completed the program. She had worked in a variety of office jobs before going into full-time ministry with her husband. Revered as one of the most effective prayer leaders and preachers in the church, Ruth has gone from an unstable family life to a stable middle-class existence where she and her husband travel frequently as representatives of the church. As church planters, they have founded half a dozen churches throughout the United States and abroad.

Having raised her seven siblings on her own, she found that settling into marriage was difficult because she was no longer responsible for others. Preparation for a traditional role as a wife required instruction from fellow Victory Outreach women who taught, by example, how to care for children and cope with the difficulties of married life. Having been raised Catholic, Ruth converted to Pentecostalism because she felt the need for a more personal religious experience. She left her office job and took up baby-sitting to be closer to her ministry, despite her husband's plea that she continue office work to help support the family.[124] For fifteen years Ruth has been a conference speaker, a prayer leader, and a women's ministry leader. Along with reinforcing the roles of women as wives and mothers, Ruth preaches to her group that they have the ability to overcome abuse, divorce, depression, and a host of other problems. She argues that they can help to keep their children out of trouble if they are good role models and pray, and that they can accomplish this without superseding their husband's role as head of the household.

A weekly women's Bible study guided her through the first five years of her marriage. Ruth brought her child to the study group, as did the other women, and it became a time to share their problems as well as to receive religious instruction from the older women. Ruth describes her experience:

> God dealt with me in a lot of different areas of my life as a woman, as a wife, as a mother, you know a lot of foundational principles were birthed there. . . . God was telling me that he was training me, but yet, I didn't want to face the fact that maybe we would go out and start a church, because that was too scary for me. But in my spirit, I knew like this was a training ground 'cause God was giving me a pastor's heart at the point where I was concerned for the people that were in our Bible studies. I mean I would literally counsel all day and not clean the house. And then I would have to unplug the phone at three before [my husband] got home so that I could clean the house.[125]

Ruth began baby-sitting to bring in additional income as her husband was not in full-time ministry at that point. For a time, after she had her second child, she went back to work as a financial officer but found that the career did not fulfill her. She explains: "For awhile, you know I got all caught up in the work thing, but then God began to deal with me and I would feel like I don't belong here."[126]

Ruth and her husband began full-time ministry in 1984. She initiated a weekly prayer meeting at the mother church in La Puente. Like many first-time church planters, they used their home as a rehab home and held Bible studies there as well. To cope with the added responsibility of living with a dozen or so people, Ruth recalled the stories of hardship she had heard from Sister Julie. "You know a lot of my discipleship, a lot of my teaching was by observing. . . . I would soak it up and just learn and apply and I'd learn from their mistakes . . . the opportunity that I had to speak with Sister Julie they were always . . . encouraging even to this point."[127] Today Ruth is involved in the administration of a Los Angeles church and is active in children's ministry. Part of her ministry also involves helping single mothers prepare for ministry. She comments on her ministry:

> They don't see no hope for themselves. They've been abused and torn apart mentally and emotionally. And I can see God building them. Giving them confidence, courage, boldness, that they could be something, they could be that leader. They could be that good mother. . . . To me the women are like the wheel, you know . . . we may not be the leaders or the heads and that's okay because I don't want that anyway. I don't want the responsibility, but I'll help bring the task to pass . . . the women's ministry is very important as far as that's concerned so that married women will learn how to work with their husbands. . . . I feel that it's very important that the women learn to be the wife. Learn their role. Learn their place.

Furthermore, for Victory Outreach women, conflict with careers, individual self-fulfillment, and political power are subsumed under a religious context. If one grand narrative exists to reaffirm the church, it is that being free from drugs, alcohol, abusive relationships, or prostitution was not accomplished by any secular organization. Overwhelmingly church members credit a supernatural experience with God for their sobriety, jobs, and reunified families. Evangelical Christianity, when partnered with practical services such as free rehab, counseling for domestic violence, and shelter for the homeless certainly fits the traditional notions of progressive social services. In its own way, Victory Outreach provides choices and avenues to mobility as church builders.

For many evangelicals, the underlying causes of social ills are not systemic. If they once believed that their circumstances were caused by institutional sexism, racism, or economic injustice, conversion has reoriented their world-view to look to a supernatural agent as the root of their troubles. As such, Sherry's response to years of domestic abuse will not be political action but, rather, ministry to other female victims. The answer to societal ills for Sherry and other Victory Outreach members lies in the practical application of faith that rebuilds their lives and, in turn, builds the church.

The issue of politics and how Latino evangelicals become grafted onto the larger evangelical political ethos, which tends to be conservative, does not oc-cur in every case of conversion. Luís León's work with a Spanish-speaking, largely immigrant Victory Outreach church found that, on issues like affir-mative action and immigrants' rights, many of his respondents supported both causes. But when the topic veered to abortion, unanimously León's re-spondents were opposed. From this and other findings, León concluded that, although Arguinzoni personally does not support many political causes and implicitly does not support his church's involvement in such matters as immi-grants' rights, individuals in Victory Outreach do support such causes.[128]

If my many conversations and observations can be quantified, it is fair to say that Latino evangelicals are consistent with their Euro American counter-parts regarding social issues. It is not uncommon to hear sermons like Julie Arguinzoni's jeremiad on secular culture and its perceived desiccating spiri-tual influences. It is also common practice now among organizations like the Christian Coalition and the California-based Traditional Values Coalition to seek out Latino pastors to network for various political causes. Reverend Martín García, Executive Regional Director of La Amistad, the Spanish-lan-guage equivalent to the Traditional Values Coalition, provided details of the growth of this organization since its founding in 2000.

García notes that La Amistad's mailing list currently contains sixteen hun-dred Latino churches. Recent events in which La Amistad has engaged would certainly place the organization in ideological stead with other evangelicals. La Amistad campaigned successfully for passage of Proposition 22, which de-fined marriage as a bond between a man and a woman and effectively stopped the momentum gay rights activists had gained in having their relationships recognized as legal unions in California. La Amistad also supported George Bush in 2000. Currently La Amistad serves as a liaison between conservative candidates and Latino evangelicals, hosting many meetings between the can-didates and the church community. La Amistad, in the last two years, has ex-panded to Washington, D.C., Maryland, and Virginia. Invitations have been extended to open branches in Florida and Texas. La Amistad's influence reaches into the White House, where a series of conferences calls were re-cently held connecting various California churches with presidential staff.

There are also active members in Chicago, New York, Delaware, North Carolina, and Wisconsin.[129]

Other examples of Latino evangelical political activity geared toward social issues includes that of Richard Ochoa, a Vineyard pastor featured in the last chapter of this book, who successfully lead a grass-roots movement of Latino evangelicals in southern California against an effort to open a casino in Pico Rivera. Further, Isaac Canales, a prominent Assemblies of God pastor who is the president of LABI, is a spokesman for the Promise Keepers, an organization of evangelical men that stresses men's spiritual involvement in families. The question remains, would these pastors be inclined to be conservatives if they were not evangelical? What does this new political activism mean to the traditional Latino political issues that have enabled so many Latino politicians to remain in office for decades? If enough inner-city people of color within shouting distance of a storefront Pentecostal church entertain thoughts of conversion, will it follow that their political ideologies will also change? Is that an inevitable result of the re-creation of a Latino Pentecostal identity? To answer these questions, more time and study is surely required. Suffice it to say that, if the current trend continues, traditional Latino politicians may one day be facing as many friendly labor, civil rights, and immigrants' rights groups as they will be facing unfriendly opposition from well-organized Latino evangelicals driven by social concerns, a situation that has not been on the typical Latino politician's agenda until now. As is shown in the next section, and in the concluding chapters on Latino youth culture and the Vineyard, the idea of a monolithic progressive Latino political consciousness, free of spiritual impulses, has never existed. Indeed, for nearly a century, classical Pentecostals (Assemblies of God), Pentecostal social missions (Victory Outreach), and, more recently, charismatics (the Vineyard) have served as alternative vehicles for spiritual attainment and social service.

As Arguinzoni stated: "In our times of desperate trouble, today's unchurched will accept help from Christians—often warily and usually after the welfare system and the courts have failed them."[130] Victory Outreach members remain wary of the governmental approach to solving social problems because they place little hope in institutional remedies. Founder Arguinzoni spent time in a federal rehabilitation hospital, and Miriam candidly reveals that her years in prison did nothing to cure her heroin addiction: "No treatment, they treat you like a dog."[131] Church member's lack of confidence in government only deepens as converts become convinced that government programs can never solve their problems. Paramount in the newly ritualized life of the convert and the established church member alike is the evangelical idea that outside Jesus, there is no salvation.

Thus ideological exclusivity becomes another aspect of the social values privileged at the church.

What began as a private conversion becomes a public crusade because of the desire to see people convert and because of an understanding that the private behavioral transformation of church members can and should be transmitted to the larger society. One example stands out as an effective portrayal of the fervency with which church members wear their new shields of faith.

Art Blajos is a self-described former hitman for the prison gang know as the Mexican Mafia. His book, *Blood In, Blood Out*, describes his journey through the correctional facilities of California from boys' homes to San Quentin. Blajos is blunt in his depiction of jail life and critical of the society that feeds such institutions. Blajos's book, co-written with Christian author Keith Wilkerson, represents an interesting mix of confessional literature, social commentary, and evangelism. Blajos, although aware of the Chicano movement of the late 1960s and 1970s, has little to say about it. He claims to have been too busy chasing women to become involved in the politics of the times.[132] Critical of the governmental agencies who housed and cared for him, he appears interested in neither social policy nor social reform: "The State of California had raised me, fed me, housed me, and clothed me since I was a mere boy, and now it wanted to kill me" (14). Blajos notes that the state failed to change his behavior, failed to cure his heroin addiction, and, when he was on trial for capital murder, finally decided that killing him was the only remedy.

Blajos's childhood represented an endless shuffle from relative to relative before he and his brother ended up in a boys' home. Two young Euro American youth taught him that being a gang member was the only way to gain respect. Blajos sought to imitate their dress and mannerisms; he had already adopted the gang lifestyle and began abusing drugs when he was sent to live with an aunt in Norwalk, California. "On my first day at this new school, I quickly got the message: I was poor, I was behind academically, and I was the wrong race" (64). The next section of the book is a rambling social commentary of the "true" causes of social ills. Blajos writes that, while growing up, he neither watched the news nor read "social commentary." It seems clear that Blajos was uninterested in current events and was apolitical in his preconversion stance, which means that something changed during the time he has become Pentecostal. I suggest that heavy doses of socially conservative theology have altered his perception of blame and responsibility regarding social problems. Blajos's clearly expresses his current politics as follows:

> Suddenly, it was cool to be a part of an ethnic minority struggling against poverty and prejudice and injustice. The American Civil Liberties Union

was rushing in to place court decisions that were tying the hands of civil authorities. . . . President Johnson's 'Great Society' and his War on Poverty poured hundreds of thousands of dollars into the hands of anybody who could claim to help the disadvantaged or oppressed. (68–69)

Blajos blames ineffectual progressive governmental programs and meddling activists for a chaotic society, both complaints resonating today within conservative circles. Like other conservatives, Blajos blames the permissiveness of today's society on moral relativism. "We were raised being told that everything is gray—no absolute white or absolute black. Nothing completely right or wrong. Textbooks are praised if they were values free—taking no position on good or evil" (78). The removal of prayer from the public schools underlies this values-free society. "At the same time that prayer and Bible reading were banned from the public schools, an assault began from the other side" (79). The other side remains undefined, but one may assume it has to do with the "enemy." Fear of the "enemy," among some evangelicals, is so pervasive that any institution not prominently displaying God—particularly schools or other government offices—becomes suspect because of alleged secular foundations. Institutions are either morally ambivalent at best, or godless and evil at worst.

Blajos's choice of sources also illuminates his changing political ideology. Columnist William Buckley, author William Bennett, and economist Michael Novack (all Catholics) figure prominently in Blajos's writing. Blajos quotes Buckley's comments in *Forbes* magazine in 1995: "I hate to say it, but I feel the need to acknowledge the quiet triumph of secularism in the past thirty years" (79). And Blajos adds that, to him, secularism is the "removal of religion from American life." He quotes Bennett's critique of popular culture: "[Making] a virtue of promiscuity, adultery, homosexuality, and gratuitous acts of violence . . . many of our most successful and critically acclaimed movies celebrate brutality, casual cruelty, and twisted sex" (83). Echoing an often heard refrain, Blajos takes full responsibility for his actions: "Just because American society was disintegrating around me as I entered childhood and became a teen is no excuse for my behavior. I still had the ability to say no. But I did not" (83–84). He blames personal moral failings, not systemic social ills, for the loss of social cohesion in American society.

In his book Blajos also discusses his time in California prisons. Aside from a graphic depiction of prison life, Blajos the evangelist continues to preview his conversion event. Before this event, he talks of the racism he felt and how prison life heightened his own racism. He describes, on leaving prison, his racial intolerance of African Americans and how "all become racists in prison." He became a member of the Mexican Mafia because to him it meant instant respect—it gave him an alternative to a powerless life behind bars. "[It was] the ultimate for a kid like me. Out on the streets, I had suffered the sting of racism. Limitations had been placed on me because I was Hispanic and born poor" (83, 94). Unlike other Chicanos who came of age in the 1960s, Blajos did not view political action as a way to reverse the limitations he felt racism imposed. He continued to work for the Mafia until a contract killing in prison went awry.

In the late 1970s Blajos was converted while trying to carry out a hit on a Mafia enemy. Blajos came very close to killing the person, but he failed to carry out the hit. He knew the consequences of such defiance but was allowed to leave prison unharmed. He left prison and entered a rehab in northern California. Life in rehabilitation signaled a sea change in his life, as he learned about, and eventually accepted, Christianity.

On one occasion Blajos's home director asked him to pray with his hands up, "like you're surrendering to the Holy Spirit" (150). Blajos had a difficult time with the ritual life of Pentecostalism, especially the loud singing and emotional prayers. Nevertheless, he came to embrace the faith: "In that short time Jesus Christ did more for me what seventeen years of prison, psychiatrists, lawyers, drugs, money, power, and sex had been unable to do. He gave me a new heart" (152). Blajos felt called to minister in Great Britain, where he is one of the church's most popular evangelists. Because of Blajos, other members of the Mexican Mafia have gone through rehab and become popular, if controversial, spokespersons for the church.[133]

The last facet of reorienting converts to Pentecostalism, and especially reshaping their religious identities to become synchronous with the founder's vision, requires theological education beyond the Bible studies the church offers. To conclude this examination of how Victory Outreach inculcates new social values, I turn now to the work of the Victory Outreach School of Ministry (VOSOM).

It is often necessary for Victory Outreach to change a person's belief system. The inner city is plagued by a widespread breakdown of the family. Many of the people in Victory Outreach came from broken homes, where parents had dropped out of school themselves. Completing homework or showing any form of educational discipline was not a high priority. Most young men in the inner city grow up more interested in joining a gang or making a name for themselves than going to school. When they become adults, Victory Outreach has to get them to think differently. Thus education is vital to the future of this ministry.[134]

Del Castro, the head of VOSOM, is in charge of systematizing and bringing existing educational standards to a level where other Bible institutes, colleges, and seminaries will accept VOSOM's transfer credits. Founded in 1984 as Victory Bible School, it soon became the Victory Outreach School of Ministry and shortly thereafter began granting certificates and diplomas. Like LABI, VOSOM wants to implant a vision and a sense of mission to its students, and, like LABI, many of its students are ill equipped educationally to take full advantage of a Bible school. It is Castro's job to create a curriculum that supports what he calls the "cutting edge" philosophy of ministry. In his words:

> You get away from that [cutting edge] and then you begin to get people that are not . . . you could tell that it doesn't have that cutting edge and that is how come we train them like that, because we have learned throughout thirty years what works and what doesn't. Some cities are Victory Outreach cities, some cities are not . . . that is just the anointing of what God has given us . . . we believe that there are a lot of other powerful ministries that are doing great works, Calvary Chapel, the Vineyard, but they all have their philosophy.[135]

One of the major obstacles Castro faces is the generally low educational levels of VOSOM students in their ability to grasp theological concepts. He notes that most VOSOM students are high school dropouts.

> This is a challenge for me because a lot of them, you know, we see that the reason why they don't get involved in school is because, you know, they are lacking their [education] and they feel inadequate. And so that is where I need to develop some curriculum . . . that would not be so intimidating . . . and help them along as I am working with a brother right now . . . working with some new learning machines that they can learn on . . . at least like to get their GED . . . and with a machine, they don't get so intimidated as in a classroom.

In order to encourage students to further their education, he rewrites the curriculum, stripping it of its theological jargon: "First of all, they don't understand these big old theological or philosophical words, but then at the same time, you don't want to shy away from them. . . . You want to challenge them so they can be familiar with these words . . . so they won't get intimidated when they do get raised up." When students confide in Castro that they cannot handle school, he challenges them with the idea that they cannot break out of the spiral of drugs and gangs that often captures generations of their families unless they begin to think of themselves as capable and changed people. "They come into another realm, another environment that is foreign to them and they feel intimidated. . . . Lot of times, they just click amongst themselves where they go to get out and begin to associate with the black brother, with the white . . . all are in Christ." Castro teaches that becoming a Christian changes not only self-destructive behavior, but it begins to change the levels at which people tolerate one another. He sees it as his job to mentor students not only in terms of education but also in discipleship. Adding the "cutting edge" to that sentiment, Castro says: "We already have it in us per se, that loyalty and that faithfulness that we had to our neighborhoods and our gangs and we just turned that around for Jesus." Loyalty and a sense of mission require the proper pedagogical instruments to bridge the levels from novitiate to pastor. This delicate balance between practical theology that reaches a predominantly undereducated class and the desire for theological and educational acceptance will become even more important as the church has begun the difficult process of retaining its second generation of members, who, for the most part, are in a different location socially and educationally.

Throughout its thirty-five-year history, Victory Outreach has seen itself as the outsider. Indeed, church members thrive on the idea that "normal church can't take them." From the mid-1970s, when only a handful of churches existed, all in California, Victory Outreach has grown to nearly three hundred churches worldwide, in such far-flung places as Madras, India, Dublin, Ireland, and the sacred city of Jerusalem. The leadership, with the exception of the founder Arguinzoni (who is Nuyorican), is self-consciously Mexican American, reflecting a shared cultural heritage. How Mexican American church leaders manifest their ethnic identity when planting churches abroad is an intriguing area for future research. However, the church's second generation has begun to change the church and to widen its circle of influence to include unchurched youth and adults, college-educated professionals, and people of color; in short, the second generation has begun the process of seeking people who look like themselves to minister to their peers. Searching for the nuances of a Latino Pentecostal identity requires that we move into what creates a crucial tangent of this identity—youth and their ability to carve out a special niche which I call a Latino Evangelical youth culture.

4

Slipping Into Darkness:
"God's Anointed Now Generation" and the
Making of a Latino Evangelical Youth Culture

Victory Outreach is in a bind in its efforts to grow and evolve, and to widen its circle of potential members, because of its desire to retain its distinctiveness as a specialized mission. By modernizing and accommodating to the second generation, the church may become just another denomination in a disparate world of evangelicals offering recovery services as part of its menu of ministries. Because second-generation members want to reach their peers, they construct and co-opt cultural forms and social entities that they believe will attract disaffected youth. In other words, the making of a Latino Pentecostal identity needs to be remade with every generation in order to continue to grow, and, like ethnicity, religious identity is an identity one chooses. I suggest that, over thirty-five years, Victory Outreach became transformed from a largely Mexican American church of former drug addicts and ex-gang members to a worldwide denomination incorporating Europeans, East Indians, Asians, and Latin Americans, and, in the process, has raised a generation of young people in the church.

To accomplish this transformation, the church has begun to resemble one of the hundreds of contemporary charismatic churches in existence—replete with pop culture, modern technology, and marketing. Currently the church is involved in creating a Latino evangelical youth culture able to compete effectively for its youth against all other options in the evangelical landscape. To explore this current effort, this chapter examines several Victory Outreach ministries so as to uncover the ways in which this youth culture operates within the church.

The leadership mantle was passed in 1997 from Arguinzoni to his eldest son, Sonny Jr. Born in Boyle Heights in 1969, Sonny Jr. displayed little interest in ministry despite being reared around his family's ministry, often living with recovering addicts in the family's Aliso Village apartment. Arguinzoni Jr. had originally wanted to play professional baseball and did play semiprofessional ball, trying out for the major leagues as a pitcher. He describes himself as having been a rather introverted young man, uncertain as to whether the ministry was for him. At age nineteen, however, Arguinzoni Jr. experienced a radical conversion experience that solidified his call to ministry.

While on a personal retreat in Amsterdam, Arguinzoni Jr. reports receiving a prophetic word calling him into ministry. He did not immediately believe what had happened, and so he asked God for a sign as proof of the prophecy. Arguinzoni Jr. reports receiving a scriptural passage (Hab 2:1–4), and, in an incident he considered miraculous, he received the same passage in a Christmas card. Thus Arguinzoni Jr. became an evangelist, attended Life Bible College (a Foursquare Institute), and received a B.A. degree in biblical studies. Arguinzoni Jr. then led the moribund youth group at the La Puente church, which began with twenty members, then grew to more than two hundred members, and, after eight months, had as many as eight hundred members who met weekly. In 1997 Arguinzoni placed his son in charge of the adult ministry at the La Puente church, and three years later his son became head pastor of the mother church. Since then, the second generation has begun to place their imprint on the church.

Arguinzoni Jr. knew that the transition would be difficult for several reasons: Would the Old Guard respect him as a leader? Could he relate to his father's constituency? How could change be implemented to help the church grow beyond its traditional boundaries? To recapture the vibrancy of the early years, Arguinzoni Jr. began to restructure the local church leadership, adding younger leaders to his staff and removing thirty years' worth of ossified bureaucracy. He comments on the transition: "I have a lot of people that have been in leadership for so long now, they know how to do it one way and that's the way they do it. So we are introducing new ideas, new things, and implementing change is a very delicate issue."[1] Local restructuring at the La Puente church occurred because church membership had stagnated for several years. Arguinzoni Jr. recognized that static leadership stifles avenues for promotion. Currently more than three thousand people attend the La Puente church, and Arguinzoni Jr. plans to increase that number to more than four thousand. In broadening the church, Arguinzoni Jr. realizes that the church will begin to incorporate members outside the church's original sphere of influence. He comments on the church's new look and how he intends to minister to his flock:

> We are broadening as a kind of by-product of reaching the inner city, you are going to have other types coming . . . you are going to have people, their children, that never experienced all that . . . I've been out there but I never was a heroin [addict] . . . I wasn't a drunk. Got drunk a lot but I wasn't a drunk . . . that is what our challenge is, to relate with that group as well as influx of the new [people] that are coming from the streets still and blending [with] them.

Moving into new realms of ministry does not mean abandoning the basic premise of becoming a Victory Outreach member—experiencing a personal conversion experience and being loyal to the church hierarchy. To accomplish this, Arguinzoni Jr. emphasizes education and tighter organization:

> Now everyone has to go through the "foundations of faith" . . . then begin to channel them to a leader . . . then begin to channel them to the right ministry that they can fit that matches . . . you've got to be faithful to the church, you've got to be loyal to God, loyal to the vision, loyal to your pastor, loyal to your leaders, loyal to one another.

For Arguinzoni Jr., keeping the vision pure represents his greatest challenge: "Keeping it focused as the ministry continues to grow and [keeping] the uniformity of those values and principles that I referred to earlier because the more reproduction, the more things get lost. . . . without compromising the word and without watering down the message, got to keep that pure, but as far as practice, of how we do things and how we go about doing certain events." Fear of dilution keeps Victory Outreach hierarchy in a bind. For the church to grow, it needs to broaden its base but, in doing so, new ideas may be brought into the church that the hierarchy does not approve of, ideas that may question the vision of the founder. In addition, the church hierarchy fears stifling institutionalism and professionalization that might destroy the sense of family in the church that was so crucial to its past growth. Fearing the church might begin to function like a business, Arguinzoni Jr. treads lightly on taking the church too far from its grass-roots beginnings.

When Arguinzoni Jr. began his pastorship at La Puente, he describes this fear as paralyzing; he worried that he could not relate to his constituency: "How am I going to relate with the gang member, shaved heads and tattoos? I never had a tattoo. All I had was a little dot, it looks like a tattoo, but it didn't work, you know, it's a pencil mark. So all these things came to my mind. I don't dress like them. I don't talk like that." Arguinzoni Jr. knows that he has upset some church members but that their criticism remains unspoken: "I assume that they [criticisms] are spoken about 'cause I'm not dumb . . . I wonder what they think, but then, I can't let that consume my thoughts because that would paralyze me . . . I don't think there is a week that goes by that I don't think of the scariness of this whole thing, you know, but then again, at the same time, I know God is with me." Rather than forcing himself into his father's mold, Arguinzoni Jr. began incorporating the ideas he learned at Life and at modernized church organizations, using models based chiefly on the work of Bill Hybels at Willow Creek.

Arguinzoni Jr. mandated that anyone who wanted to become part of the ministry had to take basic theological education courses. Partly because of his emphasis on education, Arguinzoni Jr. believes that more young people are training for ministry at VOSOM and Facultad Teologia. This professionalization of the laity and ministry, particularly if many students follow Arguinzoni Jr.'s lead and attend Life and Fuller Theological Seminary (where he is currently enrolled in a Masters of Divinity program), will have profound consequences for the church. Because of Arguinzoni Jr.'s ideas of professionalization, his view of female pastors, and his instituting small groups, I suggest that Arguinzoni Jr.'s tenure marks the beginning of a move away from the classical grass-roots Pentecostal social mission to professionalized, service-based, evangelical Christianity, that is, from a church of marginalized people to a church serving marginalized people led by professionals legitimized by theological training and social mobility. Victory Outreach struggles on two fronts: It is desperate to secure its unique vision while avoiding what I term a "maintenance tradition." This terminology, used to describe mostly liturgical traditions, I use here in reference to evangelical traditions. A "maintenance tradition" is any religious tradition that sees its role in the life of adherents as a fixed, inherited system of beliefs and practices that secure faith confessions and, more important, serve as a location for rites of passage that reinforces religious and often ethnic identity. Normally viewed as a liturgical tradition, akin to ethnic Catholicism or Orthodoxy, I suggest that maintenance traditions are not limited to liturgical faiths but that certain forms of Protestantism operate in the same way.

Victory Outreach may, in the next generation, become like many fundamentalist denominations, which, for sixty-odd years of self-imposed separation, have retained their vision and tradition but have not reached anywhere near the numbers of their cousins once removed, namely, evangelicals. An example of this is the Independent Fundamental Bible Association. The IFCA is a collection of churches that separated from denominations they viewed as capitulating to the modernist tendencies of their former churches. Vowing to be protectors of doctrinal purity and separation from the world, they came together in 1930. Whereas these Euro American IFCAs have grown throughout the twentieth century and currently number more than one thousand, the Latino churches have not fared as well.[2] For example, there are approximately ten Latino churches in California and an even smaller number throughout the rest of the United States. The church stresses separation from non-fundamentalists, does not usually cooperate with evangelicals, and, rather than accommodating to what they view as modernism (contemporary music, worship, and nonliteralist biblical exposition) and risking a theological taint, they have chosen to retain their unique vision and have grown in infinitesimal ways.[3] Another possibility is that Victory Outreach will become like dozens of other evangelical traditions that differ from fundamentalists in that they are not separatist, are usually not literalist, and are more willing to co-opt popular culture in ministry. Victory Outreach may soon become part of the larger evangelical world, becoming evangelical in faith, contemporary in style, charismatic in worship, and fluid in organization; in effect, those in Victory Outreach may become like everyone else.

Arguinzoni Jr.'s education at Life changed his ideas about female pastors. In his words: "It is acceptable in unique situations, yeah, it is acceptable to me . . . I can't build a case against it biblically . . . It's [Foursquare] influenced me a lot." Arguinzoni Jr. believes in women leaders and preachers, but he realizes that women pastors need to gain the respect of Victory Outreach churches. Arguinzoni Jr. has not committed himself to the idea of women pastors as a goal of his administration. If Victory Outreach moves to ordain women, Arguinzoni Jr. will have come a long way toward joining other Pentecostal denominations like the Assemblies of God, Foursquare, and other Protestant denominations that ordain women. However, such a theological shift can only be hypothesized as it has not yet come into practice. However, Arguinzoni Jr. has implemented several new measures that bolster my contention that the church will experience changes over the next decade or so.

Arguinzoni has established small groups that are geographically specific home missions that meet weekly for Bible studies, prayer, and fellowship. This addition to the church organization serves several purposes: It makes this three-thousand-member church more personal and more accessible to its members. It also provides a place where church members can discuss and contribute to the agenda of the church, thereby democratizing a usually closed process of engaging with church leadership. One example of this occurred at a meeting I attended, where complaints about the church leadership were aired. Apparently, a lay leader grew tired of the group's constantly changing schedule of assignments. The criticism was aired and the leader of the small group, while acknowledging the difficulty of changing schedules, proceeding to lecture the group on their insolence and lack of gratitude. That such a critique was aired before an outsider (me) represents a marked shift in hierarchical power. Together with the ongoing professionalization of its young leaders through Bible colleges and especially through seminaries, the next generation of Victory Outreach leadership will face even more scrutiny from both its members and its trained pastors.

When Arguinzoni Jr. visited Bill Hybels's innovative pioneering seeker-sensitive church, Willow Creek, he brought back with him the idea of small groups and an idealized notion of church growth as envisioned by Hybels, whose own church has grown from 150 people in the late 1970s to more than 20,000 members today. Arguinzoni Jr. looked to Willow Creek as a model of megachurch growth and management, but he has not examined the broader implications that seeker-sensitive churches have had on the life of his church. One doubts that diluting the often strong and strident message of Victory Outreach, which focuses heavily on reaching hurting people with debilitating pathological conditions, will work as effectively as Willow Creek's model of making evangelical Christianity palatable to lapsed Christians and non-Christians seeking to understand the faith.

Seeker-sensitive churches began as worship services in some churches, blending worship and mixing traditional and contemporary styles. More than twenty years ago, seeker-sensitive churches began to fill the nondenominational church category so prevalent in contemporary evangelicalism. For a Pentecostal church like Victory Outreach to become a seeker church, there would be fewer charismatic practices, if any were even allowed, and usually such practices as speaking in tongues, prayers for healing, and prophecy would be segregated to a special weekly service or to a small group. There is no evidence that Victory Outreach has moved into this seeker model. Seeker churches are designed to remove all nonessential barriers to faith so that the services are normally light on religious imagery, symbolic jargon, and other traditional expressions of faith.[4] The common assumption is that baby boomers, suspicious of tradition and authority, were drawn to churches like Willow Creek, because it offered evangelical Christianity free of their parents' language and symbols. Evangelical Christianity became redefined for a generation with no need for a usable religious past.

When examining Victory Outreach as a possible candidate for seeker status, this denomination falls short in that its message of rehabilitation and restoration continues to target a certain audience, but, stylistically, Victory Outreach may qualify. For example, services are contemporary, held in all manner of spaces: homes, storefronts, strip malls. Younger members usually dress casually, but many younger and older members dress in their Sunday best. The church's religious imagery, symbolism, worship, and jargon revolve around themes of redemption, forgiveness, and loyalty, reinforcing both the vision of the church and evangelical theology.

Sociologist Robert Wuthnow's observations about post-1950s American spirituality augment this discussion about religious seekers. Wuthnow describes the shift from post-1950s spirituality, characterized as dwelling spirituality, to seeker spirituality, characterized by sacred spaces without barriers, a lack of emphasis on membership and inheritance, and a perpetual sense of marginalization—from spiritual producers to spiritual consumers. As Wuthnow notes:

> They [churches] used to produce offspring for their churches . . . send out missionaries and evangelists to convert others, and spend their time working for religious committees and guilds; they now let professional experts—writers, artists, therapists, spiritual guides—be the producers while they consume what they need in order to enrich themselves spiritually. In other ways, the shift from dwelling to seeking influences images of what it means to be spiritual. Faith is no longer something people inherit but something for which they strive. It provides security not by protecting them with high walls but by giving them resources, by plugging them into the right networks, and by instilling the confidence to bargain for what they need.[5]

Putting Victory Outreach into this equation, I argue that although the church's message has not changed under the new seeker-sensitive model, the structures were in place for such a change to occur. Victory Outreach wants to produce offspring, plant churches, and evangelize but it specifically wants to preach a vision. This vision, guarded closely by the Arguinzoni family and church elders, within a generation, will be placed in the hands of a professionalized class, most probably people trained outside the confines of the church's institutes. More important, the second generation does not live in the same social (dis)location as their elders; thus to inculcate the same passion for an unchanging vision to a generation without a similar point of reference is a daunting task.

Simply put, in order for Victory Outreach to retain the second generation, and, in effect, pass on their faith through inheritance, it must offer some aspect of a maintenance tradition that sacralizes Christianity as much as it sacralizes the church vision. The downside of that is that evangelical Christianity usually works against such implementation. Ideally it works against the notion that faith can be inherited, arguing specifically that it cannot. Additionally, through a series of rhetorical flourishes that mark its ingenuity, it insists that spirituality, tradition, and religion are different, and are basically meaningless without commitment to Jesus. Ideally the only entity that is sacred in evangelical Christianity, and hence capable of being sacralized, is Jesus; particular visions of various movements are human inventions that cannot begin to reach the heights of the sacred cannon, lest evangelical Christianity descend into heterodoxy—*sola scriptura*. Therefore, for Victory Outreach to accomplish this feat, it needs to incorporate the parts of evangelical Christianity that secures its tradition, while growing beyond its original audience. Observations of Arguinzoni Jr.'s preaching style illuminate this point.

Comparing the preaching style of Arguinzoni Jr. to that of Charlie Moreno, La Puente's other assistant pastor, demonstrates the different styles these generations represent in the church. Moreno, in his forties, has retained many stylistic accoutrements of his past gang life: well-coiffed, slicked-back hair and a well-groomed, thick mustache. His gait and cadence leaves no doubt as to his past. He speaks in clipped phrases while sermonizing about how one can be trapped by the thoughts of one's own history. Moreno stresses loyalty to pastors, especially to Sonny Sr., and to the church. He occasionally uses slang and shuffles as he walks across the stage. During the sermons, Moreno rarely quotes from the Bible.

Arguinzoni Jr., like Moreno, is well-dressed and very enthusiastic. Before preaching a sermon, he joins the worship team and exhorts the audience, participating on stage in the praise and worship time; he speaks in tongues before beginning his sermon. He appears much more polished, making constant references to biblical passages, interspersing Greek translations of certain words. Substantively there seems to be little difference between the sermons of Moreno and Arguinzoni Jr. Both deal with submission and loyalty, both decry the individualism that keeps people from volunteering to do less glamorous jobs like setting up the chairs and tearing down the stage. He remains a charismatic figure who has the attention of many in the eight-hundred-member audience.[6] How do these two styles coexist in this church?

Another member of this Gen-X leadership, Mando Gonzales Jr., represents still another side of Arguinzoni Jr.'s leadership team. Gonzales Jr. grew up in a family often on the verge of disintegration, filled with drugs and gangs. He recalls his mother contemplating suicide and his father using drugs in front of him. His desire, even at the age of five, was for his father to quit using drugs. Gonzales Jr. describes this pivotal event in his young life:

> At five years old, I prayed for my father. I was real close to my dad, and I prayed for him and when I laid hands on him . . . I really didn't know . . . I just prayed you know . . . that he would get saved. . . . The next day, when he woke up, he didn't have no desire for alcohol, for drugs, and he forced the desire. But when he went and used alcohol, the drugs, he didn't get no high, no buzz, no nothing.[7]

Shortly thereafter, his parents became involved in Victory Outreach as rehab home directors. Gonzales Jr. was raised in the church, but it was not until 1996–97 that he displayed any interest in ministry. Gonzales Jr. describes his teen life as one of parties, drugs, and drinking. One night he saw his friend walk through a glass door and severely cut himself. Such incidents propelled Gonzales Jr. to move toward ministry. He began working with Arguinzoni Jr.'s youth ministry and is now worship leader at the La Puente church. He also remains the overseer of the reentry homes in southern California.

Having grown up nominally Catholic, Gonzales Jr. adapted quickly to his new religious life as a Pentecostal. What bothered him was the strict lifestyle: "I just found it hard to live by, from my own life, because I felt that I had not had the problems my parents had. I was not into drugs . . . I just wanted to have a girlfriend." Part of reorienting Gonzales Jr.'s religious identity toward the piety of evangelicalism lay in the theological reinforcement provided by his studies at LABI and VOSOM.

Like many in the church leadership, Gonzales Jr. credits the longevity of the ministry to the deeply guarded vision of the leadership. The belief rests on building a drug rehabilitation ministry not sullied by faddish trends or whims. "His vision was East L.A. for Jesus . . . Now, the world for Jesus." Gonzales Jr., like many church leaders, wants the vision to signify geographical distance as well as distancing from its roots as a drug rehabilitation ministry catering primarily to Chicano ex-convicts and gang members. Gonzales Jr. says that he has not thought about the idea that prospective church members might be attracted to the church because of the preponderance of Latinos in its leadership and membership: "As you're telling me about it, I think that it is attractive, you know, for the Latinos to see other Latinos that have the same problem, that come out of the same generational curses."

Like many evangelical missions, Victory Outreach uses a personal touch. Its members are not afraid to walk through neighborhoods, to meeting people and evangelize door to door—praying with those who desire it, handing out flowers on Mother's Day, making a church van available for those who lack transportation. Under Arguinzoni Jr's leadership, the church has become more cognizant of what is called follow-up ministry: phone calls, inviting people back for a second visit, sending out thank-you letters, and, occasionally, organizing a special luncheon for newcomers.

Because Victory Outreach, under Arguinzoni Jr.'s leadership, wants to retain its vision as a place for drug rehabilitation while expanding its membership base, the church has had to include in its outreach services traditional evangelism programs that take the church beyond its original circle of potential converts. As essential as these outreach ministries are for expanding the base of the church, the "bread and butter," as it were, of the church's continued growth comes from its outreach to gang members and substance abusers.

Under Arguinzoni Jr.'s leadership, church members are younger and enter church with a more diverse set of problems.

Two time-tested strategies have worked well as a means of introducing people to Victory Outreach and helping them find a place where they can feel comfortable: These are the street dramas, a staple of Victory Outreach's ministry, and the new youth ministry, appropriately called G.A.N.G. (God's Anointed Now Generation). Both these ministries demonstrate that in order to replace its first generation, Victory Outreach has had to move beyond its traditional strengths. In so doing, it has entered a realm of specialized ministries and conferences, and has added layers onto their ministries because not to do so would signal an unwillingness to move away from its grass-roots phase into its current phase.

Victory Outreach seeks to evangelize Latino youth in disparate ways using street dramas, plays, rap, and rock music. In doing so, popular culture serves several purposes: it sacralizes usually "dangerous" forms of secular entertainment, and it re-creates the notion of "dangerous" youth by providing the cover of religious legitimacy to their modes of expression. Within this framework, Christian expressions of rap, drama, and rock music become evangelistic tools in retaining youth. Christian rap, in particular, serves its dual role as an African American cultural form that "attempts to negotiate the experiences of marginalization . . . within the cultural imperatives of African American . . . history, identity, and community."[8] But in the context of evangelism within a Latino church setting, rap denounces the other "enemies" of youth: drugs, gangs, premarital sex, hopelessness, and other assorted "ill vibes" of urban culture, exhorting youth to "represent a multiethnic faith to your peers."[9] As is the case in the context of urban evangelism, rap is the common language that allows Latino youth to worship with African American youth, as is also the case with Victory Outreach. But before rap, street dramas provided the church's most effective means of reaching out to youth.

Victory Outreach's drama ministry began before it officially broke away from Teen Challenge in 1967. Since the days of performing street theater in New York, dramas have been an integral part of its evangelism. One pre–Victory Outreach group called "Addicts for Christ" presented a drama in 1968 called "The Junkie." This Latino group consisted of future leaders of Victory Outreach and evangelists loosely affiliated with the church. The playbill announces: "The most shocking portrayal of dope addicts ever witnessed by an audience. Once you see this drama, you will be able to better know the horrors that a drug addict goes through."[10] The playbill pictures an addict shooting heroin. Teen Challenge and Victory Outreach performed the drama throughout the early 1970s.[11]

Dramas became very important to the church when it moved from its home in Boyle Heights to a nearby high school auditorium in the mid-1970s and soon afterward to a banquet hall. LaCrue says that dramas were held regularly at both locations, and as a result the church experienced major growth throughout the 1970s. The plays succeeded in reaching young people as no other evangelistic technique had done up to that point.[12] The long-time member and church elder Ed Morales wrote the church's first drama, entitled "Duke of Earl," to reach a wider audience.

The "Duke of Earl," like most of Victory Outreach's dramas, is laced with references to gangs and their music, lifestyles, and destructive behavior. The Chicano gang culture of the late 1960s to the late 1970s in southern California, according to the anthropologist James Diego Vigil, reflects the "tendency among adolescents to develop new modes of dress and speech. Chicano gangs have adapted a distinctive street style of dress, speech, gestures, tattoos and graffiti. This style is called 'cholo,' a centuries-old term for some Latin American Indians who are partially acculturated to Hispanic-based elite cultures."[13] The earliest roots of gang-style dress can be seen in the African American adaptations of the "Zoot Suit," but much of the fashion style in the "Duke" video emanates from an acquaintance with institutions such as prisons. Vigil notes that the generally low incomes of barrio youth also influenced the dress habits of gang members. The basic style, comfortable shirts, durable pants and shoes are practical and long-lasting. The khaki pants became fashionable after Chicano war veterans from World War Two and the Korean War continued to wear their military garb. Jeans worn with tennis shoes became part of cholo attire as a residual effect of jail and prison wear. Other residual effects of prison culture are the close-cropped hairstyles.[14] A brief synopsis is in order before examining how this drama attracts youth. The drama begins in prison where two gang members make a peace treaty between themselves on the eve of their release. Evident in this opening scene are multiple expressions of prison culture: slang, posturing, and clothing styles. The remaining scenes are interspersed with "oldies" music, which is integral to cholo party culture. Oldies are derived from the African American rhythm and blues tradition. Drinking, drugs, and fighting are are ubiquitous in this culture.[15] One oldie, Gene Chandler's "Duke of Earl," is played at the end of the first scene as the lead character leaves prison. Cisco, Duke's younger brother, eagerly awaits him, and their long-suffering, Spanish-speaking grandmother prays that her two grandsons will abandon their gang life. She tells them that Jesus is the only answer. The gang members constantly worry over retaliation and over the infractions of the peace treaty. Throughout the drama, the grandmother attempts to witness to her grandsons but to no avail.

A Euro American young woman named Robin represents another side of gang life. Robin is the "good girl," the good student who can also fall prey to gangs. Pushed into the gang orbit by her alcoholic father who beats her, Robin runs away from home to join the gang at a party. Transformed into a *chola* through heavy application of makeup, the appropriate clothing, and her attitude, Robin's transformation occurs at an Army-Navy surplus store. Ed Morales, playing himself, witnesses to Duke and others after having broken up a fight in the store. He tells them that he was a low rider, a gangster, and he understands their pain. He tries to convince them of the emptiness of gang life. "Ask God to come into your heart right now . . . Jesus died on the cross for all of you. . . . We need to get together and fight against the Devil . . . its's about the barrio [mockingly] . . . it's about God! Homeboy! Can't you handle God's love?"[16] Ed convinces no one.

After another gang fight where rivals are killed, Duke returns home and his grandmother prays over him and lays hands on him. Duke realizes that the life of the gang is not for him, and he speaks with Morales. Morales and his wife, Mitzi, lead Duke and his girlfriend in the "sinner's" prayer. Mitzi asks the Holy Spirit to come. The drama, still performed around the country, became a teleplay broadcast over the Trinity Broadcasting Network in the early 1980s.

The "Duke of Earl" portrays a completely negative picture of gang life, effectively taking all future and current gang members in the audience to task for the lives they lead; then, by unreservedly accepting them, these "outlaws" become children of God. Victory Outreach seeks to recapture "outlaws" from the margins and place them in the mainstream of evangelical Christianity. Gang members are accepted, as are all others, as souls waiting to be saved. At the same time, by using music and Chicano gang culture as evangelistic tools, Victory Outreach touches youth who are on the margins of society. Music that conjures up images of the *veterano* is used to reach the *veterano*, and that same music also reaches today's Gen-X gang member, except that hip-hop, a different kind of slang, and other fashions have become appropriated to preach to a new generation.

Victory Outreach members have written new plays in an attempt to evangelize in new quarters of the gang subterranean, recognizing that the dynamics of youth subcultures have changed since the church began performing dramas more than thirty-five years ago. These dramas continue to draw large crowds (six thousand in Riverside, California, in 1997)[17] because Victory Outreach members make modifications based on the prevailing trends of youth culture, for example, Hip Hop instead of Old School; sports jerseys, tennis shoes, and baggy pants instead of pressed khakis and flannel shirts. The church has made concessions to popular culture because, unlike other Pentecostal groups, it has never seen the need to demonize certain cultural practices. While not seeking to endorse secularism, Victory Outreach does not have the same historical animosity toward dancing, various hairstyles, clothing, and other cultural forms as have their foundational denomination (Assemblies of God). For many reasons legalism has not been part of Victory Outreach's prescription for spiritual health. One incident, in particular, illuminates the philosophy undergirding the church's lack of legalistic tendencies.

Arguinzoni describes a scene at a church which did not take kindly to the graphic representations depicted in the play, "Straight from the Hood." He describes the scene with dripping sarcasm: "The service started like every one has since the 1940s. The congregation sang from their hymnals, good old standards with phrases that nobody understands anymore, then Brother Herschel prayed in a kind of depressing monotone for a long list of people who were very ill and obviously not expected to live much longer."[18] He continues:

> Our play came to its dramatic climax. We had an altar call and a crowd of kids got saved—I mean they were streaming down the aisle, crying and asking God to forgive them. But the pastor was not looking at the kids. He was worried about Brother Herschel and Sister Maud clutching her purse and adjusting her bifocals. The church was used to hiding in their safe little Christian subculture. And they were *offended.*

Arguinzoni quotes the preacher: "God, we thank you Lord for being with us today. And we thank you for Your grace even though these methods are very unconventional and they're not pleasing before your sight, O Lord."[19]

Arguinzoni's angry tone hearkens back to the story he relayed earlier about people in his mother's church who also clutched their purses. This unnamed church's transgressions include not only its critique of the play but its conservative style—which Arguinzoni views as outmoded and ineffective. Arguinzoni intimates that the church is lifeless and powerless to change youth's lives and powerless in praying for its own members. A subtext to Arguinzoni's critique might be the racial dynamics at work in Herschel's and Maud's church. Though this church is not described, it probably was not a Latino church and, judging from Arguinzoni's depictions, was also probably not an urban church.

Arguinzoni does not indicate why such a church would host the play in the first place? One could speculate that it was an attempt by this church to invigorate its membership by offering a special youth night. In Arguinzoni's eyes, the play accomplished its goals. Church has to be pragmatic and not concerned with appearances. Clearly Arguinzoni vents his anger toward the unnamed pastor, who, rather than encouraging kids and rejoicing at the successful altar call, ignores them and focuses on the older generation, whom Arguinzoni describes as being offended and scared. This scene also signals the hidden fears of dangerous youth, perceived as stalking the urban landscape in search of prey. Although not overtly stated, that the actors were undoubtedly youth of color, stereotypically cast as the predatory class of U.S. society, surely had an effect on the church elders, who rarely encounter such "urbanness" directly. Arguinzoni continues:

> The people huddled in the pews of these churches are too religious to be effective in reaching sinners anymore. . . . Most of their growth comes from recruiting members from other churches. Most of their time goes into getting Christians who already tithe and know the Lord to switch locations. That's why these churches have a hard time evangelizing. They have forgotten how, and frankly, they have no idea what to do with the lost if they did come down the aisles and ask to become members.[20]

Here Arguinzoni echos a common critique of traditional Protestant churches often leveled by evangelicals: that spiritual stagnancy dressed as religiosity no longer reaches others because such people refuse to evangelize and have become comfortable simply maintaining the culture and the comfort of members.

In addition, this process of "stealing sheep," which Arguinzoni and other church members expressed, reveals their fear that Victory Outreach is viewed as being little more than a mid-level program that readjusts people to living in society until they can find a "real" church with more intellectual stature and tradition. This insecurity and need to protect the church from both the critical gaze of traditionalists and the opportunistic forays of other evangelicals propels the church to continue to carve out a familial, cultural, and religious space for its youth, which includes producing relevant dramas as well as the establishment of G.A.N.G., the active youth ministry headed by Arguinzoni Jr.'s brother, Tim. Before discussing the role that G.A.N.G. plays in shaping a Latino evangelical youth culture, I shall examine a recent Victory Outreach play, "Street of Dreams," to illuminate the argument that, in order to create a religious identity that both retains youth and reaches a new audience, the church needs to modify popular culture.

"Street of Dreams" focuses on a young man, who, at his brother's urging, converts and leaves behind his life as a drug dealer. In contrast to the "Duke of Earl," "Street" examines the life of a crew of drug dealers. It is urban and multiracial, and caters to the largely Gen-X and millennial audience of seven hundred to eight hundred people. The target audience has changed from cholos to crew members, the music from old school to rap, and the actors do not dress in any particular way to signify their crew.

Hearkening back to the drama Gabriel Martínez describes in chapter 2, gender roles in these dramas emphasize women as being lost without men. Men are cast in the roles of redeemer and aggressor. For example, in both "Duke" and "Street," young women are treated similarly—as sexual toys and party companions in "Duke" and as "hoochies" in "Street." In "Duke," women become victims of physical violence, and "Street" reinforces the idea that women cannot live without men's protection. In "Street," women are discouraged from attending college and are constantly reminded that, without their boyfriends or brothers to care for them, they would revert to being "tramps" and "ho's." In "Duke," the redemptive woman is the grandmother, who never stops praying for her grandsons, and, in "Street," the main character gives up drug dealing because he has fallen in love with an independent-minded, intelligent young woman.

In "Street" the trappings of youth culture abound: pick-up games, parties, drug and alcohol use, and violence. Unlike in "Duke," violence is not limited to knife fights and occasional gunfire, "Street" features extensive use of guns, and several characters die, including the pregnant girlfriend of a treacherous crew member. The life of a drug dealer, like the life of a gang member, is never glorified, and the crews describe their lives as being filled with uncertainty and backstabbing. In a way, Victory Outreach appears to have moved into what theologian Leonard Sweet calls specialized ministries based on "affinity communities."[21] The affinity communities of Victory Outreach include party crews (loosely affiliated groups who often are involved in Hip Hop culture), gang affiliates (wannabees), gang members, drug users (casual users and addicts), and second-generation members with little experience with any of these communities. Specialized ministries require leadership by specific peer representatives to minister to each community. The representatives of popular cultures in the form of Hip Hop culture, fashion, and music signal to youth that the church does not reject them, and, in fact, seeks to validate their life experiences. Victory Outreach, in particular, seeks not only to validate Hip Hop culture but also to rescue the gang member from his or her vanquished status in American culture.

G.A.N.G., the youth ministry of Victory Outreach, operates in nearly all churches large enough to support it. G.A.N.G. holds conventions and retreats, sponsors plays, and prepares other youth leaders to continue in the ministry. The message of Victory Outreach has changed to speak to those who were not heroin addicts, who did not spend time in prison, or were not hard-core gang members. Some of G.A.N.G.'s youth fit the above profile, but many simply partied their way through their teenage years or grew up unchurched. Thus G.A.N.G. members resemble much of larger society, more so than any specialized or marginalized group generally associated with Victory Outreach. How does one incorporate this new group while not alienating the Old Guard? How does Victory Outreach retain its second-generation members, who, for the most part, do not suffer from the same pathologies as their parents did? More important, how does a church that does not experience or encourage transfer growth ensure its survival into the new millennium? Part of the answer lies in the brilliant and intentional co-opting of the emblematic expressions of inner-city youth gangs to sacralize their social purpose and reclaim the idea of "gang" for a generation marred by both the violence of gangs and the constant stereotyping of all Latino youth as gang members.

Arguinzoni Jr. has reoriented the concept of a gang from a violent, predatory entity to a sacred familial entity that provides an alternative identity for Gen-X and millennial Latino youth in the church. Such co-opting also brings with it popular cultural expressions that pervade urban youth culture—Hip Hop. Historian Tricia Rose describes the role of the crew for inner-city youth and its cohesive bond with Hip Hop:

> The crew [is] a local source of identity group affiliation, and support system. . . . Identity, in Hip Hop, is deeply rooted in the specific, the local experience, and one's attachment to and status in a local group or alternative family. These crews are new kinds of families forged with intercultural bonds, that, like the social formation of gangs, provide insulation and support in a complete and unyielding environment and may serve as the basis for new social movements.[22]

G.A.N.G. serves as an alternative to street gangs and serves as an alternative family with the purpose of creating and maintaining an evangelical identity. G.A.N.G. offers a sense of local identity by telling youth that they belong to the La Puente G.A.N.G., or the Santa Ana G.A.N.G. G.A.N.G. secures the often tenuous intercultural and interracial bonds by providing venues where affinity communities can meet and mingle with other youth of color in a religious procession. G.A.N.G. also insulates youth from the harsh environment of the inner city, while empowering them spiritually to fight problems in their communities.

The 1998 G.A.N.G. convention, held at the La Puente church campus, lasted three days, with nearly three thousand young people attending. Some raised the $60 registration fee by holding fund-raisers: food and bake sales, and car washes. Others raised significantly more money in order to travel from Europe and Latin America to attend the conference. Local G.A.N.G.'s were acknowledged at the beginning of the conference when church leaders asked: "Is Fresno in the house? Is Spain in the house?" Each group responded with enthusiastic shouts reinforcing their local identity. The stage was cloaked with all the trappings of a youth rally: graphic posters warning youth to avoid drugs, teen pregnancy, gangs, and graffiti. The stage resembled a basketball court, and the crowd cheered wildly when Arguinzoni Jr. entered the stage on a motorcycle. Worship began and lasted more than an hour. The music was distinctly tinged with R&B, soul, and rap. Three rappers performed that evening to the crowd's delight. Tim Arguinzoni preached well over an hour. The message was a familiar one: a plea for youth to abandon their partying and to follow Jesus. Arguinzoni also warned those in the crowd that, if they were only attending the conference to socialize, they were there for the wrong reason. Mingling in the crowd were young men and women, African American youth and Latino youth, and smaller Euro American and European youth groups. Nevertheless, Latinos comprised approximately 80 percent of the audience.

Two church members from Connecticut and London, respectively, performed rap, as did a well-known Christian rapper and television star Deezer-D. Deezer-D's rhyme, "Ain't no party like a Christian party, 'cause a Christian party don't stop," is a take-off of a popular secular rap song. As simple as the rhyme may sound, Deezer-D's rap reflects a theme that is crucial for convincing youth to see Christianity as a substitute for the party life. The act of partying, characterized by music, dancing, and drinking, is reoriented toward the idea that, if you are a Christian, the partying never stops. In other words, Christianity is fun. Young people do not have to stop socializing and can have healthy relationships, provided they abandon drinking, drugs, and sex. As long at Hip Hop culture reinforces a Christian message, it remains a powerful evangelistic tool for reaching youth.[23]

It is worthwhile to discuss Christian rap in a broader context to demonstrate how this co-optation occurs lyrically and stylistically. Christian Hip Hop has websites and magazines, and markets itself in a similar manner as does secular rap. As with secular rap, there are commercial and underground artists. The underground magazine, *Underground Fire*, advertises clothing, churches, evangelists, and musicians. Articles cover everything from Hip Hop culture to artwork done by Christian graffiti artists. One article discusses how the traditional church should perceive Christian Hip Hop artists as co-laborers in the "fulfillment of the Great Commission" by accepting their evangelistic efforts as sincere attempts.[24]

Sales advertisements for clothing by a company called "Righteouz Cloth-ing" displays slogans such as "What Saints Wear," "One Way," and "Down for Christ." "One Way" is a particularly interesting choice, because the Jesus Movement used that slogan more than thirty years ago and apparently it still has residual power as an affirmation of faith. "Down for Christ" is lettered in Old English on a baseball cap, like a cap that would be worn backward by a musical act of the same name. Advertisements for musical acts include a management company, "Soul'd Out," representing acts as diverse as "Soneros de Alabanza" (Songs of praise) and Lakita, an African American woman who raps about abstinence.

Both Christian Hip Hop and Victory Outreach seek to accomplish essen-tially the same goal in their use of music to place inner-city youth and their cultural expressions under the cover of evangelical Christianity. Therefore, when a rapper enters a church wearing baggy pants and an oversized hooded sweatshirt, gesturing with his hands and rapping about God, the message is not one delivered by a menacing "gangsta" but rather by a believer. Depend-ing on the person' s experience, the rapper may use the occasion to vent his anger at the devil or preach about politics. One Victory Outreach rapper de-scribes his anger: "The devil hates our guts, man . . . why should I miss a chance to stick him in the neck, man? When I preach and win souls . . . that's when I put a 9-millimeter in his chest."[25] Such violent imagery disturbs some in the Christian rap community. Underground rap artist David doubts the ef-ficacy of rap as an evangelistic tool and views its use as superficial at best.

David, not associated with Victory Outreach, would probably be outside Victory Outreach's affinity communities, given his educational background (he is a graduate student at Biola University), yet his familiarity with Victory Outreach rap and dramas make him a capable outside observer of the church and Hip Hop culture. The twenty-five year old has been rapping since he was a teen. He opines that, for the most part, over 95 percent of Christian rap is "fluff."

> The thing is, what motivates churches, and the people who put out the product, is what I think is a simplistic and naïve view of evangelism. What they want to say is, "Okay, we are rapping not because we appre-ciate it as an art form and because it is an interesting cultural phenom-enon, and it is of aesthetic value—no the reason we allow rap is because you can save a soul or something."[26]

David believes that such mimicking of rap invalidates its countercultural val-ue, reducing it to a mass-produced commercial venture. David's purist vision would have churches encourage rappers as artists of other forms to develop their skills. He is highly critical of the refusal of many churches to nurture rap artists: "We don't want to nurture this because it is a skill or a gift or a craft, no, do it because you can save souls."

The graphic depiction of gang life and violence that Victory Outreach encourages in its plays and raps are subject to a particularly tough critique: "They [Victory Outreach] are used to hearing this [violence] in their music they used to listen to. Now they want to do something for the Lord so they are going to rap and they are going to turn this anger and aggression that they have because they are growing up in tough neighborhoods. They want to turn it on who they know to be their enemies" David believes that Christian rap does not encourage spiritual growth by merely substituting secular for religious words.

> I think Hip Hop needs to start engaging people's minds with issues that really matter. And so you have a Christian rapper talk about the plight of the Third World countries and not necessarily have to say anything about . . . missions. . . . God is the source of all truth . . . you get kids who start questioning this and when they reach the existential plight . . . that is when God is available and they are more immediately available to God. They realize that it's really not about sex, money, and clothes, or whatever.

David says that it is a pattern he has seen with churches that do not aspire to place youth in intellectually stimulating situations: "If there is no growth in your spiritual life, in your intellectual life . . . there is a problem and I think the church is responsible for a seventeen-year-old kid who starts out acting like that. And if he's twenty-three and is still acting the same way . . . [there are] more appropriate means of engaging our faith."

Despite David's criticisms, he understands why churches use rap. Rap's popularity and ability to meld with different styles make it irresistible to many churches. Nevertheless, he feels compelled to lend his talents to evangelistic purposes. Even within the loosely configured world of Christian Hip Hop, certain codes and standards prevent it from moving toward secular Hip Hop. David explains:

> In terms of fashion, no there aren't any [standards], but in terms of graffiti . . . some of them [Christian artists] have made a commitment not to do illegals anymore. . . . I think that running and writing on the walls . . . is probably out of bounds . . . kind of where everybody does it, and maybe

against the wall I would say it is against the law. Be careful . . . I don't know what I want to say about that . . . I would say . . . if you are going to cuss in a rap song, I would say, as a Christian artist, I would say no.

The protective barriers evangelical youth place around their use and appropriation of popular culture will be looked at again in the next chapter on the Vineyard. David's words speak to several prohibitions that are important in ensuring the holiness of the individual. Breaking the law by writing on property does not appear to bother him as much as swearing. Polluting the inner life of the person—through swearing or through illicit sexual thoughts—seems more troubling to most evangelicals because, for them, faith rises and falls on whether a person's confirmed confession of faith becomes internalized and transformative. Trespassing and defacing of property, although probably not encouraged, would render a less condemnatory verdict than were a rapper to use vulgar language during a performance. Such standards may one day be insignificant, when, as David predicts, churches begin to think that rap has outgrown its usefulness as an evangelistic tool. Until then, churches, catering to youth, appear willing to use it.

In addition to Hip Hop and the G.A.N.G. youth ministry, Victory Outreach has also seen the benefits of what the larger work of evangelical Christianity has been engaged in for a couple of decades—marketing its own line of merchandise. The G.A.N.G. youth convention is where the coalescence of old-school Victory Outreach converts and new Gen-X and millennial converts meet and where the overarching framework of evangelical marketing culture becomes most prevalent.

Providing the security are older *veteranos*, dressed in old-school style. Others are dressed more casually, with O.G. ("Original G.A.N.G.ster") sweatshirts. The majority of the crowd are young, fifteen to thirty-five, both men and women. Many have Bibles, key chains, and other paraphernalia with Christian messages. There appears to be a prevalence of WWJD (What Would Jesus Do) items. Some don WWJD neckwear, others have the acronym written on their Bible covers, or they have WWJD key chains. Victory Outreach simply puts the slogan on its own merchandise to separate their merchandise from the generic items. There are G.A.N.G. T-shirts, sweatshirts, hats, CD and Bible covers, dog tags, and wallets. One young man has G.A.N.G. engraved in his hair.[27] Judging from the cost of the items, from $30 for a sweatshirt to $15 for a CD cover, Victory Outreach has begun to capitalize on the multimillion dollar Christian apparel industry that, under the cover of evangelism and church building, has developed tens of thousands of youth producers and consumers of the evangelical material culture.

The practical success of the conventions and plays are difficult to assess. Victory Outreach has made a concerted efforts to follow up on those who answer altar calls and on visitors who fill out information calls. The church rarely discloses such information, but, based on journalistic accounts and some candid assessments, success appears mixed.

The youth conventions of the past years have been well attended—three thousand in 1998 and two thousand in 1996; six thousand attended a play in Riverside, California, in 1997. Journalists who reported on the conventions and dramas, and my own fieldwork at both dramas and conventions, confirm the initial findings that more interest in the La Puente conference appeared to come from youth at the front of the church rather than those in the back. Journalists who reported at the Fresno convention noted a considerable amount of disinterest. The three-hour prayer session that closed the convention proved tiring to many youth. Isolated skirmishes among rival gangs tainted the event as well. A young woman opined that her friends attended the convention to socialize, hoping to meet gang members. I also noticed pockets of individuals socializing and just wandering around, especially at the "Street of Dreams" presentation. Every church member I have spoken to over the last several years lauds the effects of the dramas as evangelistic tools. However, one member doubted the long-lasting effects of dramas if follow-up did not include church attendance and Bible study. However, there should be no doubt that, at the convention and drama performance, there were altar calls that drew hundreds of youth who answered the preacher's call to "give your heart to God."

One final example of how G.A.N.G. hopes to broaden its base within Victory Outreach is through its website. The website advertises merchandise, provides a schedule of upcoming events, and offers a detailed guide to G.A.N.G. initiation. Initiation begins with the acceptance of Jesus. Rules for those wanting to join this gang include bringing their "weapons," their Bibles, with them to church and reading the Bible every day. Interestingly, G.A.N.G. members are asked to attend a Christian church in order to seek more recruits by witnessing. That no one need attend Victory Outreach or recruit others to the church seems a remarkable statement considering the importance of conversion growth to Victory Outreach. Using a website also represents an outreach to youth of a different class than those in the first generation and even some in the second. The Gen-X leadership of Victory Outreach appears ready to reach out beyond the traditional base of inner-city drug addicts and gang members, even if it means that those who convert will find another church. The strategy hopes to broaden the appeal of the church to a more middle-class and better-educated committed Christian.

By emphasizing theological education, innovative uses of popular culture, technology, and marketing, the second-generation leadership of Victory Outreach has effectively brought their movement closer to the larger, diffuse family of faith called evangelical Christianity. By so doing, it has gone a long way to ensuring its survival beyond the first generation and has loosened itself from its grass-roots moorings. Evangelicals, after all, exhibit an almost limitless ability to harness their message to nearly every facet of popular culture: bobby soxers, hippies, cholos, the tattooed, body-pierced college students searching for God—if there is a song to be co-opted, a style to be transformed, a corporate logo to be refashioned, evangelicals will seek to do just that.

5
Worlds Apart:
The Vineyard, La Viña, and the
American Evangelical Subculture

Entering the fray to try to find a middle path away from the dogmatic and often legalistic theology of classical Pentecostalism and the often noncharismatic, historic evangelical traditions were a loosely knit group of evangelicals who wondered, aloud, what would happen were they to offer evangelical theology and charismatic worship in their services. What would happen if their pastors dressed down and broke up the sermon with an occasional rock and roll song and a coffee break, and preached authentically in personal and spiritual matters? Would such a movement be effective beyond the casual baby-boomer base that earlier had spawned the Jesus Movement?

A former Foursquare minister, Chuck Smith, began a ministry to hippies and surfers in southern California in 1965, a ministry that eventually became Calvary Chapel. For nearly ten years, these autonomous ministries brought hundreds of countercultural youth into the fold of evangelical charismatic Christianity. As often happens with many Protestant movements, the Calvary Chapels began to experience splits, and it was one such division in the late 1970s that produced the Vineyard. The Vineyard, born in 1982, was the result of a merger of two wings of a church, an independent church in West Los Angeles founded by Kenn Guilliksen and a Calvary Chapel church in Orange County, California, under the leadership of a charismatic former jazz musician, John Wimber.

John Wimber, born in Peoria, Illinois, in 1934, earned his living as a musician for the Righteous Brothers through the early 1960s, leading a life of drugs and rock 'n roll. In 1963 he converted at a Quaker-led Bible study and, from then until 1974, he embarked on an evangelistic trek where he ministered to hundreds and led them to convert. In 1974 he began his ministry at the Evangelical Friends Church in Yorba Linda, California, but his charismatic leanings disturbed the worship life of the Quaker church, and, in 1977, he and his Bible study split to form a church affiliated with Calvary Chapel. Controversy over charismatic expressions like healing, speaking in tongues, and prophecy, which Wimber's group practiced, again divided the group, and his wing left in 1982 to join Guilliksen's Vineyard church.

Almost immediately Wimber's religious innovations, his teachings, and the Vineyard's style began to filter through the evangelical world and soon revolutionized the style and substance of evangelical Christianity in the United States and Great Britain.[1] In addition, Wimber became one of the most controversial preachers in evangelicalism. In its short history, the Vineyard has passed through several phases that have brought the church much negative publicity. First, Wimber's writings attracted the attention of evangelical theologians and scholars, and his influential book, *Power Evangelism*, espoused his most controversial ideas about charismatic experiences. Wimber's chief argument in the book was that Christians should evangelize in a spiritually empowered way. Spiritual gifts should be used to demonstrate God's power and to demonstrate Christian truth.[2]

Wimber spent most of his years in ministry trying to bridge the worlds of evangelical and Pentecostal Christianity. He wanted to assure evangelicals, who had experienced the gifts of the Spirit, that there was room for them in the evangelical church. At the same time he wanted to break the long-standing doctrinal stranglehold that Pentecostals had on spiritual gifts and their insistence that the initiation of those gifts began when people spoke in tongues. Although Wimber spoke in tongues, he stressed healing. Ironically he lived most of the last years of his life with a myriad of health problems, including cancer, and he finally succumbed to a cerebral hemorrhage in 1997.

Wimber's program for evangelism resulted in rapid growth. Within its first six years the Vineyard grew to include 140 churches, most of them in the United States and Great Britain, with nearly forty thousand members.[3] The Vineyard was first characterized as the "signs and wonders" movement, based on a New Testament idea that miracles would presage the second coming of Jesus. In 1982, before Wimber began to exert his leadership over the Vineyard, he taught a class at the evangelical Fuller Theological Seminary entitled MC510 "Signs and Wonders." In the class Wimber taught his "power evangelism" concepts, and the optional laboratory featured healing clinics. The class became so controversial that it was canceled in 1986. Wimbers's overt charismatic style and leadership lent an uneasy feeling to the seminary, at least according to media reports of that time. *Christianity Today* writer Tim Stafford said that the "signs and wonders" movement was a different religious entity, outside the bounds of evangelical Christianity, with its own theology, terminology, music, and style. Within many Vineyards a time that was labeled "ministry time," or healing time, began to take center stage. Healing time occurred before or after service and included groups of prayer teams that prayed for people's physical and emotional conditions. The Vineyard's emphasis on healing continued to attract controversy.

Wacker's critique of Wimber's theology was rooted in Wimber's lack of social mission: "There are problems of that sort that are endemic to virtually all forms of Pentecostal piety. One is the absence of ethical and social concern. There is no evidence that hunger, poverty, or oppression play any role in Wimber's theology."[4] If one were to limit the study of Wimber to his writings, hoping for a systematic approach to Vineyard theology, then Wacker would be correct in his assertions. However, in considering some of the Vineyard's ministries, especially the food pantries and feeding programs (which Wimber did not systematize in theological canons), Wimber did practice social mission in some form. In fact, some of the attractiveness of movements like the Vineyard is that they do not operate like traditional churches do—there are no "Institutes of Christian Religion," no "Dogmatics." In denominations like the Vineyard, preachers have not seen the need to canonize their theological musings because, like classical Pentecostal denominations, the church life is rooted, in part, in the continued inspiration of the Holy Spirit and is therefore difficult to codify.

Similar academic examinations by historians and sociologists, in particular, focus on examining the Vineyard's growth. Probably the most thorough study to date is by sociologist Donald E. Miller, who examined three movements he believes to be part of a larger post-denominational movement within Protestantism. Miller's empathic analysis found that his self-described "new paradigm" churches are more effective, more lively, and generally more successful at adapting to the needs of adherents. His descriptions of the Vineyard's social ministry—its efforts to distribute food and clothing, its prison ministry, and the help it offers single mothers—contradicts Wacker's assertion that Vineyard theology contained no references to social mission, implying that it must not have been part of the church since the leader of the church had not written about it.

Unfortunately all the literature on the Vineyard suffers from the same myopic approach, as does nearly all scholarship on evangelicals regarding race and ethnicity. Neither Miller's work nor any of Wimber's theological critiques mentioned the small but growing number of Latinos and Asians in the church. This is surprising, because sociology and theology have examined the Vineyard as a small cottage industry. For example, Miller's conclusions that the phenomenal growth of the Vineyard does not occur at the expense of other churches (he cites the Episcopal church as a reference point) might be true if one examines Euro Americans exclusively, but this simply is not true of Latinos.[5] Latinos are overwhelmingly Catholic (66–77 percent) and the rest belong to various Protestant denominations (22–33 percent).[6] Latinos are simply not joining mainline traditions. That Miller did not factor in Latinos in the "American Religious Economy" says more about what academics think that term means and why Latinos and Asians rarely find themselves part of the landscape in the literature, even though they make up part of the movement. Hence the title of this chapter. When scholars of evangelicalism and evangelicals alike discuss American Evangelicals, they mean Euro Americans. Specialists discuss the black church or the new Latino presence in Protestantism, but rarely are these groups included in a holistic approach to discussing what American Evangelicalism is—it is not white, though its proponents often speak of it as if it is a separate entity from churches of color. My use of the term *American Evangelical* is intentional. What exists in the varied subculture of evangelicalism are really several subcultures operating in separate spheres that occasionally merge to portray a larger picture: Televangelists are of all colors, and some of the highest-profile leaders are African American. Thus, when discussing the American evangelical subculture, I am referring to the large percentage of denominations, colleges, publishing houses, and marketing entities that cater to and are comprised of whites. To analyze how Latinos fit into this subculture, one must move the lens examining the Vineyard away from southern Orange County to northern Orange County and further north to the working-class neighborhoods of Los Angeles County. Although these represent a small presence in the church (twenty to thirty churches are either U.S. born Latinos or immigrant churches), they nevertheless deserve mention and study.

Many of the churches that have a large number of Latinos are called La Viñas. There are a smaller number of predominantly English-speaking Latino churches and other Euro American churches that have at least 20 percent Latino attendance. In this chapter I present only the first two examples because such churches, specifically three—a small church plant in San Francisco, a mid-sized U.S. Latino church in Pico Rivera, and a larger immigrant church in Downey, California—were chosen because of their chronological importance. La Viña Downey was founded by one of the Vineyard's first Latino leaders, Joe Castaños. The "Lord's Vineyard" in Pico Rivera was an adoptee, from Calvary Chapel to the Vineyard, and has operated since the mid-1980s. Finally, La Viña San Francisco is a relatively new church plant, having spun off from its larger Euro American parent church just over two years ago. But before examining these three churches as case studies to uncover the historical development of Latinos in the Vineyard, and how they go about constructing their faith lives within this Euro American context, I wish briefly to note the theological innovation the Vineyard brings to the evangelical table.

The Vineyard, as a newer denomination, has few formal ties to classical Pentecostal denominations. The Vineyard's experimentation with charismatic practices began from its intermingling with other ministries during its formative years, deciding in its nascent stages to become part of an effort to bridge the Pentecostal and evangelical worlds. The Vineyard describes itself as evangelical and charismatic—not insisting on any evidence of Spirit baptism but allowing for charismatic experience and, in some churches, encouraging that experience. The Vineyard is evangelical in the sense that one has to have a personal relationship with Jesus as the prerequisite to salvation. Belief in Jesus' virgin birth, death, resurrection, and second coming, along with acceptance of the Trinitarian view of the Godhead, represent the church's basic doctrines. Many Vineyard doctrines are not codified beyond this point. It is charismatic in that they practice charismatic worship and believe that one can operate in the gifts of the Spirit without separating, which signals Spirit baptism.

So why would an overwhelmingly Euro American church, rooted in the suburbs of Southern California, attract Latinos? By its own admission, the Vineyard has never sought to target Latinos, but the ever-changing demographics of the United States made such an outreach inevitable. Part of the answer lies in the social milieu that many Vineyard leaders experienced growing up in the baby-boomer generation of the 1960s and 1970s. Many Vineyard leaders, if not all, are baby boomers, and, despite their normally conservative social outlook, they express tolerance of ethnic and racial differences and have sought to open the Vineyard beyond its original base. Leadership, like that provided by Mark Fields, has shaped the view of the churches about ethnicity and race.

A pastor for fifteen years, Fields leads a church in Pomona, California, formerly a Calvary Chapel that adopted into the Vineyard in 1983. His interest in ministering to Latinos began because of his desire to rid himself of the prejudice he harbored toward them. Fields "distrusted" Latinos and had difficulty relating to them. He began to confide in a fellow pastor of a local church, who opened Fields' eyes to what it meant to live in the United States as a Latino. Fields explains: "That really kind of shook me, I mean, I'm white, I'm educated, I'm male, I'm everything that has power in this society."[7] Fields has since dedicated part of his time to Latino ministry and Latin American missions.

A characteristic of many post–Jesus Movement churches is that their leaders have a more confessional style—that is, they do not appear to be afraid to tell their members that they, too, are sinners and in need of forgiveness, and often they do not place themselves above the reach of the congregation's own collective piety. This helps people to see their pastors as authentic. Fields, for example, described his prejudicial feelings toward a fellow pastor who spoke with a heavy Spanish accent. Bothered by the accent, and by feelings the accent revealed, Fields asked the pastor to pray for him.

Fields believes that a spirit of openness in the Vineyard led the church to see the importance of developing Latino leadership. Since the beginning of the Vineyard, Latinos have participated in the church, though admittedly their numbers were small. Joe Castaños remembers being one of only a handful of Latinos ever to attend the first Vineyard church in Anaheim in the early 1980s. The organization of the Latino leaders of the Vineyard began about five years ago. The process, according to Fields, was supposed to empower Latino leaders so that they would lead their own churches: "The goal was one of the commitments of the Vineyard, is not to have an Anglo leading . . . in leadership over Latinos. The desire is to have a Latino leader." This was the goal because the Vineyard had seen too many examples of a pastoral power structure that often wanted Latinos to become part of the church, but rarely, if ever, were Latinos able to participate in leadership positions.

Surrounded by Latino neighborhoods, many in the Vineyard leadership only recently saw a shift in attitude toward Latinos, "[which] is evident now in the hierarchy of the Vineyard in terms of sensitivity." Fields participation in a "Missions Task Force" signaled to some Latino leaders that they were being viewed as a mission field. Fields says: "[Pastor Abel Mata] threw out a couple of things to me, and one of those is, he said, 'maybe you ought to quit calling it missions because we had a church here [Latin America] for a hundred years' . . . what needs to be different is not the word, but our attitude." Fields and others struggle with how to shed the traditional model of Euro American missionaries lording over Latinos as overseers. Further, Fields has tried to figure out how the Vineyard can be different with regard to U.S.-Latino leadership: "I have a number of friends that are in the Hispanic Assemblies of God community, and most of them are not really happy, the younger folks." Fields believes that more traditional classical Pentecostal denominations suffer from two crucial problems: (1) the perceived stagnation of Latino leadership in churches like the Assemblies, and (2) the entrenched Euro American leadership insisting on overseeing Latino churches without giving them resources and autonomous leadership to empower them to make their own decisions for their ministries. Fields believes that the former is why Latinos find the Vineyard attractive: "I think the Vineyard has a lot of life and youth in it." The legalism of many classical Pentecostal churches does not help retain youth attracted to the casualness of the Vineyard's style of worship. To ameliorate the historical inequality of Euro American leadership overseeing Latinos, Fields

wants to establish autonomy, possibly by separating Latino churches and placing them under Latino leadership.

Fields's work has been complicated by the untimely death of Vineyard
founder John Wimber and the subsequent years of transition. Fields elaborates:

> We have a bit too much territorialism and control and so when you have
> people of color that are not part of that system, then they're perpetually
> excluded as one of the newer folks. And so I think the question is, can
> there really be positions of power offered to new people? . . . And that
> to me is the challenge, because if we have no identifiable leaders of col-
> or, then it is not going to be really a diverse movement. . . . We see it in
> our church here [Pomona]. We're finally moving past the 20 percent
> non-white, and critical to that has been visibility of people that are not
> white in the church and not doing it in any way that's just a token kind
> of thing. . . . They see that the guy that is leading that week is Latino,
> that makes a huge difference to people and understandably so. And so
> I think it's got to be culturally sensitive. I mean I hear all kinds of com-
> plaints from people from Latin America about the Vineyard . . . just not
> being sensitive to cultural differences.

Two strategies, one programmatic and one attitudinal, mark stark depar-
tures from classical Pentecostal denominations of the past. First, the Vineyard neither requires nor suggests that Latino Catholics need to convert in
order to attend a Vineyard church. Unlike the anti-Catholic rhetoric of the
past that marked Protestant denominations, the Vineyard does not tell people that they need to pick one denomination or the other, although Fields
concedes that "people are choosing to be more 'biblically based' "—a not so
subtle hint that even if one remained Catholic, one would naturally become
more evangelical in one's reading of scripture. My research confirmed
Fields's comments that people who consider themselves Catholic attend the
Vineyard because they like the worship and the sense of community, but
they do not feel the need to formally convert. Such tolerance may serve the
Vineyard well, as it has grown from one La Viña in Anaheim in the early
1980s to more than fifteen churches in the United States and several in Latin
America (in Costa Rica, Chile, Venezuela, Nicaragua, and Guatemala).
Though this should not reflect a hesitancy on the part of the Vineyard to receive converts should Latinos make that decision, the Vineyard most certainly is willing to accept converts and has by the thousands. It is also willing
to facilitate that choice by promoting, as Fields did, the fact that, in the Vineyard, one will receive instruction that is more "biblically based" as opposed

to Catholic teachings, which are largely viewed as being overly influenced by traditions outside the Bible.

There are many reasons for this shift away from anti-Catholic rhetoric, but much of the evidence is anecdotal. One theory posits that the emergence of the Catholic charismatic movement in 1967 and the movement's growth within the Church, and even mainline Protestantism, created a connection among Catholics and Protestants in what sociologist Corwin Smidt calls the "spirit-filled" movement. In surveying more than four thousand Christians, Smidt found that "social distances between 'spirit-filled' and other Christians have eroded both physically and psychologically. . . . Religious radio and television, media heavily influenced by these movements, have produced a cross-fertilization of different religious traditions, denominations, and local churches further reveal[ing] the influence of these charismatic movements."[8] In short, charismatic practitioners, of whatever denominational stripe, are bound by their spiritual experiences, and that forms a kind of common self-identification while at the same time allowing the groups to retain their theological distinction. For example, Catholics report, probably to the surprise of Pentecostals, that charismatic experiences have deepened their appreciation of the Mass and of Mary.[9]

I contend that the growth of the charismatic movement within the Catholic Church in the United States, and especially in Latin America over the last thirty years, has made Catholicism more palatable to Protestant charismatics. In turn, Protestant charismatics have probably seen the futility of asking Latino Catholics to convert; or perhaps they do not see the need for them to convert, because, by not asking them to convert, the Vineyard helps Latino Catholics avoid the often tumultuous decision to leave behind not only a faith tradition but a maintenance tradition that marks the births, marriages, and deaths of millions of Latino Catholics. Finally, I suggest that the evangelical movement's ingenious use of a lexicon of salvation has insulated the movement from the critique that it has abandoned the cause of conversion—what is important is not one's religion, one's tradition, or denomination. What evangelicals speak of is not inviting people to join an organization but rather to know Jesus. Understanding that the charismatic movement privileges the work of the Holy Spirit, especially as seen in the work of Jesus and what charismatics view as the ability to replicate the miraculous, helps to explain why evangelicals can accept Catholics despite their theological differences.

The Vineyard began Harvest Bible College five years ago, with the expressed purpose of training people, mostly Latinos, for pastoral leadership in urban areas. The impetus for founding the school came, as Fields describes it, from Vineyard pioneer Bob Fulton, who has led much of the shift toward serving ethnic communities and building up local leadership. Half the people who teach at Harvest are Vineyard pastors, but the students represent forty denominations. In its attitude Harvest is markedly different from LABI and, indeed, from nearly any other evangelical Bible school in that it does not seek to enlist students into its specific denomination. In addition, in its mission statement, Harvest acknowledges that people come from different learning environments and cultures and that, for many of Harvest's students, oral traditions are to be valued, not viewed as inferior modes of learning.

Harvest Bible College shares space with a myriad of programs at a church in the Pico-Union area near downtown Los Angeles. Its mission statement is the following:

> The key to changing society is the presence of the Kingdom of God. Its presence comes as the people turn to Christ, churches are formed, and believers live and do the works of Christ. This includes prayer, righteous living, evangelism, serving others, feeding the poor, healing the sick, teaching the Word, working and speaking out against evil, [and] church planting.[10]

Harvest's courses were designed to be practical and authentic:

> Harvest is designed to develop character, Bible knowledge, relationship with God, and ministry competency. It uses only teachers who are spiritually mature and have ministries themselves. . . . Harvest is designed for working people with families who are active in their own churches and therefore do not have great amounts of time for schooling.[11]

This is the essence of what many evangelicals believe to be their work in society. The unique aspect of Harvest's mission statement follows, for it breaks with nearly every mission statement of any charismatic Bible college I have encountered. Demonstrating the social milieu that shaped the Vineyard's leadership ideas about race and ethnicity, this statement expresses a dramatic departure from the past:

> Harvest leaves people's ethnicity and socioeconomic identity intact. It is a multiethnic school that helps each group develop its own approach to reaching its people for Christ. Harvest is designed for regular people who will never be able to afford a major Bible college education; for people who come from oral traditions cultures and therefore do not fit

well with the white academic establishment; and for people who have been marginalized by the system for any number of reasons.[12]

Simply contrasting this statement to Luce's "supervisory" attitudes toward Mexicano converts and Arguinzoni's authoritarian tone toward his followers shows a marked shift toward autonomy and acceptance. Moving away from the missionary attitudes of many Christian denominations of both the past and present, the Vineyard's Bible college and leadership do not appear to see the link between Protestantism and Americanization but rather are seeking to break with past practices. Harvest's ideal is not to superimpose a methodology for evangelization that strips the unique contribution Latinos bring to the Vineyard of its ethnic roots. The school appears to understand that, to be successful in attracting ministerial candidates of diverse language, economic, and ethnic backgrounds, it needs to come to terms with why it has to offer such an apologetic statement in the first place. The Vineyard leaders who wrote this statement seem to understand something that many Christian leaders failed to grasp over the years, namely, that the conversion process became intimately tied with becoming "American." Exchanging Spanish for English, escaping the "darkness" of Catholicism for an enlightened Protestantism, Latino converts were being asked to leave behind a culture that was somehow not as morally uplifting as the one being offered by Euro American missionaries. Conversion equaled changing behavior, behavior often viewed as innately cultural and racialized, and reflecting a genetic disposition toward drunkenness, gambling, and sexual vice.[13] By divorcing the evangelical faith from the notion that to be Protestant means to be or become "white," churches like the Vineyard represent what many evangelicals of color hope is not an isolated case but a trend that will spread to the rest of the movement. I shall turn to the question of whether such a trend is evident in the conclusion of this book.

Like Victory Outreach members, many Vineyard members do not ascribe any validity to secular methods of changing society. To support these beliefs, the Vineyard cites several success stories. One story recounts how two Harvest students changed their neighborhood, causing gang activity and drug sales to recede, by praying over the street. "We can crush the devil's party where we live too." Empowerment comes in the form of religious exercises: prayer, harnessed to strict interpretations of biblical scripture and buttressed by social and moral expectations.

Sociologist Christian Smith astutely observes that, as committed as evangelicals are to winning the world one person at a time—what Smith calls the "personal influence strategy"—this approach remains largely ineffective in bringing about large-scale social change. Instead, evangelicals rely on what

Smith refers to as the "miracle motif," where all social ills disappear if people convert. Smith adds: "Relationists have difficulty recognizing the potentially transformative power of countercultural communities and alternative collective identities and practices which challenge systems."[14] Ironically, evangelicals think that Christian morality should be the primary authority for American culture and society, and simultaneously think that everyone should be free to live as they see fit, even if it means rejecting Christianity. As difficult as the "personal influence strategy" is, nearly all charismatics interviewed for this study supported it as the only means to change society. Thus Vineyard members, including those being trained at Harvest, tend not to see large-scale change as their goal but generally tend to see personal evangelism as their way of changing society.

Returning to examine Harvest's mission statement for a closer examination of why the Vineyard's approach is so radically different than the Bible schools of the past, one need look no further than the statement that "Harvest leaves peoples' ethnicity and socioeconomic identity intact." This statement presumes that other theological educational models have not done so, but it does not comment on why? Harvest acknowledges the validity of oral cultures and that the "white academic establishment" has rarely validated such a culture. More revealing, Harvest admits that many people who avail themselves of Harvest's services—working-class people, Latinos, and Asians—have somehow been marginalized. It is safe to assume, from my discussions with Vineyard pastors, that one reason they remain unwilling to mention why people have been marginalized is because, like Fields, they are not comfortable with the jargon of what they view as political correctness. Furthermore, because many evangelicals do not wish to privilege political solutions to marginalization, the less said about the non-spiritual causes of poverty, racism, and sexism, the better. For now, let us return to what Harvest teaches, and how, by making theological education accessible, affordable, and practical, the Vineyard addresses an essential element in training Latino clergy.

There are six departments at the school: biblical studies, theology, language, character, ministry, and evangelism. The courses are taught in both English and Spanish. It takes one year to complete a certificate in biblical studies, two years to receive an Associate of Ministry degree, and three years for a ministerial diploma. The school also offers a B.A. degree and, upon accreditation, will offer master's and doctoral degrees as well. Several courses deal with urban problems and social ministry in a cross-cultural context. Language programs include Greek, Hebrew, and Bible English and Spanish. The school has mercy ministries to the poor based on the premise, "How can we empower them in this wicked world and yet not make them dependent on us?"[15] The class on healing and deliverance denotes the charismatic nature of Harvest's Vineyard influence. There is also a section for multicultural education that includes customs, cultures, and urban areas. In order to build knowledge of the Bible and character, students are asked to read the Bible at least twice a year and to pray at least ten minutes a day.[16] Moral codes, similar to those at LABI, are intended to regulate behavior and build character consistent with evangelical beliefs. "Each student must abstain at all times from illegal drugs, alcohol, gossip, sexual activity outside marriage, things needlessly offensive to others, and whatever else the Bible says Christians should not do."

Affordability appears to be one of the attractions of the school. The application fee is $10, and each course unit costs $37.50, so that the average class costs $75. Taking from one to eight classes per quarter would cost between $75 and $610 per year; taking three to twenty-four classes would cost between $225 and $1,830 per year. Installment payments are also possible.

Signs indicate that Harvest officials wish to empower Latino clergy in making decisions and in guiding the school in a different direction. Four of the five individuals on the board of directors are Latino, as are seven of the twenty-three faculty members. There is also a Spanish-only extension in Huntington Park, and, in Santa Ana, Harvest offers English, Spanish, and Korean classes. By its accessibility, affordability, and moral codes, and its language of inclusion, the stage seems to be set for Latinos to mobilize their religious space within the Vineyard. The following three case studies demonstrate how Latinos go about re-creating themselves religiously and how, in the process, they are affected socially and politically as well.

Joe Castaños is pastor of La Viña Downey. A Chicano baby boomer raised in Southeast Los Angeles, Castaños grew up as an active member of the Assemblies of God. He remembers his extended family viewing his family as "traitors" for leaving the Catholic Church. In high school, Castaños rededicated his life to God when he heard Nicky Cruz speak at a high school rally. Castaños began attending LIFE Bible College to train for the ministry. He originally attended LABI but found it too confining. At LIFE, Jack Hayford, a nationally recognized leader of the Pentecostal movement, trained Castaños. From there, Castaños grew tired of the traditionalism of the Assemblies and, influenced by the charismatic renewal of the 1960s, began to move into a more ecumenical charismatic direction. In the late 1970s, he began attending the Anaheim Vineyard. La Viña Downey opened in 1991, and Castaños became its part-time pastor, still keeping his job as an engineer, until he became a full-time pastor in 1996.

La Viña Downey began when people began gathering to discuss certain issues, to socialize, and to hold Bible studies. This nucleus of about forty people came from churches with internal political disputes, and thus they sought a common place to worship. They rented a hall, which they soon outgrew, then rented a church, moved to a gym, and finally moved to a larger church where they currently remain. Today La Viña Downey is a Spanish-speaking church with more than three hundred members. The church, I argue, represents a bridge for immigrant Latinos to find community, religious experience, and networks in order to establish themselves in the United States. As such, a Latino Pentecostal identity has been reshaped to resemble a charismatic identity; the Vineyard plays down the legalism of Latin American Pentecostalism and the traditionalism of Roman Catholicism, which helps immigrants to establish a relationship with the larger evangelical world. Castaños explains the Vineyard's attractiveness: "I think it's going to [grow]—and as it grows, I think it's going to attract second-generation youth—and there on, third I think what's attractive is its—there's a casualness about the Vineyard that does not demand a certain sense of appearance. It's laid back in the sense that there's no emphasis on dress codes of any kind."[17]

Castaños's casual attitudes often conflict with the expectations of those in his congregation, who tend to be more traditional and legalistic concerning worship, dress, and behavioral codes. In worship music, Castaños uses translated Vineyard songs, classic Latin American hymns, and praise songs, many of which are original compositions written by his church members. The music, a mixture of contemporary Christian pop, is intermixed with more traditional *coritos* (Spanish Protestant hymns). Several Vineyard standards may echo a soft-rock style, but then the strong beat and tambourine of a *corito* like *Jehova es mi Guerrero* (Jehovah is my warrior) turns this very modern-looking church, with pews, into a storefront with folding chairs: Women dance in the aisles, some with flags, while the crowd claps enthusiastically, and many respond to the singing with shouts of "Gloria a Dios," and "Alleluya."

Castaños and the congregation help to translate materials and train missionaries. Castaños serves as a liaison between Vineyard leadership and the Latino churches and is the de facto leader of the Latino Vineyards in the United States. Vineyard co-founder Bob Fulton has encouraged multicultural practices by securing funds for Harvest Bible College and by supporting church plants in geographic areas where Latinos might be able to strengthen their presence in the Vineyard. Castaños believes that a transnational component may indeed help build churches in Latin America and attract newly arrived immigrants who are already familiar with the Vineyard: "I've been on several trips to Latin America. . . . It's very appealing to them, because of the emphasis on the value of a person, and not so much trying to create a Vineyard tradition in other countries. . . . There's a high degree of awareness of the differences and . . . a very good effort to respect that. . . . I think a lot came out of the civil rights movement in valuing other cultures." Ninety percent of La Viña Downey is comprised of immigrants, drawn from Latin American countries like Chile, Peru, Venezuela, Guatemala, El Salvador, and Mexico. Based on a survey that asked members of this congregation about their social, political, and religious experiences, La Viña Downey appears to be the most charismatic of the three congregations. For other demographic information gleaned from this survey, see the appendix.

In examining the theme of religious identity and how Latinos accomplish this in the Vineyard, let us turn to the female respondents to this survey. The survey revealed that more women had converted from Catholicism (twenty-nine out of thirty-five) than from any other faith. The other eight women had converted from various Protestant faiths. All the women described themselves as having been born-again; of these, eleven are long-term converts, meaning that they became born-again at least ten years ago (of these, eight came out of the Catholic Church). Many of the women (sixteen) had attended La Viña for seven to ten years; that is, they attended before La Viña became an institutionalized entity at its present location. All but one responded that they attend church more than four times a month, and all but three indicated that they were very satisfied or satisfied with their church.

In terms of their beliefs about the Bible, fourteen women believe that the Bible is the inspired word of God and is free of error. Twenty women take a more literal approach, believing that the Bible is the actual word of God and thus should be taken literally. Regarding charismatic gifts, very few of the women experienced all such gifts. Only five reported receiving visions, speaking in tongues, receiving words of knowledge, and being healed. Twenty-five reported often speaking in tongues. Aside from asking for and receiving prayer, tongues represented the most often reported spiritual practice. Visions were the least likely manifestation reported. Eight women said that they had never had such an experience. These numbers are not surprising, given that speaking in tongues is the essential component of the charismatic experience and is used both as a private devotion and a public prophetic gift. Only five women reported never speaking in tongues. One of the Vineyard's characteristics of ministry is its belief in healing, so, not surprisingly, twelve women reported being healed on a regular basis. Six reported never being healed, but, of those six, only one never witnessed the healing of another person.

The element of the church that La Viña women find important reveals much about what they value. For example, they do not appear to be interested in politics, partly because of their citizenship status. Three women classified themselves as conservative Republicans; seventeen had no political affil-

iation; and twelve considered themselves to be liberal to conservative Democrats. Of all these women, most never voted or cannot vote. When asked
about jobs, volunteer work, and evangelism, all the women who responded
considered evangelism very important. Twenty women also expressed a high
regard for volunteering. Only sixteen of the women considered job success
very important.

Regarding the male respondents, twelve men had converted from
Catholicism. Five had converted from other Protestant denominations. All
but one defined themselves as born-again and nine were long-term converts,
having been reborn more than ten years ago. Men's attendance rates were
the same as women's, and all but one attended church at least four times a
month. Five men have been active churchgoers for between seven and ten
years. Like the women of the congregation, men appear very satisfied with
their church. Unlike women, men tended to be less literal, believing that the
Bible is inspired rather than the actual word of God. With regard to charismatic experiences, men were much less likely to have consistent experiences. The most common such experience among men was speaking in
tongues, reported by seven men. Only three men reported that they often received words of knowledge. Several men responded that they had not had
any charismatic experiences in any category; five had never spoken in
tongues. Only two men reported having been healed and having often witnessed healing.

There may be something to the mechanics of worship that accounts for
this lack of charismatic experience. In Vineyard churches, there is usually a
ministry time where manifestations occur in a consistent manner. By cordon-
ing off ministry time to either before or after the service, the appropriate time
is usually segregated by gender, meaning that women pray for women, men
pray for men. It may be that men are intimidated by the public display of such
manifestations. Ironically, it is usually under the authority of a male pastor
that charismatic ministry occurs. It may also be that women, as the support
system for evangelical churches, are more likely to support the church, to attend Bible study, to volunteer, and to attend church. Also, women are less intimidated by public displays of emotional worship.[18]

When it comes to issues like jobs and politics, nine men reported no political preference and little or no interest in politics. Of those who stated a
preference, six considered themselves liberal to conservative Democrats, and
four reported they were Republicans. Twelve men reported voting occasionally. Like women, men overwhelmingly rank evangelism as their priority. All
but two men hold evangelism to be very important. Men split evenly on the
notion that job success and volunteering are very important.

Analyzing these findings places the La Viña Downey congregation in common stead with most of evangelical Christianity. In terms of charismatic experience, the range of experiences is quite typical of most self-identified charismatics. My survey findings support Smidt's findings that speaking in tongues should not be a definitive marker of charismatics. Smidt reported that 23 percent of the American public self-identifies as charismatics, but only 9 percent speak in tongues. Such responses tend to support Smidt's findings that the more charismatic a person was, the more "orthodox" he or she was, meaning that the person tended to believe in miracles, the infallibility of the Bible, and a host of other markers of "orthodoxy."[19] Regarding job success, volunteer time, and evangelism, La Viña Downey respondents are similar to Smith's survey of evangelicals. Smith found that evangelicals were more likely than mainline Protestants, Fundamentalists, or Catholics to evangelize others, defend a biblical worldview, volunteer for community programs, and work hard in their daily lives to set Christian examples for others.[20]

The major distinction between La Viña Downey and the evangelical community focused on politics. While Smith's subjects were more likely to vote, lobby political officials, and work hard to educate themselves about social and political issues, my respondents exhibited little interest in politics.[21] Perhaps the sense of a lack of ownership in the U.S. political system forms a barrier that made politics inconsequential. The citizenship status of many respondents explains their lack of political engagement. These findings are important because they support my contention that, by serving as a bridge to the larger evangelical community, La Viña Downey serves as a mediator between two traditions, the evangelical and the Pentecostal; by placing charismatic experience at the center of worship, the church offers its acceptance.

However, there is more mediation at La Viña Downey. The church mediates between at least two cultures, that is, Euro American and Latino, by creating a space for Spanish to be the worship language for adults and by securing a space for U.S. Latino youth. Finally, the church mediates between generations. Through language and through the use of popular culture and innovative forms of worship, the Vineyard succeeds in being many things to many people while using evangelical theology to bind its members together and tie them to the larger Euro American evangelical community.

La Viña Downey services are distinctly tinged with Latin American influences, even with regard to the food served during Bible study. The adults of the congregation can feel comfortable worshiping in their own language, while at the same time, their children, from nursery age to young adults can receive religious instruction in English. At La Viña, a half dozen different Latin American countries are represented with generational, cultural, and linguistic differences, which makes the youth ministry challenging. Castaños asserts that La Viña seeks to "create a contemporary environment where [youth] . . . can identify with and dwell in, in a sense."[22] Castaños sees the problems of Latino youth to be compounded by a lack of opportunity and a pervasive sense of isolation. He notes: "a lack of identity in feeling that they are a part of this society, so we created our own . . . subcultures." To counter these feelings, Castaños bridges the worlds of traditional Latin American hymns with contemporary Vineyard standards.

For Spanish-speaking young adults, the Sunday service provides contemporary worship and a chance for them to dress casually. Much of the older and some of the younger people are formally dressed in suits and ties. Those not wearing their Sunday best are nevertheless made to feel comfortable. Castaños notes that one of the generational and cultural gaps that he has tried to mend in the church are the legalistic tendencies of some older, and newly arrived members who came from countries where dressing informally for church is considered disrespectful. Castaños tries to change this attitude by dressing casually himself. He would love to make the service even more casual, copying other Vineyards, who have an intermission in the service for a coffee break—but he fears that too much informality too soon may irritate his constituents.

As the young adults and youth of the church become more acculturated to life in the United States they need to find something for themselves: English services, rock music, drama, and dance ministries are used to keep them interested in church. These activities also provide the added benefit of keeping the second-generation in an immigrant church rather than losing them to an English-speaking, Euro American church. Paul Castaños, Joe's son and the youth pastor of La Viña, presides over the youth service held in the main sanctuary on Wednesday nights. Dimly lit, and attended by fifty to seventy-five youths and young adults, the service begins with praise and worship—and rock and roll. The music represents a mix of Vineyard standards, Christian rock, and slower ballad-like songs. Paul follows with a message, relevant to youth, and the service ends with ministry time, where people pray for one another.

The music, this evening, is a rendition of "We Wanna See Jesus Lifted High." People lift their hands and many sing. There is an overhead projector with the lyrics displayed, but few need to use it—as many of the songs played that night are familiar throughout the evangelical community. Occasionally, the music is accompanied by a dance performed with flags. In the past, Paul has spoken on the potential dangers of secular music, but, instead of condemning secular music entirely, Paul distinguishes between secular music and music he believes supports occultism. The rock performer Marilyn Manson

was singled out for his critique.[23] Part of creating and maintaining an evangelical youth culture, Latino or otherwise, means that co-opting rock music has its
drawbacks. How does one sacralize music one believes accomplishes one's religious purposes while at the same time warn of the dangers of other rock music? Lyrical content becomes the standard by which La Viña members measure the extent that they will co-opt music for worship. Musical styles—rock,
rap, and techno-industrial—are all rearranged and used by churches, provided
that the content conforms to the religious message.

La Viña seeks to help Latino youth find their identity in the larger American society through spiritual transformation. Charismatic/Pentecostal Christianity provides a place where youth can participate in the supernatural spirituality that remains the faith's most inviting attraction. Sharing such beliefs
and experiences with others and creating community bridges the same liminal space as the rehab home does for Victory Outreach. The Vineyard,
though, has other methods that accomplish this bridging of cultures besides
church settings—many of their Latino pastors are immigrants and committed
to helping Latino immigrants in southern and northern California. It is
through their narratives that the creation of a Latino religious identity becomes transmitted and experienced.

William Pinedo pastors a church plant previously attached to the larger
Vineyard in Anaheim. Pinedo, now in his thirties, was born in Colombia but
was raised in New York. Pinedo teaches while waiting for his chance to pastor full-time. Raised Catholic, Pinedo converted in college, when his room-
mate invited him to a Bible study. What impressed him was "the relationships, the sense of community that I saw there, the love, the peace.[24] After
college, Pinedo attended a local Bible college and began attending the Vineyard. Attracted to the expressive worship and the availability of ministry to anyone, Pinedo joined the Vineyard in 1984. He became involved in a Vineyard
feeding program called "Lamb's Lunch." He also ministered by taking food to
local residential hotels that housed single mothers and their children, as well
as ministering to prostitutes that frequented the hotels. In 1992 La Viña Anaheim was started under Pinedo's leadership, separating as an independent
church in 1998.

At first Pinedo had no interest in working with Latinos. In fact, he was
adamantly against it: "I really didn't want to do anything with that part of
my culture, okay . . . I ended up going and when I was there the Lord really touched me and broke my heart. . . . And for the first time, I knew God
was calling me to work with Hispanics." La Viña began in 1998, and a year
later forty-five adults and twenty children had joined. Pinedo continues his
ministry to the poor, leading the church and visiting the neighborhood.

Occasionally he will take up a special collection for a family that cannot pay their rent.

Several aspects of the Vineyard philosophy of evangelism bolster the Latino ministry and its ability to work within the denomination without abandoning the language or culture. The first is the church's extensive missions movement around the world. Thus an immigrant can experience familiarity with a Vineyard in his or her home country. This transnational link eases the traumatic move to the United States, as it provides an immigrant with a place to call a spiritual home. Conversely, immigrant converts in the United States often want to use their religious knowledge to return and plant a church back home, thereby securing that they have links back home. For example, two of Pinedo's congregants are on missions, one to an orphanage in Baja, the other to a church plant in the troubled region of Chiapas, Mexico.

Also helpful is that many of the Latino pastors of the Vineyard do not come from one geographic or cultural group: they are Cuban, Puerto Rican, Guatemalan, Chicano, Mexicano, Colombian, Venezuelan, among other nationalities, who can cross cultures and pastor pan-Latino churches. Pinedo notes that he has no difficulty relating to the predominantly Mexican and Central American group that comprises his congregation.

La Viña Anaheim's services are in Spanish, but the youth services are in English. Pinedo asserts that the young feel more comfortable in English. Practically and spiritually, young people can have their spiritual needs met in the same church as their parents, or, if they are so inclined, they can become part of the evangelical landscape through a church that uses the Spanish language and affirms the culture of their family.

Pinedo points out that, in addition to helping out in the community and offering casual worship, one of the most attractive aspects about the Vineyard is its egalitarian attitudes toward its congregants. The ability to pray for others, operate in charismatic gifts, and minister to others is not limited to a priesthood or appointed laity—anyone can and should minister. As passionate as the Vineyard is to meld Pentecostal and evangelical worlds, it apparently has little desire to be dogmatic about converts changing their religious labels. Pinedo notes that this attitude has helped him deal with his parents. Though his mother is more accepting, his father is less so: "My dad, he's kind of funny, 'cause he kind of looks at it as a hobby. This is my hobby. . . . I think that was one of the things of the Vineyard, too, was that you know you're still in the church, whether you're Catholic or Baptist." This nondogmatic nature may also be why youth are attracted to the Vineyard in general.

Although much of the Vineyard's social mission develops outside the churches, it should be noted that Pinedo's priorities are spiritual. "I want to impact the Hispanic community for God. And working here . . . we've got Anaheim . . . I keep hearing L.A. at 2010 they [Latinos] will probably be 50 percent of the population. . . . If there is a group of people who are bound up in idolatry and witchcraft, in all kinds of stuff, it is the Hispanic people." In Pinedo's estimation, churches can never shift into spiritual areas viewed as non-Christian—that would be an unacceptable price to pay for inclusiveness. Pinedo does not describe what he means by idolatry or witchcraft, but it is safe to assume that such elements as Catholic icons, palm reading, fortune telling, and curanderos would be applicable. Protestant Christianity has historically drawn the line in acknowledging that the indigenous roots that many Latinos incorporate into their larger religious world are valid expositions of faith. For Pinedo, rooting out beliefs which he views as unorthodox are all part of becoming evangelical.

If one were to view Vineyard pastors in a spectrum, Pinedo would be considered more conservative stylistically, and Ryan De La Torre, a youth pastor at the Vineyard in Monrovia, California, would fall on the other end of the spectrum. De La Torre, a young man in his mid-twenties, has dyed blond hair and wears several earrings and tattoos. He prefers to minister at barbecues or coffeehouses. He is a blended Chicano, having a Mexican father and Irish mother. Raised in the American Baptist Church, De La Torre began to look for a church that was more accepting of charismatic experience when his own church began to discourage his gifts. The Vineyard's nondogmatic approach to charismatic experience and its orientation toward missions appealed to him. He attends LIFE Bible College and is training to pastor his own church.

The Vineyard Monrovia meets in an elementary school auditorium. Its congregation is 95 percent Euro American and includes between 100 and 150 adults and young people, De La Torre begins the service by worshiping as part of the larger congregation; when the worship service ends, he leads his youth group outside to lunch tables. De La Torre's stint as a youth pastor began more than two year ago, and he as seen the group grow from only a few high school students to include thirty-five to forty college students as well.

De La Torre has always been active in youth ministry, but he admits to not living up to his role as a leader: "I was kind of doing my own thing at the same time. I was living in the world . . . didn't really have a problem with it either."[25] He did not have a problem with it until a youth pastor from another church confronted him: "God gave him a word." This other youth pastor told De La Torre that God wanted to work with him but that De La Torre had to deal with his own problems first. "I mean, he had told me things here and there before, like through people, I didn't pay attention. . . . Because I wanted to be a businessman and make a lot of money." De La Torre describes how it felt to be confronted by his own insolence: "Probably one of the life changing things of my life. God was just speaking in my heart. . . . I just couldn't stop crying for like hours." De La Torre's next move was to find a church that accepted charismatic practice; his old church helped him and recommended the Vineyard. Still, De La Torre did not yet leave his denomination. Instead, he began a summer camp for American Baptist youth that emphasized charismatic practices, but he did not receive support from his own denomination. He left the church soon after and joined the Vineyard, because it suited him best theologically and philosophically. After a rather rebellious youth, he has developed a nonjudgmental approach to his charges:

> I have never put any kid down for anything they've ever done. . . . I've done a lot worse than a lot of them have. I had it rough. Had a rough time growing up . . . kids aren't evil. They do evil things. . . . But God created them in His image . . . they're no different. I mean, they might not know who God is. They might not know exactly who they are . . . I see them as kids who need help.

Part of the growth of the Vineyard as a whole lies in its ability to cultivate pastors who are confessional, authentic, and accountable. In addition, De La Torre notes: "We shouldn't add to the world what the world thinks of as putting kids down. We should help, be helping them up." De La Torre's tolerance for his youth is almost unlimited. For example, he knows that music is part of a young person's life, and so he knows that there is little use in telling a young person not to listen to music.

> I remember growing up, my youth pastor . . . telling us not to listen to this music. We'd brush them off, because they don't understand what we're listening to. . . . We have to accept them, these kids will listen to stuff whether we tell them to or not. . . . If you're just going to tell them that their music is bad and stuff, they're not going to want to listen to you from day one. . . . It's almost like putting them down again. You know, you can't accept the music I listen to, you can't accept me.

So how does De La Torre protect the youth of his congregation against secular music? He takes them through the songs of a particular artist and explains why the songs reflect un-Christian lyrics. He expresses his concerns about Marilyn Manson's values, which are reflected in the lyrics, rather than talking about the style of music. He hopes that by uncovering the lyrical content he can discourage young people from listening, but he knows that may not be the case.

De La Torre's methods also extend to dress codes: He does not believe in them and encourages the youth to dress as they wish. Yet, at LIFE, students cannot wear shorts or sandals. "I can't have my earrings in," says De La Torre; they cannot dye their hair, except in natural colors. Still, almost any form of expression is acceptable. De La Torre is not bothered by body piercing, so long as the parents are informed first. Although he is not terribly enthusiastic about tattoos, he has three himself. Most important, he is adamant that the Vineyard accept the youth with all their foibles, since accommodation is the only way to reach this generation. He relates a story in which the Vineyard founder John Wimber told him that the Vineyard's baby-boomer constituency would pass and that De La Torre would have to reinvent what the Vineyard means to his generation. In response, De La Torre offers an explanation of why he found a home in the Vineyard. "I'm in this denomination because [of what] the Vineyard believes, what their belief system is, is the closest to mine of any denomination I've been to. . . . I wouldn't even go to a church . . . that compromises who Jesus is." The Vineyard's nondogmatic approach to charismatic practice greatly impresses him:

> Belief in the gifts. But not belief in the gifts because they have to be there in order for God to work. . . . [I] don't believe you have to have these gifts. . . . Foursquare, in their belief system, speaking in tongues, is the evidence . . . [of] the Holy Spirit. Of being filled with the Holy Spirit. Well, I don't believe that, and a lot of Foursquare people don't believe that either.

Along with a casual attitude about style and dogma, De La Torre describes his coffeehouse model but notes that it will not be successful everywhere. He describes a Gen-X church, of the Foursquare denomination near his church, that has a coffeehouse atmosphere, and he noted the racial difference: "It's more of an Anglo kind of [thing]." De La Torre believes that the socioeconomic and cultural factors of the community need to be taken into account when beginning a ministry. He believes that coffeehouses will not work in predominantly African American neighborhoods, for example, because it is more of a "middle-class, white thing."

Part of the Vineyard's growth lies in its ability to be different things to different people. For De La Torre, it is to relate to his youth, to bring in the small group of Latinos, to introduce them to the already established Anglo group while making sure they are all involved in ministry. De La Torre believes that youth are looking for "spirituality." "I mean, whether they find it in a bottle, or in partying, in sex, or in Jesus Christ, people are going to look for things . . . like I know our generation, everyone's got so much, into like . . . looking at their spiritualness. They go to Buddhist, New Age, and psychics . . . they're just looking in the wrong place."

One tends to believe that the blended ethnicity of De La Torre, his dyed hair, his tattoos, would do better in Los Angeles because he looks like the people in his group. What seems conspicuously absent from De La Torre's discussion is any hint that he is conscious of his ethnicity—or that such things matter for the purpose of ministry. Echoing back to Toulis's argument, and as evidenced by the students at LABI, one's religious identity as a Christian tends to supersede one's ethnic identity, and, in the Vineyard, one's identity as a Christian supersedes denominational labels.

De La Torre's lack of emphasis on ethnicity is not the result of a lack of awareness, but of his current work in a church that lacks diversity. He seems keenly aware that the overwhelmingly Anglo presence of Vineyard leadership has much to do with how ministry develops—and that such homogeneity will not work in diverse neighborhoods because of the inability of leadership to relate to its clientele. Indeed, there seems to be a growing realization within evangelical youth that their generation does not place the same importance on ethnicity because they grew up around diversity and are comfortable with difference. This may be true of youth of color who are raised or schooled in diverse neighborhoods and schools. But is this true of youth who are raised in homogeneous communities that have not experienced an influx of diverse populations and who, for the better part of several generations, have not experienced socioeconomic dislocation? When we profile the Lord's Vineyard in Pico Rivera, California, we should keep these questions in mind. For now, let us leave individual profiles behind and examine another congregation, a second type of La Viña, a church plant that has spun off from the Vineyard in San Francisco, one that considers itself a bilingual, bicultural congregation working in the mission district of the city.

La Viña San Francisco, a church plant founded in 1998, began when a group of Spanish-speaking Latinos broke away from the larger English-speaking church. This bilingual and bicultural church of about thirty-five to forty people met at first in a recreation room that also served as a place where neighborhood children played games after school but has now recently moved to a new building.

Similar to La Viña Downey, the San Francisco church has benefited from the decades-long exodus of Latinos from the Catholic Church. All but seven members left the Catholic Church and now attend La Viña, although one respondent said that she still considers herself Catholic but attends La Viña because of its worship and sense of community. Many of the church members are new converts; only five have reported a significant number of years intervening between the time they reported having been born again and their decision to attend La Viña San Francisco.

Perhaps because of a host of factors—newness, youth, the generally liberal attitudes of many in San Francisco—this congregation has more moderate views on political and spiritual matters. Spiritually the San Francisco church appears to be less charismatic, only three members reporting having received visions and only five that they spoke in tongues often and received a word of knowledge. No respondent reported having been healed more than once and only three said that they had frequently witnessed healing. Regarding biblical authority, thirteen responded that the Bible was inspired, and this was the largest number of such respondents in all three surveys. Of these, one believed that the Bible contained errors. Many of the respondents can be described as new believers based on when they converted. Only one Catholic convert, now in her thirties, noted that she was born again between the age of eleven and eighteen. The other long-term converts, of which there were seven, were Protestants. All respondents reported that they were either satisfied or very satisfied with their church. These responses tend to contradict Smidt's findings that the more charismatic a person is, the more "orthodox" that person is, meaning that such people tend to believe in miracles and the infallibility of the Bible. Therefore, despite the one respondent who did not follow suit, La Viña San Francisco appears to be in the evangelical fold.

Respondents exhibited more interest in politics than other churches. Eight said that they were at least nominally interested, and five identified with political parties; all but one reported being a Democrat and six voted regularly. Regarding the last section, the San Francisco church did not differ significantly from the others. Of the three categories ranked for their importance—jobs, volunteering, and evangelism—the most important remained evangelism. The higher rate of political involvement may reflect the citizenship status of the congregation, since more people report voting regularly. Regardless of this, the congregation's political activity supports Smith's findings that evangelicals are more actively involved in politics than Catholics, fundamentalists, or mainline Protestants.

The pastoral care of the church has fallen to a Venezuela native named Alex Vargas, a thirty-year-old former missionary who wanted to continue in that field until he was asked to take the helm of this new church plant more than three years ago. Raised as a Catholic, Vargas converted in college and became a Presbyterian. He began attending San Francisco Vineyard church to train for mission work. He joined the church because he liked the balance the Vineyard gave to evangelical theology and Pentecostal experience; he also liked the casual atmosphere of the church.

Many of the first members of La Viña, which began as a small church plant of Spanish-speaking members from the San Francisco Vineyard, were from Guatemala. Now the church has a more mixed Latino immigrant and U.S. Latino congregation. "Since we started coming [to the United States] that was one of the reasons to come to an American church, to learn the culture, to learn the language. And bridge two cultures, between the Latinos and the Americans."[26] Vargas echoes the sentiments expressed by Castaños, who, though not consciously, is also bridging cultures. "They don't belong to any— they don't have a sense of belonging to a culture, like, for example, they can't say they are Americans, because although . . . they speak very well [*sic*] English . . . the faces . . . the looks."[27] Despite his earnestness, Vargas expresses disappointment that there has not been more growth. He notes several difficulties: from a generally nonreceptive atmosphere in San Francisco to conservative evangelicals and noncooperative relationships with other Latino churches, especially those who find the Vineyard's nondogmatic approach to charismatic gifts a betrayal of deeply held Pentecostal beliefs. Similarly noncharismatic Latino evangelical or fundamentalist churches that do not support charismatic practice are not comfortable with the Vineyard's willingness to allow public or private displays of such practices. Despite Vargas's trouble with minimal growth or cooperation, the health of the church seems secure. Financially the church recently bought a building, and church members support Vargas and his family through their tithing.

A final example of Vineyard San Francisco leadership highlights the complexities of integrating the disparate parts of a religious and ethnic identity, especially when other factors such as sexuality play such a prominent role. The church that gave birth to La Viña is home to the assistant pastor Bill Hernández, a son of Mexican- and U.S.–born Mexican migrant farm workers. Hernández received a scholarship to Berkeley to study the Ancient Near East. Though he was raised Catholic, he converted to evangelical Christianity in college, prompted by the campus ministry, Campus Crusade for Christ. Hernández appreciates the role that Campus Crusade played in teaching the Bible and disciplining him, but he had other difficulties that kept him from embracing the faith completely. "I needed something more because I was dealing with a lot emotional problems and stuff and sexual identity issues and stuff like that. And so I fell away for about three and a half years. And then the Lord started bringing me back into the Bible."[28] After reading the Bible and studying for a year, Hernández says: "I had reached the end of my rope. I had gotten involved in drugs and was very depressed, suicidal . . . I was hit by the Holy Spirit and just had this incredible experience, very miraculous. I heard His voice and He said 'I want to be your God, I want to take care of you.' " Hernández became involved in healing ministry and became licensed at a nondenominational charismatic church in northern California. For Hernández, unfortunately, there was a "ceiling" to what the church was willing to accept as charismatic practice. Hernández was led to the Vineyard, where, especially during Wimber's leadership in the early 1980s, there were very few ceilings. By 1989 Hernández was a part-time pastor at the San Francisco Vineyard. "I started doing some groups, support groups for men and women and dealing with sexual identity issues and relational issues." In 1997 Hernández became a full-time pastor. Although he considered becoming a licensed counselor, he decided to work under the cover of a church so that he could inject religious advice into the prescription: "I can talk about the Bible, I can break some rules. I can talk about sin, I can cast out demons." Regarding homosexuality, Hernández explains his philosophy of ministry as follows:

> People will come very obsessed or very anxious about their homosexual identity and I get them to accept it, the struggle, and to try to get them to normalize that so they won't be so focused on the fact that they are dealing with homosexuality . . . that person might still be dealing with homosexual feelings and stuff for, you know, five years later, but they may start becoming very functional in other areas and being healed.

Hernández relishes the fact that the Vineyard allows such counseling without stigmatizing the participants—"where they can confess and talk about the brokenness, the sexual brokenness . . . to have a place where people can talk about all their dysfunctional issues." However, in our interview, when the subject turned to Hernández's role as a Latino member of the Vineyard, he seemed to be more hesitant and more aware of an obvious weakness of the Vineyard, if not of evangelicalism, with regard to issues of race and ethnicity.

Hernández had grown up in an overwhelmingly Euro American neighborhood and had never given much thought to his ethnicity. Approached by Chicano activists at Berkeley, he declined to join them because he never felt part of that movement. His ethnic consciousness did not become manifest until he began pastoring at the Vineyard where he heard church workers make racist jokes about Mexicans. "I just started to become conscious and realize . . . You know, this is a humiliation of me . . . I eventually spoke up and I just said 'you know, when you guys joke like that, it does bother me, it hurts.' " The joking stopped. As part of the Vineyard's realization that it could not grow unless it became more open to diverse groups, Hernández says that the San Francisco Vineyard has prayed for more diversity in the congregation. "I'm not here because I am Mexican but because I have worked hard." Hernández eschews the focus on gaining members from particular ethnic groups, but he believes that, because of his upbringing in a Euro American neighborhood, "that is part of my problem, because I didn't see myself as Mexican American, but I am and I like that part of me."

Two of the most contentious issues evangelical Christianity has encountered in its contemporary life are its stance in homosexuality and the ways that it has treated people of color. Because of the unwieldy and diffuse nature of the movement, it is almost impossible to generalize about it. Nevertheless, it will serve us well to make at least two assumptions about groups like the Vineyard: First, there exists a deeply rooted theological prohibition against accepting homosexuality as a fixed sexual orientation equal to heterosexuality; and, second, aside from denominations and movements built by people of color (African American, Asian, and Latino denominations aside), evangelical Christianity, only until recently, has "discovered" that its mostly Euro American churches are increasingly surrounded by people of color.

Diversity, for many evangelical churches, was not a planned goal of building a better church but a demographic inevitability. The incidental Latino Bible group came about because neighborhoods changed—social missions to Latinos historically were seen as missions to Latin Americans outside the United States. Historically many evangelical denominations refer to the departments that support Latino churches as "home missions." Multicultural ministry appears a recent concept and more a product of a few people like Vineyard leader Bob Fulton and Latino leaders like Joe Castaños. That the Vineyard in San Francisco invests time and money in ministry to reorient gays and lesbians, while allowing racial jokes to be a part of workplace banter, reveals more about the sociopolitical leanings of the congregants and the kinds of demons evangelicals have chosen to cast out.

So why would Hernández subject himself to this treatment? Why have Latinos been satisfied with their position as a mission field? One reason is because, as they have entered the realm of their evangelical world, their internal lives have changed. Hernández reports that God spoke to him in wholly personal terms: " I want to take care of you." Admonitions to change the society, to take up the cause of ending racism, to promote causes seen as "ethnic," in an era where the therapeutic personalism that makes charismatic Christianity one of the fastest growing faiths in the world, resonates less than personal appeal.[29] Latino evangelicals—like the LABI students, like De La Torre and other Vineyard members—subsume their ethnic identity under a religious identity that, for many of them, is new or different from the one in which they were raised. Charismatic experience solidifies, in an existential way, that they are changed people—they live differently, pray differently, read the Bible differently. Their worldview, which may or may not have included strong ethnic consciousness, has either been channeled to focus on the cultural accoutrements of ethnicity (festivals, language, food, or music), or it has dimmed to the point where only a searing remnant of prejudice reminds them that they often do not feel like they belong. The Lord's Vineyard in Pico Rivera, California, represents perhaps the most revealing example of ethnic consciousness vying for a place at the table with charismatic Christianity.

The Lord's Vineyard, located in a working-class area of Pico Rivera, is an English-speaking church dedicated to neighborhood evangelism and ministry to youth at risk. The Lord's Vineyard, in contrast to the San Francisco church, is an older congregation, and larger, with about 150 adult members. It is composed of many baby boomers and also many older people who all seem to know one another.

The Lord's Vineyard, like the other churches profiled, has grown at the expense of the Catholic Church. Eleven of the fourteen respondents reported being raised Catholic. Only four of the respondents reported being born again for any significant amount of time, and only two of those were from a Catholic background. Fewer than half the respondents belonged to the church for five years or more, meaning that at least some of the church growth has occurred in recent years. Regarding the authority of the Bible, of the fourteen respondents, ten said that the Bible was the actual word of God, intimating a more fundamentalist interpretation; only one viewed the Bible as inspired, and another said that the Bible contained errors. Of all three of the Latino Vineyards, the Lord's Vineyard has the least amount of charismatic activity. Not one person reported continual charismatic activity. Nine reported never receiving visions, eight spoke in tongues only once or not at all, and three reported never receiving or witnessing healing. These results would seem to contradict Smidt's findings that the less charismatic people are, the less "orthodox" they will be, and vice versa. Though the Lord's Vineyard was not overtly charismatic during Sunday services, the church maintains a belief in certain theological ideas that would place it in a more orthodox position. Congregants expressed a belief in miracles and quite often reported, during testimonial times at church, events that they believed to be miraculous in nature, such as healing, help with job seeking, and rescue from serious injury in car accidents.

Politically eight respondents called themselves Democrats, three called themselves Republicans, and seven indicated that they voted often. When it came to categories such as jobs, volunteering, and evangelism, evangelism was considered the most important. These findings would also seem to support Smith's findings that evangelicals are more likely to be politically involved, lobby for causes, and evangelize than any other Christian tradition. An added component to the Lord Vineyard's heightened awareness of politics emanates from the pastor, who is very involved in civic affairs in the community and is active with other local pastors in lobbying for more church involvement in political campaigns that focus on "traditional family" issues.

One can make sense of these numbers regarding charismatic practice and other items by examining the brief history of the church and its current leadership. It should also be noted that it was in surveying this church when I received my first and only dissatisfied comment when asking church members to rank their level of satisfaction. This person, who had little experience with charismatic practice and who believed that the Bible contained errors, claimed not to be satisfied with the Lord's Vineyard but declined to elaborate.

The lack of charismatic gifts may be directly related to the fact that this church began as a Calvary Chapel in the mid-1980s. Between Calvary Chapel and the Vineyard, the latter has, until now, taken the most charismatic road—allowing charismatic practice to occur during the services and setting aside a portion of time before or after the service for more intense experiences. Calvary Chapel, on the other hand, has not been open to charismatic manifestations during the service, suggesting that these practices are best kept to private prayer times. It would seem that the Lord's Vineyard has adopted many of its predecessors' ideas about charismatic practice. In four months of fieldwork at the Lord's Vineyard, I witnessed no charismatic practices or separate ministry time that occurred on Sundays. There were charismatic styles of worship characterized by the raising of hands and expressive worship. However, the laying on of hands seemed to be reserved for special occasions, usually performed by the pastor. Another reason for the lack of charismatic practices may be the leadership of the Lord's Vineyard under Richard Ochoa.

Born in Los Angeles in 1944, Ochoa is a father of four and grandfather of five. His father worked in the produce industry as a truck driver, and his mother was an electronics assembly line worker. Before becoming a pastor, Ochoa drove a truck for a local market for ten years. He has Pentecostal roots, his grandfather having been a pastor in East Los Angeles. Richard grew up in church but, by his early teens, began to get into trouble and drifted away from church. "You know, looking back, I know God was touching me and God, grandma prophesied over me when I was eight years old."[30] By the age of sixteen, he had begun hanging around with gangs and soon landed in the California Youth Authority for a year and a half in 1962. In 1963 Ochoa met and eventually married Cecelia; he also became an atheist.

Through the resuscitation of his premature son, Richard's wife Cecelia became a Christian, but that event did not solidify his newfound faith, as he continued to gamble, drink, and do drugs. However, he did become attracted to a brand of Pentecostalism called Word of Faith.[31] On one occasion, when he wanted to go home and get high after work, Ochoa realized he had had enough. "At that precise moment, I felt the presence of God come over me again. I was all by myself and this time there I was, I just surrendered . . . fell onto my knees and began to weep." Ochoa became a zealous evangelist, witnessing to his coworkers and over the CB radio in his truck. He began pastoring at his church six months after his conversion experience. Ochoa did not find the support he wanted at the Word of Faith church and left to attend Calvary Chapel in 1983. Shortly thereafter, that particular Calvary Chapel became a Vineyard, and Ochoa became the head pastor in 1985.

The Lord's Vineyard began, as with many Vineyards, as an informal gathering for Bible studies, meeting in a park auditorium. The church soon moved to a local high school, and, in 1996, the Anaheim Vineyard gave them financial support to purchase a renovated two-story, Spanish-style house. Ochoa started the Vineyard phase of the church with about a dozen people, since many of its 120 members left the church when the Calvary Chapel folded. Ochoa refused to acquiesce to the congregation's desire for more experience-based faith life in the church. He wanted to keep his church away from the controversial happenings that surrounded much of the Vineyard's first two decades. Ochoa says that the period was "craziness" and filled with "tangents," intimating that the prophetic years and the Toronto Blessing were distractions from the church's real work.

Richard Ochoa focused the energies of his church on inner-city problems and youth at risk. A glimpse at his homiletic style offers clues to his ministerial concerns. At a service, Ochoa passionately described how he presided over a funeral of a gang member who died during a particularly bloody month of drive-by shootings in the city. His solution to such violence is twofold. He actively participates in a character-development program at a local continuation high school, and he invites his students to church and hopes that conversion will help to stem the violence. Ochoa has been teaching character development since late 1998, and, though he cannot preach, he uses the time that he has with the youth to invite them to church; on several occasions, they have attended. In one instance a group of young men attended and sat together, unsure of what to expect. When the worship began, they stood but did not sing. When many of the people raised their hands to worship, they did not. They looked uncomfortable and waited for a suitable moment to sit down. By the end of the service, Ochoa attempted to signal to the congregation, with these young men in mind, that anyone wishing to accept Jesus should make a private statement.[32] However, Ochoa's strong personal pleas may not be sufficient to reach the youth, since the Lord's Vineyard has not incorporated any popular cultural forms that might serve as a bridge to the gang subculture. For example, music at the Lord's Vineyard is almost exclusively Vineyard worship standards, with an occasional gospel song for emphasis. Unlike Victory Outreach, the music does not appear to resonate with gang members, and, aside from Ochoa's outreach, the church supports no other formal programs. Gang members attend the Lord's Vineyard largely because the pastor is an ex-gang member who does not bother to hide his tattoos. Ochoa invites them and tells them he understands.

Teresa Arce and her husband preside over youth ministry at the Lord's Vineyard. Raised Catholic, Teresa Arce converted in 1981 after, having been invited to church, she found that the service helped her to cope with her father's death earlier that year from cancer. Arce comments on what the Vineyard offers her and her husband: "I know what draws us—what keeps us coming to this particular church was the way people accepted us . . . my husband [did not] have to wear a shirt and tie and go to church . . . but he could come here and be comfortable, and be himself in shorts and a T-shirt, and be happy."[33] The Arces' first church experience had been unsatisfactory because they felt uncomfortable. "Just by walking in there and just seeing the way people were dressed and kind of looking at you . . . you know, it was like I kind of felt I had to live up to that—to that kind of standard." Casualness and acceptance are values Arce transfers to her youth group.

Arce, like De La Torre, believes that youth can be reached only by being their friend, not by judging their behavior. She seems to know something that many people who do not work with youth do not know—that the young people care and have a heart. Arce is drawn to their compassion. Unlike Ochoa, Arce did not have a troubled childhood, but she does not think that this limits her ability to relate to youth. In some way she believes that the youth she works with represent the children that she and her husband tried to have but without success. Keenly aware of the problems youth experience, Arce sees her role as providing an alternative:

> [It is a] low-income area, and I think that's important; these kids have something other than what's out there now . . . I think that it's important . . . to have . . . a Christian youth group, where these kids can come in and just be themselves. . . . we don't say you can't to this, you can't do that. You know, you can be yourself. And we talk about anything. And I think that's very important, especially with the drugs and the sex and everything.

Arce serves as a role model for young women, and her husband mentors the young men of the group. The Arces have found that many of the youth come from difficult family situations, many from single-parent homes. Acceptance helps form a bond with youth that builds trust, even though Arce has little experience with many of these problems. The Vineyard, through its reliance on lay leaders, helps to create a relational atmosphere that makes church a safe place, free of the traditional notion that only good people belong there. Arce explains: "These teens need to know that they can go somewhere, that they have a place to go, to stay, you know, and I've always told them, I don't care what it is. You know . . . you can always tell me and not have the fear of 'she's going to tell my parents.' " Although she is not required by law to keep anything that is told to her confidential, Arce takes her role as a lay minister seriously; she knows that sometimes her young people confide in her and that such confessions need to be preserved. What makes Arce effective, too, is that she has broken with the age-old prohibition against having discussions on sex and the like. "I think it's more of any open atmosphere. And I don't hold back from that because I know that's what they're hearing. Other than using profanity—of course."

Traditionalists, however, have some fears regarding the open atmosphere that both Arce and De La Torre offer youth. To traditionalists, it is a kind of moral slippery slope. If ministers allow clothing to be worn that is less than proper and then also begin to talk openly about sex, profanity and profane behavior cannot be far behind. To help combat this argument, Arce's role is twofold: She is the counselor and pedagogical leader who inculcates evangelical theology onto the *tabula rasa* represented by many youth's religious templates, and she is also the gatekeeper of traditional evangelical notions of virtue. Arce's two prohibitions, profanity and gossip, have become the proverbial lines in the theological sand. Such is the power shift from the priestly tradition of the Catholic Church, where the hierarchy held much of the power as gatekeeper. In evangelical Christianity, the laity hold the key to which aspects of the secular world are allowed to seep into their once hermetically sealed existence.

Like De La Torre, Arce's philosophy of ministry seeks to create an authentic spiritual place for her youth group. She explains: "We're all sinners . . . so sin is going to make us say you're out of our group. We can't do that . . . only the Lord can judge them." Somewhere along the line, through the varied streams that comprise contemporary evangelicalism, the Calvinist idea of sinners, eternally separated from a deity forever removed from human experience, was replaced by a gracious, merciful deity that insisted one come in as a sinner and receive forgiveness. This tolerant deity gained wider acceptance within contemporary evangelicalism, because he was more attractive to nonbelievers than the fire-and-brimstone Old Testament deity and because this generation of evangelicals began to realize that worldly renunciation and isolation were simply not effective strategies for living, or for evangelism.

Co-opting language, culture, and secular therapeutic models have made Arce's job easier:

> We tell them . . . the world's definition of cool isn't cool. . . . Even though your friends may look at you kind of weird, because, you know, it does say in the Bible that you will be persecuted for your beliefs. . . . People may look at you funny and say, oh a Jesus freak. That's a good thing. Don't let anybody ever tell you that's a bad thing . . . you need to feel good about yourself. And what better than to share them with the Lord. I mean, He accepts you for you.

The evangelical youth have their own clothing, music, language, and cliques, which, in effect, has created an oppositional culture, which the church hopes will form a fortress against the secular culture. Preparing youth for the rejection and derision they might experience at home and in school provides two crucial lessons: (1) the people with whom you surround yourself, date, and marry should agree with your beliefs; and (2) suffering for a cause and self-denial tie youth to the New Testament idea that one's life belongs to Jesus and therefore one needs to live differently than others, setting examples of self-control, humility, and suffering.

To inculcate such ideas, Arce leads her group in Bible studies that cover basic Christian doctrine laced with references to daily living. She began her study by trying traditional forms of pedagogical exercises, but this effort failed because the group was not familiar with the most rudimentary of biblical concepts. Arce toned down the lessons and made the studies a more casual affair: "We tell them, you should read your Bibles at home, not just, you know, for Larry and Terry. Just read your Bibles for yourselves." She tries to make her Bible study part-lesson and part–counseling session:

> We're not saying you're going to be sin-free because you're coming to this youth group, you know. But what we are saying is when you do sin, you know . . . that God will forgive you and that there's somebody here you can talk to. . . . And we've shared with them that once you do have the Lord and you really have the Lord in your heart, you will be convicted in your heart, you know, when you sin—you will have the conviction.

Arce also attempts to inculcate social values discouraging vanity that comes with teenage territory. She tries to get them to think about the plight of the less fortunate, and she relays stories about the homeless problem.

Wanting to promote sexual purity in her group, Arce took the group to hear a woman speak on abstinence. Arce represents the ideal Christian woman so as to attract young girls, and thus she must promote the idea of chastity before marriage. Her chief problem lies in facing those awkward moments when someone in her youth group will ask her if she waited until marriage. Arce acknowledges that she did not live a Christian life before marriage, but she believes that if she is honest, questions about hypocrisy will not derail the larger goal of discussing how much better abstinence will be for her youth. Placing Arce's ministry in the context of the larger evangelical subculture helps to contextualize where the Lord's Vineyard stands in this subculture and how, through ministries like Arce's, Latino youth are prepared to enter this new world.

Evangelicals know who they are and who they are not. Smith observes: "They possess clear symbolic borders that define the frontiers beyond which one is not an evangelical. The implicit distinction between us and them is omnipresent in evangelical thought and speech, so much so that it does not often in fact draw to itself much attention."[34] Smith continues that evangelicals suffer from a sense of displacement meaning that they perceive themselves as being under attack by the media, public schools, and from a culture that has, in Smith's words, like a lover, spurned evangelicals' affections. "Evangelicals are forever passionately pursuing a culture which increasingly disregards and mistreats them. But the more they are spurned, the more evangelicals believe they need to pursue and influence the culture."[35] Gen-X pastor Todd Hahn encapsulates this idea:

> A scriptural view of the church shows us as likely to endure persecution, rejection, and hostility. In our culture, we were comfortable with being the leaders of this consensus worldview. This is no longer true and it frightens us. In response, we have lashed out. . . . People who are not believers should be expected to view Christian ideas as bigoted and angry. . . . How easily we forget that nonbelievers are casualties of the true war—the spiritual war.[36]

Part of creating this subculture means that evangelicals need to create oppositional structures so that youth have a place to have fun, meet other like-minded youth, and replicate as much of their social lives as possible without falling prey to secular teen-age life. One of the most effective methods the Vineyard has to accomplish its goals lies in its music.

The Vineyard Music Group (VMG) is one of the most influential outlets for contemporary Christian music over the last twenty years. VMG publishes, produces, and distributes worship music for its churches and for countless churches worldwide. To promote its music, the Vineyard relies on hundreds of local musicians who have incorporated songs into the evangelical canon. Today Vineyard songs can be heard in hundreds of non-Vineyard churches, across the world, crossing denominations, even being reprinted in such unlikely places as United Methodist hymnals. No study of the Vineyard would be complete without incorporating the narrative of a musician about his role in the church. However, what began as an interview about the role of music soon turned to the more intriguing question of the ambiguities of what it means to be a Latino evangelical.

Born at the Los Angeles County General Hospital in the late 1940s, John Luna is married with four children and works as a driver for a nonprofit community health clinic. He grew up in a nominally Catholic home; his grandmother rejected organized religion, as did his mother. Luna, raised by his single mom, grew up in the Maravilla housing projects, living on welfare. His family's lack of religious faith did not deter Luna from attending church. For a while, he found solace from his "wayward" ways at a Boyle Heights church where a progressive nun impressed Luna with her commitment to help youth in the neighborhood. This introduction to Catholicism so affected Luna that he raised his children as Catholics.

The death of his grandmother impressed on him the need for faith, and Luna went back to church, attending Victory Outreach in East Los Angeles in the early 1980s. Luna and his wife became very active in church. He played guitar with the worship team. Attracted to the church because of its interest in at-risk youth and gang members, Luna believed that any church that allowed ex-convicts to be preachers suited his taste for progressive faith. However, he did find that something was missing at Victory Outreach, and eventually he stopped attending.

The Luna family moved to Pico Rivera, California, where they discovered the Vineyard. It seems that the specter of traditional family living away from the old neighborhood gave Luna the impetus to settle down. He settled into the church and says of his family, "We're like the Cleavers. You know, you see my wife and me walking up the street with a couple of Bibles."[37] Apparently aware of the 1950s sitcom stereotype of WASP America, the Lunas found their place in the comfortable casual atmosphere of the Vineyard. When I interviewed Luna, he and his wife had attended the Vineyard less than a year, but both were heavily involved in ministry.

Luna has not found it necessary to investigate the doctrines of the Vineyard. What draws him to the church is the pastor, whom Luna knew before Ochoa began to pastor, when Ochoa "did a bunch of crazy stuff." Authenticity, not doctrine, appears more important, because Ochoa symbolizes authority. In post-denominational churches, there is more theological capital in being real than being right. "He [Ochoa] is for real. And he won't tell you one thing and do another. He won't lie to you . . . he is an honorable . . . when he preaches, he preaches truth and you know." Despite Luna's appreciation of Ochoa's leadership and his own ministerial role as a musician, Luna's ambivalence about fully engaging in the larger role of evangelical Christianity displays the ambiguity rarely seen on evangelicalism's public face.

Luna expresses great distress at the conservatism of his fellow evangelicals, because he came of political age in the 1960s. He marched in support of the United Farm Workers and boycotted lettuce and grapes. He was also a member of the La Raza Unida Party and was active in socialist and communist politics. "I was beat up by the police in sixty-eight, sixty-nine . . . as a matter of fact, I was ready to leave [for Vietnam]." Luckily, as Luna tells it, he broke his ankle in a barroom brawl and was deferred when he did not pass the physical.

Luna did not shift political leanings when he converted. He still considers himself a progressive and is dismayed by the lack of political allies he has in the evangelical movement. He explains: "Well, I've found it very interesting that a lot of Chicanos, I don't know why they call themselves that anymore? . . . have a relationship with Christ and are in the church . . . are overwhelmingly Republican, it blows my mind!" Luna's politics have become a sore point between him and his wife, but Luna feels compelled not to co-opt that part of an evangelical identity: "I can't go to sleep politically because if my nest is feathered and my lot is full, I know there is [sic] a lot of people that don't have those blessings." Luna's social concerns are rooted in what he sees as the marginal existence of the passengers who ride the van he drives, dropping off patients at free clinics throughout Los Angeles. Luna also finds support for his politics in his faith. "Christ would . . . He says in His word that we should care as you do to the least, you do to me. So the least are often times people that we don't find attractive for whatever reason. . . . God has blessed me . . . but, you know, we have to remember." On this day, Luna was especially upset about the growing anti-immigrant sentiment that culminated in the passage of a controversial California proposition, Proposition 187, in 1996. Luna is near tears has he describes how many of his passengers would not have met the criteria for basic medical care if the courts had ruled Proposition 187 constitutional. Luna believes that, in the heyday of the Chicano movement, such propositions would have been unheard of. He notes: "There was a kind of unity, there was a unity through the antiwar movement . . . there was unity through social change with Cesar Chávez. . . . I think that is one of the problems; kids don't have a common goal. There is nothing. They're just indulging themselves."

The startling aspects of these statements are Luna's omissions. It is a given that evangelicals would mention the need for God to ease social ills. Luna did not mention God, and, furthermore, he cited politics as an answer to social ills. His attitude reveals the broadness of Latino evangelicalism. Luna encourages his youth to take classes in Chicano studies and to develop a heart for Latinos: "I'm still a world person in that we're all the same, we're all equal in the eyes of the Lord, but there is a place in my heart for Latinos." Luna longs for the church to be a moderate voice for social change, to be a vocal proponent against injustice: "It would be interesting to see if a church could walk a picket line or be willing to do a sit-down. I don't think so . . . you would have to come to that medium where you feel you know what your conscience tells you and where it fits with biblical teachings and principles. I think that Christ was a heavy radical." Our conversation concluded with a stark example of what Luna views as evangelicalism's capitulation to a blind faith in authority that has silenced its protests.

One Sunday, Ochoa related a story of police brutality committed against his deaf son that brought the service to a silent shock. His son had been pulled over for a traffic violation and was perceived by the local police as being noncooperative because he would not heed demands to be searched. Either Ochoa's son could not communicate to the officer that he was deaf, or the officer ignored his pleas. Either way, the incident ended with Ochoa's son in the hospital. Having been beaten with a club, he was bleeding from several gashes to his head. The officer cited him for resisting arrest and, despite the elder Ochoa's protestations that his son was deaf, the officer did not drop the charges. Ochoa had attempted to relate to the officer as a pastor, but the officer mocked Ochoa's religious fervor and refused to apologize for the incident. Instead of becoming angry, filing a lawsuit, or protesting against police brutality, Ochoa prayed for forgiveness and used the story to ask his congregation to submit to authority. Luna, to this day, cannot believe Ochoa did nothing of a worldly nature. Luna knows that he himself would not have been gracious, forgiving, or a pacifist, because this kind of submission to authority is alien to his political nature. Luna ends the interview apologetically: "Maybe my faith is not as great as other peoples' in that . . . we have to pray for people in authority and God will guide them. Maybe I don't have that kind of faith sometimes."

The ambiguity Luna displays in his faith life says much about how Latino evangelicals go about forming and re-forming their religious identity to complement their ethnic identity. But for as many Latino evangelicals, Pentecostals, and charismatics who tend to subsume their ethnic identities to their religious identities, there are others like John Luna. Luna's political consciousness, forged in the 1960s, cannot be easily subsumed to a faith which he believes does not offer resistance to social injustice. Luna continues to play the guitar in a rock band, to his wife's dismay. His paradox represents a microcosm of the evangelical paradox. Evangelicals want to live in a culture without becoming corrupted by it; they want to change the culture but lack effective strategies to do so. The rhetoric of "being in the world, but not of the world" is viewed as a biblical command that few ever attain. However, in the Vineyard, people are determined to engage in the culture and have abandoned their predecessors' strategy of retreat. They may very well be playing rock music in a bar on Saturday and then playing in the worship band on Sunday.

The fluidity of engagement that Latino evangelicals pursue is in marked contrast to the legalism that characterizes much of Latin American Pentecostalism and more dogmatic forms of U.S. Christianity. The Vineyard serves as a bridge to the larger world of evangelical Christianity as much as it is a way out for others. Critics of post-denominational Christianity lament the accommodation the Vineyard has made to modernity, but such criticism, according to Smith, requires "that religious groups have a fixed number of orthodox 'goods' to try and protect, which are gradually depleted through accommodation. The truth is, religious actors are quite capable of reclaiming and reinvigorating lost and dormant sacred themes, traditions, and practices; of generating new religious goods while relinquishing others."[38] The Vineyard provides Latino charismatics a place to accommodate to American culture without accommodation to their essential theology. The Vineyard has reinvented itself, appealing to immigrants and to second-generation youth while holding onto its original base of baby boomers, as it experiences the essence of a faith and piety that evangelicals hold to be the core of their lives.

Epilogue

Studying communities of faith has its inherent problems; I believe that I faced them all over the last five years. More times than I can remember, I was asked about my own faith preferences, quizzed about the purpose of my work, and viewed suspiciously as an interloper in private church matters. I was asked if I had ever been in prison, presumably because only if I had been in prison would I understand the significance of the meeting I attended. More often than not, these queries were not intended to stifle my research but simply to understand where I was coming from. It is the lens through which most evangelicals view the world, and I understand that, for many scholars, it is an unwanted gaze. Because I am familiar with this subculture, I was not offended. Although I was approached to convert to a particular faith tradition a few times, I understand the impetus behind this. It has been my task in this book to try to explain to a broader audience the evangelical subculture and how Latinos operate in it.

I would like to be able to say that, through my many personal conversations and formal interviews, I made great strides in breaking through the various defense levels I confronted, the God-talk, the testimonials, bringing the conversations to introspective discussions on ethnic and religious identity. The truth is, however, that ethnic and religious identity is not the topic most evangelicals are interested in; moreover, the historic anti-intellectual strains that run deep in Pentecostalism make such exchanges nearly impossible. Faith, for the subculture, resembles something alien that has inhabited one's body; it is planted there and grows. There are no extenuating factors that form this faith aside from Paul's explanation that it is a gift—the substance of things hoped for, the evidence of things not seen. Looking for the tributaries that flow from that faith—social location, ethnic background, familial ties, and cultural adaptations—requires more than simply taking my informers at their word. Such probing no doubt distressed them, because they were telling me the truth, at least the truth I needed to hear: Why is it necessary to pick such a pristine thing apart with intellectual analysis? As my friend Enrique Zone overheard once at a Pentecostal leader's meeting, "what we want is people filled with the Spirit, not people with Ph.D.s."

People in this subculture are guided by the need to protect their faith — from the unorthodox, from the critic, and from doubt. Ambivalence is tantamount to disbelief and is discouraged in all quarters. The fact that people choose religious identities, reinvent their own, or borrow someone else's and discard it only to start all over again is a cultural and social process for which evangelical theology has no answer, except that it is to be avoided because it smacks of disloyalty. But such events occurred historically with Latinos, who, often having converted from a Catholic background (viewed positively), became members of a Trinitarian Pentecostal tradition, and then chose to become part of the Oneness Pentecostal tradition (viewed negatively). Within the various denominations, Latinos struggle with problems similar to those with which many religious traditions struggle: How do you keep your children in church? Religious identities change and adapt to cultural shifts and generational changes, and, quite often, they routinize into bureaucracies. Listening to Victory Outreach members discuss their desire to retain their uniqueness, to remain untainted by the lack of inner-city vision they saw in other denominations, remaining the same while changing to reach a new audience, it would have been easy to discuss Weber's routinization theory, if they believed that Weber would have helped them in their mission of faith; otherwise, such theories were lost as one more analysis bereft of soul. Perhaps because the Vineyard was birthed in the Jesus movement and is relatively young and innovative, it has less interest in maintaining traditions. Basically, the Vineyard you get depends on what part of the country you live in. Latino Vineyards are no different. They can be heavily Chicano-oriented, immigrant-based, and nationality-specific — each having its own approach to faith, politics, and society. Despite the Vineyard's more progressive trajectory, my work there did not veer too far away from the testimonial, though it was the one place where I received the most introspective and analytic discussions with members.

What concerns me about this attitude is that the protective shield of faith with which Pentecostals cover themselves often descends into anti-intellectualism, legalism, and insularity. Is there any doubt that one reason it took so long for someone to write a scholarly work on Latino Pentecostals is because apparently such a study was of no interest to the thousands of pastors, ministers, and lay workers? And is it any surprise that the few books that will be published over the next few years will have emanated from insiders or former insiders? I wish to borrow an analogy from another problematic area that has given me great concern over the course of my young academic career, namely, the ghettoization of ethnic minorities in the evangelical press. Authors of color overwhelmingly write about topics that they presumably know best, but where are they when it comes to expounding on theological issues that scarcely touch on racial or ethnic issues? Pentecostals have fallen into our ghetto and, as they know full well, once you're in the 'hood, it's hard to get out.

It is not solely the sin of omission that has kept these stories out of the academy for all these years; it is also a sin of commission, where people in the subculture have steadfastly refused to view their faith lives as being open to scrutiny. In one of the more influential books of the last two decades, Mark Noll's *Scandal of the Evangelical Mind* (Grand Rapids, Mich.: Eerdmans, 1995), the author took his own people to task for their lack of intellectual depth. Perhaps if we in the academy take up the task of becoming evangelists of a different kind, insisting on the broadening of our minds, the feeding of our intellectual curiosity, and the opening of our faith to interlopers, we will go a long way to completing the triad of commands the Lord has asked of us: Love the Lord with all your heart, all your soul, and all your mind. To me, it is a command worthy of our efforts.

Appendix

Survey Results for La Viña Downey

The survey was conducted between January and March 1999. Following are the results:

Like many evangelical churches, most of the more than three hundred congregants are women. All respondents but one indicated that they were Mexicano, Latino, or Hispanic; one woman identified herself as Cuban.

Of the fifty-one respondents, women outnumbered men by three to one.

The women of the congregation are young; of the thirty-five women respondents, twenty-two were between twenty and forty-five years of age. Women split equally among the following categories of education:

eight had less than a high school education;

eight had attended some college;

eight were high school graduates.

The younger women, between twenty-one and forty-five years of age, had the most exposure to education, with only one not attending high school.

Twenty of the thirty-four women were married.

Women held a variety of diverse occupations.

Seven held positions as teachers and instructional aides in both Christian and secular education.

Thirteen worked at home.

All the single-parent respondents were women.

Seventeen women were either separated, divorced, or declined to give their marital status.

Six were widowed.

Of the married and single women combined, there was an average of between one and four children.

Men accounted for a much smaller number in the survey, with seventeen responding. Of these, thirteen were between the ages of twenty-one and forty-five; like women, they are young baby boomers and Gen-X Latinos. Concerning education:

Eleven men had either some college or a college degree.

Fourteen of the men are married.

Their employment varied from technical or industrial-related jobs.

Survey Results for La Viña San Francisco

The San Francisco survey was conducted between January and March 1999. Following are the results:

Like many evangelical churches, of the thirty-five to forty members, at least 50 percent are women.

The members represent a Gen-X and baby boomer constituency.

The group as a whole is better educated than those in the Downey church.

Sixteen of the twenty respondents have postgraduate, college, or some college education.

Seven of the twenty respondents are single.

Two respondents are divorced; all the others are married.

A diverse range of occupations is represented in various service industries:

Office work, delivery, sales, and a few professions, such as administrators, financial consultants, and school principals.

There are two female single parents.

There is one woman divorced with children.

Many of the children are young, between the ages of six and twelve, and they attend church with their parents.

Survey Results for The Lord's Vineyard–Pico Rivera

The survey was conducted between January and March 1999. Because there was a very low response rate—only fourteen responded—it was necessary to combine my fieldwork with the survey to garner the following results:

Many of the church members are married; this is supported by six of the fourteen respondents and many informal conversations with church members.

Most, if not all, respondents and members had some employment in the service industry, though there were a few professionals such as an assistant principal. Respondents offered little information on children.

Notes

1. El Aposento Alto

1. Larry Eskridge, " 'One Way': Billy Graham, the Jesus Generation, and the Idea of an Evangelical Youth Culture," *Church History* 67 (March 1998): 85.

2. Vicki L. Ruiz, "Dead Ends or Gold Mines? Using Missionary Records in Mexican American Women's History," in *Unequal Sisters*, ed. Vicki L. Ruiz and Ellen Carol Dubois, 2nd ed., 304 (New York: Routledge, 1994).

3. Timothy M. Matovina, *Tejano Religion and Ethnicity: San Antonio, 1821–1860* (Austin: University of Texas Press, 1995), 54.

4. Randall Balmer, *Blessed Assurance* (Boston: Beacon, 1999), 87.

5. Grant A. Wacker, *Heaven Below* (Cambridge, Mass.: Harvard University Press, 2001), 75–76.

6. Reuben Torrey, quoted in Wacker, "Travail of a Broken Family: Radical Evangelical Responses to the Emergence of Pentecostalism in America, 1906–1916," in *Pentecostal Currents in American Protestantism*, ed. Edith L. Blumhofer, Russell P. Spittler, and Grant A. Wacker, 31 (Urbana: University of Illinois Press, 1999).

7. Ibid., 34.

8. John H. M. Laslett, "Historical Perspectives: Immigration and the Rise of a Distinctive Urban Region 1900–1970," in *Ethnic Los Angeles*, ed. Roger Waldinger and Mehdi Bozorguehr, 41–42 (New York: Russell Sage, 1996).

9. Michael E. Engh, *Frontier Faiths: Church, Temple, and Synagogue in Los Angeles 1846–1888* (Albuquerque: University of New Mexico Press, 1992), 2.

10. Ibid., 14.

11. Engh, *Frontier Faiths*, 22.

12. Ibid., 16, 69.

13. Ibid., 16.

14. George Sánchez, *Becoming Mexican American* (New York: Oxford University Press, 1993), 71–72.

15. Engh, *Frontier Faiths*, 47; Clifton Holland, "Appendice I," in *Hacia una Historia de la Iglesia Evangelica Hispana de California del Sur*, ed. Rodelo Wilson (Montebello, Calif.: Hispanic Association for Theological Education, 1993), 199.

16. Holland, "Appendice 1," 199.

17. Engh, *Frontier Faiths*, 55.

18. Ibid.

19. Ibid., 176.

20. Gregory Singleton, *Religion in the City of the Angels* (Ann Arbor: University Microfilms Inc. Research, 1979), 84.

21. Board of Stewards, quoted in Singleton, *Religion*, 91.

22. Ibid.

23. Ida L. Boone, quoted in Engh, *Frontier Faiths*, 206.

24. Jane Atkins Vasquez, "La Iglesia Presbiteriana Unida," in Wilson, *Hacia una Historia de la Iglesia Evangelica Hispana*, 66.

25. Ruiz, "Dead Ends," 203.

26. Ibid.

27. "A Sunday Service in Pisgah Tabernacle," *Word and Work*, 28 September 1918, 7.

28. Wacker, *Heaven Below*, 204.

29. A. G. Valdez, *Fire on Azusa Street* (Costa Mesa, Calif.: Gift, 1980), 25.

30. Sánchez, *Becoming*, 151.

31. Ibid., 165.

32. Ibid.

33. Holland, "Appendice I," 199–202. Holland's preliminary research for this appendix appeared originally in his 1974 work, *The Religious Dimension in Hispanic Los Angeles* (South Pasadena: William Carey Library, 1974).

34. Ibid., 200–201.

35. Sánchez, *Becoming*, 156.

36. Holland, "Appendice I," 199–201

37. Robert M. Anderson, *Vision of the Disinherited* (New York: Oxford University Press, 1979), 43.

38. Ibid., 148.

39. Donald W. Dayton, *Theological Roots of Pentecostalism* (Peabody, Mass.: Hendrickson, 1987), 126.

40. Robert M. Anderson first articulated this "disinherited" theory of Pentecostal success. Grant Wacker's work examining the same early Pentecostal era has cast doubt on Anderson's theory because he found that, although many Pentecostals were from the rural poor classes, many Pentecostal leaders and later converts were not very different than average Americans at the time in terms of educational attainment and income. See Wacker, *Heaven Below*, esp. chap. 9 ("Leadership").

41. Ibid., 35.

42. Anderson, *Vision of the Disinherited*, 50–52.

43. Joe Creech, "Visions of Glory: The Place of the Azusa Street Revival in Pentecostal History," *Church History* (September 1996): 405–10.

44. Ibid., 405.

45. Ibid., 406.

46. Rodney Stark and Roger Finke, *The Churching of America, 1776–1900* (New Brusnwick, N.J.: Rutgers University Press, 1992), 18.

47. Ibid., 73, 76, 84.

48. Ibid., 17, 19.

49. William Seymour, "Missionary Notes," *Apostolic Faith* 1, no. 3 (November 1906): 1.

50. Frank Bartleman, quoted in Cecil M. Robeck Jr., ed., *Witness to Pentecost: The Life of Frank Bartleman* (New York: Garland, 1985), 25.

51. "When the day of Pentecost came, they were all together in one place. Suddenly, a sound like the blowing of a violent wind came from heaven and filled the whole house where they were sitting. They saw what seemed to be tongues of fire that separated and came to rest on each of them. All of them were filled with the Holy Spirit and began to speak in other tongues as the Spirit enabled them" (Acts 2:2–4).

52. Harvey Cox, *Fire From Heaven* (New York: Addison Wesley, 1995), 46.

53. Valdez, *Fire*, 47.

54. Vicki Ruiz has reported similar findings of conversion in her study of the Houchen Settlement House in El Paso, as has Robert M. Anderson in his history of American Pentecostalism. Ruiz found that many Protestant converts did not begin in the Methodist Church, but, in fact, converted earlier in their lives to other mainline Protestant churches. See Ruiz "Gold Mines," 307. Anderson concluded the same, that the first Pentecostal converts came from Holiness denominations: "The steady shift away from the more formal, established denominations toward the newer Holiness institutions intimates the predisposition of those in the leadership sample to some such movement as Pentecostalism" (*Vision*, 109–10).

55. *Los Angeles City Directory*, 1920 (Los Angeles Public Library: Los Angeles, microfilm), 1024; Cecil M. Robeck Jr., "Evangelization or Proselytism of Hispanics? A Pentecostal Perspective," unpublished paper, 1996, 5.

56. William Seymour, "Missionary Notes," *Apostolic Faith* 1, no. 10 (October 1906): 4.

57. Little else is know of the Lopezes or of their fellow Mexican convert, Brigido Peréz, except that he received the Pentecostal baptism in November 1906 and soon left to the mission fields of San Diego. It is hoped that Mel Robeck's new research on Azusa Street and forthcoming book will illuminate the roles of Latinos in the revival.

58. William Seymour, "Missionary Notes," *Apostolic Faith* 1, no. 11 (November 1906): 3.

59. Wacker, *Heaven Below*, 48. I have recently been told of another incident of this gift that occurred when a noted Pentecostal educator was trying to preach a sermon to a Spanish-speaking audience. The person reports being able to speak Spanish in order to exhort his audience.

60. William Seymour, "Missionary Notes," *Apostolic Faith* 1, no. 11 (November 1906): 4.

61. Ibid., 1.

62. The Oneness movement began in 1913 at the World-Wide Pentecostal camp meeting held in the Highland Park section of Los Angeles. The Canadian

Pentecostal R. E. McAlister delivered a sermon proclaiming the baptismal formula in Acts 2:38 as the preferred method. This method required that all Christians be re-baptized in the name of Jesus.

63. *Los Angeles City Directory*, 1912 (Los Angeles: Los Angeles Public Library, microfilm), 1236.

64. Manuel Gaxiola-Gaxiola, *El Serpiente y la Paloma* (South Pasadena, Calif.: William Carey, 1970), i–xi, 6–7.

65. Holland, *Religious Dimension*, 356.

66. Ibid.

67. Daniel Ramírez, "Pentecostal Praxis: A History of Latino Immigrants and the Apostolic Assemblies," paper presented at the annual meeting of the Society for Pentecostal Studies, Lakeland, Florida, 5 September 1991, 1–5.

68. Holland, *Religious Dimension*, 356–60.

69. Ramírez, "Pentecostal Praxis," 6.

70. John Preston, "Calixico, Calif.," *Pentecostal Evangel*, 28 December 1918, 10.

71. Ramírez, "Pentecostal Praxis," 12–13.

72. William Seymour, "Missionary Notes," *Apostolic Faith* 1, no. 9 (September 1906): 3.

73. Abundio López, "Spanish Receive the Pentecost," *Apostolic Faith* 1, no. 10 (October 1906): 4.

74. Ramírez, "Pentecostal Praxis," 5.

75. "Flocking to See Mystic Santa Teresa," *Los Angeles Times*, 15 December 1902, 8.

76. Gene Fowler, "Don Pedrito and Dr. Mud," in *Mystic Healers and Medicine Shows*, 51 (Santa Fe, N.M.: Ancient City Press, 1997), 51.

77. Ibid., 53.

78. Frank Bishop Putnam, "Teresa Urrea: The Saint of Cabora," in *Mystic Healers and Medicine Shows*, 40–49 (Santa Fe, N.M.: Ancient City Press, 1997).

79. Fowler, "Don Pedrito," 56.

80. Robeck, "Evangelization," 9.

81. Allen Figueroa Deck, *The Challenge of Evangelical/Pentecostal Christianity to Hispanic Catholicism in the U.S.* (Working Paper Series: Cushwa Center for the Study of American Catholicism, 1992), 14.

82. Most of my students are nominal Catholics of various ethnicities. Among the Latinos, there appears to be little interest in maintaining a religious identity beyond a symbolic one, but, as they tell me, their moms would kill them if they ever left the Church.

83. Ruiz, "Gold Mines," 311.

84. Portes examined four factors to determine at what levels acculturation occurred: (1) history of the immigrant, first generation; (2) pace of acculturation among parents and children and its bearing on normative integration; (3) the barriers, both cultural and economic, confronting the second-generation youth in

their quest for successful adaptation; and (4) family and community resources for confronting those barriers. Based on these factors, second-generation immigrants can enter society on one of three levels: (1) dissonant acculturation where there is racial discrimination, a divided labor market, no answer to inner-city subcultures, and downward assimilation; (2) consonant assimilation where there is family support, parental guidance and family resources, countermeasures to inner-city subcultures, and mostly upward assimilation; and (3) selective acculturation that is filtered through ethnic networks and community support, jobs supported through family and community resources, countermeasures to inner-city subcultures, and upward assimilation and possible biculturalism. See Alejandro Portes and Rubén G. Rumbaut, *Legacies: The Story of the Immigrant Second Generation* (Berkeley: University of California Press, 2001), 45–46.

85. Robeck, "Evangelization," 9.

86. J. Gordon Melton, *Biographical Dictionary of American Cult and Sect Leaders* (New York: Garland, 1986), 208–9.

87. Anderson, *Vision*, 71–74.

88. Jennifer Stock, "George S. Montgomery: Businessman for the Gospel," *A/G Heritage* 9, no. 2 (summer 1989): 12–14, 20.

89. Information on the anti-Catholic nature of nineteenth-century American Protestantism is copious if one were to look at the various journals and magazines for the denominations. For scholarly treatments, the best is Ray Allen Billington's *The Protestant Crusade* (Chicago: Quadrangle, 1964). Or, for a more regional examination, see Laura Maffly Kipp's *Society and Religion on the California Frontier* (Berkeley: University of California Press, 1994).

90. Francisco Olazábal, "Speech to the 9th Annual Convention of the Los Angeles District of the Epworth League," in *El Rdo. Olazábal* (Brownsville, Tex.: Latin American Council of Christian Churches, 1986), 192–93.

91. Ibid.

92. E. V. Neimeyer, "Anticlericalism in the Mexican Constitutional Convention of 1916–17," *The Americas* 11 (July 1954): 35.

93. Deborah Baldwin, *Protestants and the Mexican Revolution* (Urbana: University of Illinois Press, 1990), 35–37.

94. Olazábal, "Speech," 194.

95. Ibid., 196.

96. Henry Ball, "*Historia*," *Luz Apostólica* (April 1966): 2.

97. Olazábal, "Extracts from Missionary Letters," *Triumphs of Faith* 40, no. 6 (June 1920): 142.

98. Olazábal, "Work among the Mexicans," *Triumphs of Faith* 38, no. 3 (March 1919): 71–72.

99. Ibid.

100. "The Needs of Mexico," *Pentecostal Evangel* October 15, 1921, 3.

101. J. R. Flowers, "A Bible School for the Mexican Workers," *Pentecostal Evangel*, 6 January 1923, 13.

102. Ibid.

103. Miguel Guillen, *La Historia del Concilio Latino Americano de Iglesias Cristianas* (Brownsville, Tex.: Latin American Council of Christian Churches, 1982), 82–83.

104. Ibid., 106.

105. Glenn Gohr, "A Dedicated Ministry among Hispanics," *A/G Heritage* 9, no. 3 (fall 1989): 8.

106. Ball "Historia," *Luz Apostólica* (April–May 1966): 3.

107. Guillen, *La Historia*, 93. Bazán eventually returned to the Assemblies of God.

108. Gastón Espinosa, " 'El Azteca': Francisco Olazábal and Latino Pentecostal Charisma, Power, and Faith Healing in the Borderlands," *Journal of the American Academy of Religion* 67, no. 3 (September 1999): 603–4.

109. Olazábal, "Carta Abierta al Hermano Richey," in *El Rdo. Francisco Olazábal*, 3.

110. Olazábal, *El Rdo. Olazábal*, 6.

111. "Hundreds Pray All Night at Unique Healing Service," *Cleveland Daily Banner*, 12 September 1936, 421.

112. Spencer Duryee, "Great Aztec," *Christian Herald* (August 1936): 5.

113. Ibid.

114. Roberto Almaraz, interview by author, tape recording, Santa Fe Springs, California, 27 July 1997.

115. Jesse Miranda, interview by author, tape recording, Azusa, California, 6 May 1997.

116. Anderson, *Vision*, 149.

117. Ibid.

118. Olazábal, "Preguntas y Repuestas," *El Rdo. Francisco*, 207.

119. Anderson, *Vision*, 217.

120. Holland, *Religious Dimensions*, 356.

121. Enrique Zone, conversation with author, Azusa, California, April 11, 2000.

122. Alice Luce, "Mexican Work along the Border," *Christian Evangel*, 15 June 1918, 11.

123. Luce, "Encouraging Report of Mexican Work," *Pentecostal Evangel*, 24 January 1920, 11.

124. Henry Ball, "A Call for More Laborers for the Mexican Work," *Weekly Evangel*, 24 March 1917, 13.

125. Samuel Ortegón, *Mexican Religious Population of Los Angeles*, masters thesis, University of Southern California, 1932, 10. It should be noted that Holland's numbers differ significantly from Ortegón's. Holland found more than a dozen churches in East Los Angeles by 1932, fourteen by 1934.

126. Ibid., 11.

127. Ibid.,39–40, 50.

128. Ibid., 46–47

129. Victor De Leon, *The Silent Pentecostals* (Taylors, S.C.: Faith Printing, 1979), 59.

130. L. V. Kenney, "An Appeal," *Weekly Evangel*, 21 April 1917, 13.

131. Demetrio and Nellie Bazán, with Elizabeth B. and Don Martínez Jr., *Enviados de Dios* (Miami, Fla.: Editorial Vida, 1987), 26.

132. Holland, *Religious Dimensions*, 347.

133. Holland, "Appendice I," 199–202.

134. Holland, *Religious Dimensions*, 347.

135. Paul Barton, "Inter-Ethnic Relations Between Mexican American and Anglo American Methodists," in *Protestantes/Protestants*, ed. David Maldonado, 74–76 (Nashville, Tenn.: Abingdon, 1999).

136. Mario T. García, *Desert Immigrants: The Mexicans of El Paso, 1880–1920* (New Haven: Yale University Press, 1981), 88, 90–91.

137. Luce, *Missionary Report*, 1920, Assemblies of God Headquarters, Springfield, Missouri, 1.

138. Ibid.

139. Josué Sánchez, *Angels without Wings*, ed. Monte R. Madsen (New Braunfels, Tex.: Atwood, n.d.), 49.

140. Luce, "Mexican Work in California" *Pentecostal Evangel*, 1 September 1923, 13.

141. Luce, "Portions for Whom Nothing Is Prepared," *Pentecostal Evangel*, 9 December 1922, 6–7.

142. Ibid..

143. M. M. Pinson, "A Mexican Tent Meeting," *Weekly Evangel*, 28 July 1917, 12.

144. Ball, "Historia," *Luz Apostólica* (October 1966): 3.

145. Ibid.

146. "Report of Trip Through Texas," *Pentecostal Evangel*, 12 June 1920, 10.

147. Ball, "Writing from Ricardo, Texas," *Weekly Evangel*, 15 July 1916, 15.

148. Ball, "Historia de La Luz Apostólica," *Luz Apostólica* (July 1972): 8.

149. Ball, "The Mission to the Mexicans," *Weekly Evangel*, May 27, 1916.

150. F. A. Hale, "Mexican Work at Ricardo,Tex.," *Weekly Evangel*, 12 February 1916, 11.

151. Compilation of totals for Henry Ball's mission for 1916 from "Distribution of Missionary Funds," *Weekly Evangel*, 17 June 1916; 4 November 1916; 2 December 1916. The Assemblies of God published these lists periodically and in a 1917 column explained how the monies were distributed. The Assemblies did not want to overlook anyone, and, in order to make distribution more equitable, in the spring of 1917 the Assemblies of God began to ask churches to donate to a missionary fund and choose what mission they wanted to support.

152. Ball, "Historia," *Luz Apostólica* (April 1966): 2.

153. "The Present Condition of the Lower Mexican Work," *Weekly Evangel*, 20 October 1917, 9.

154. Ball, "Mission to the Mexicans," *Weekly Evangel*, 27 May 1916, 12.

155. Bazán, *Enviados a Dios*, 31.

156. "The Apostolate of Women," *Weekly Evangel*, 18 March 1916, 6.

157. Nellie Bazán, "'50 Años de Cristiana y De Ministerio Cristiana," *Luz Apostólica* (October 1967): 4.

158. Nellie Bazán, "Conclusion," *Luz Apostólica* (June 1968): 9.

159. Anderson, *Vision*, 93. The Azusa Street magazine, *Apostolic Faith*, carried one such account in its June–September 1907 issue. A Witchita, Kansas, girl died and her body was prepared for burial: "She says she was taken to heaven in a cloud accompanied by two angels." She was healed by Jesus and returned to earth to preach about her experiences (4).

160. Sánchez, *Becoming*, 40–43.

161. There are seven specific spiritual gifts: word of wisdom, word of knowledge, working of miracles, prophecy, discerning of spirits, diverse tongues, and interpretation of tongues (I *Corinthians* 12:14–40). As many as twenty spiritual gifts can be cited for Pentecostals to seek, but the ones listed above represent the core of Pentecostal belief.

162. Almaraz, interview.

163. Lillian Valdez and Berta García, "Historia," *Luz Apostólica* (June 1967): 3.

164. Stella Cantú, interview by author, tape recording, Los Angeles, California, 3 April 1995.

165. Simón Melendres, interview by author, tape recording, La Puente, California, 9 July 1997.

166. Anderson, *Vision*, 149–50.

167. Miguel Sánchez, interview by author, notes, Los Angeles, California, 22 June 1997.

168. Ball, "Historia," *Luz Apostólica* (September 1966): 1.

169. Ibid.

170. Until 1973 district policies were not codified. Henry Ball was the last Euro American superintendent.

171. Gregory S. O'Brien, "A Short History of the Pacific Latin District of the Assemblies of God," unpublished paper, Assemblies of God Theological Seminary, Springfield, Missouri, March 1994, 2–4.

172. Henry Ball and Alice Luce, *Glimpses of Our Latin American Work in the United States and Mexico* (Springfield, Mo.: Foreign Missions Department, 1940), 5–7.

2. Workers for the Harvest:
LABI and the Institutionalization of a Latino Pentecostal Identity

1. Eldin Villafañe, *The Liberating Spirit* (Grand Rapids, Mich.: Eerdmans, 1997), 122.

2. Edith Blumhofer, *Restoring the Faith: The Assemblies of God, Pentecostalism, and American Culture* (Urbana: University of Illinois Press, 1993), 31.

3. Ibid., 150.

4. Alice Luce, "Strangers within Our Gates," *Latter Rain Evangel* (December 1930): 22.

5. Ibid., 18.

6. "Veteran Missionary Dies," *Pentecostal Evangel*, 30 November 1955, 30.

7. Luce, "Bible School Opens in San Diego," *Pentecostal Evangel*, 13 November 1926, 4.

8. Figures compiled from the "Distribution of Missionary Funds" for the years 1926–28, *Pentecostal Evangel*, various pages.

9. Alice Kessler-Harris, *Out to Work: A History of Wage-Earning Women in the United States* (Oxford: Oxford University Press, 1982), 262–63.

10. Ibid., 257.

11. H. May Kelty, "Needs of Bible Institute," *Pentecostal Evangel*, 27 August 11 1927, 11.

12. Luce, "The Latin American Pentecost Work," *Pentecostal Evangel*, 25 June 1927, 6.

13. Ibid., 7.

14. Luce, "Scriptural Methods in Missionary Work," *Pentecostal Evangel*, 9 May 1931, 8–9.

15. De Leon, *The Silent Pentecostals*, 63.

16. "Berean Bible Institute" *Pentecostal Evangel*, 21 July 1928, 3. The graduates were Ursula Riggio, D. Addie Sugg, Maria Grajada, and Bueno.

17. Mable Bax, "San Diego Bible School," *Pentecostal Evangel*, 13 July 1929, 11.

18. Devra Weber, *Dark Sweat, White Gold: California Farm Workers, Cotton, and the New Deal* (Berkeley: University of California Press, 1994), 48, 53.

19. Ibid. Weber notes that the workers' children sang songs about the Mexican flag at school and occasionally wore the flags' colors at public events as a display of national pride.

20. Luce, "Latin American Bible Institute," *Latter Rain Evangel* (December 1930): 17–18.

21. G. H. Thomas, "The Value of the Bible School in the Latin American Work," *Pentecostal Evangel*, 28 March 1931, 10.

22. DeLeon, *The Silent Pentecostals*, 70. The LABI faculty were composed of veteran missionaries: Luce, Ralph Williams, Richard Williams, Mabel Bax, G. H. Thomas, Eva R. Gonveia, Lellian G. M. Lee, and Francisco Nevarez.

23. Hong Yeun-Cheng Yang, "Formation of Pentecostal Spirituality through Theological Education toward Effective Ministry," (D.M. diss., Ashland Theological Seminary, 1992), 71.

24. Ibid.

25. Luce, "Commencement at Latin American Bible Institute," *Pentecostal Evangel*, 6 June 1936, 9.

26. "Latin American Bible Institute," *Pentecostal Evangel*, 13 December 1937, 7.

27. Yang, "Formation of Pentecostal Spirituality," 70; Synan, *The Holiness Pentecostal Tradition* (Grand Rapids, Mich.: Eerdmans, 1997), 91. Ozman's testimony of speaking and writing Chinese for three consecutive days has become one of the most well-known testimonials in early Pentecostal history.

28. Luce, "Latin American Bible Institute," *Pentecostal Evangel*, 6 June 1942, 7.

29. Ball, "Signs of Crumbling Walls," *Pentecostal Evangel*, 5 June 1943, 10.

30. DeLeon, *Silent Pentecostals*, 73.

31. Ibid., 75.

32. Luce, *Probad Los Espiritus* (San Antonio: Casa Evangelica de Publicaciónes, 1900), prologue.

33. Luce cites the following groups as contributing to this biblical prophecy: Oneness, Spiritism, Roman Catholicism, Calvinism, Christian Science, and Mormonism. The biblical quotation Luce used should be placed in context. In Revelation, seven angels are sent to the world to pour out the last plagues before Armageddon; the sixth angel pours out the second to last plague. The demonic forces against God are poured out of the mouths of a dragon, the beast, and the false prophet. These demons fool worldly leaders into thinking that they are performing miracles, but, in reality, according to Revelation, the demons are preparing to fight the army of God. See Walter A. Elwell, "Revelation," in *Evangelical Commentary on the Bible*, ed. Walter A. Elwell (1197–1229), 1220–21 (Grand Rapids, Mich.: Baker, 1989).

34. Wacker, *Heaven Below*, 182.

35. Stephen J. Land, *Pentecostal Spirituality: A Passion for the Kingdom* (Sheffield, England: Sheffield, 1993), 41.

36. Jackie D. Johns, "Pentecostalism and the Postmodern World View," *Journal of Pentecostal Theology* 7 (1995): 90.

37. Luce, *Probad*, prologue.

38. Ibid., 17.

39. Luce, *El Mensajero y Su Mensaje: Manual Para Obreros Cristianos*, rev. ed. (Springfield, Mo.: Casa de Publicaciónes Evangelicas, 1953 [1920]), 12. The original 1920 version was published in English by the Assemblies of God. It cannot be stated with accuracy that this book was used at LABI, but, considering its tone and that Luce was a teacher at LABI till her death in 1955, it can be stated with some measure of confidence that this publication, with its question-and-answer section, was one of the texts used at LABI.

40. Ibid., 15.

41. Ibid., 22–23.

42. Ibid., 59.

43. Jesse Miranda, interview by author, tape recording, Azusa, California, 31 March 1998.

44. LABI, *1948–49 Catalog* (La Puente, Calif., LABI, 1948), 1.

45. Ibid., 11–12. The other "disciplines" included more creedal than moral re-

quirements than bear repeating here to reinforce the idea that LABI's mission to create Pentecostals relied heavily on orthodoxy and spiritual maturity. The other requirements of students were outward evidence of a righteous life, water baptism, the Lord's Supper, the Promise of the Father, evidence of the Baptism of the Holy Ghost, entire sanctification, the church, ministry, and evangelism, Divine Healing, Blessed Hope, Millennial Reign of Jesus, Lake of Fire, and the new heavens and new earth.

46. Historian Vinson Synan comments on the early years of Pentecostalism where, at Azusa Street in 1906, African Americans, Euro Americans, Latinos, and others worshipped together when such gatherings were anathema to many in U.S. society: "In an age of Social Darwinism, Jim Crowism, and general white supremacy, the fact that Pentecostal blacks and whites worshipped together in virtual equality was a significant exception to the prevailing attitudes and practices. . . . Even more significant is the fact that this interracial harmony occurred among the very groups that have traditionally been most at odds—the poor whites and poor blacks" (Synan, *The Holiness Pentecostal Tradition*, 167). Synan did not mention the role of Latinos in the early days of Pentecostalism.

47. Wacker, *Heaven Below*, 65.

48. For a comprehensive examination of the Repatriation Era, see Francisco Balderrama and Raymond Rodriguez, *Decade of Betrayal: Mexican Repatriation in the 1930s* (Albuquerque: University of New Mexico Press, 1995), 122. For a large-scale picture of the lives of Latinos in the United States, with particular reference to Los Angeles, see Richard Griswold del Castillo and Arnoldo de León, *North to Aztlan: A History of Mexican Americans in the United States* (New York: Twayne, 1996), 76–77, 80, 92, 111–13.

49. Villafañe, *Liberating Spirit*, 114.

50. Ibid., 95.

51. Ibid., 139.

52. Virginia Sánchez Korrol, *From Colonia to Community: The History of Puerto Ricans in New York City* (Berkeley: University of California Press, 1983), 77, 155, 211.

53. Villafañe, *Liberating Spirit*, 115.

54. Nicole Rodriguez Toulis, *Believing Identity: Pentecostalism and the Mediation of Jamaican Ethnicity and Gender in England* (Oxford: Berg, 1997), 270.

55. Sánchez, *Becoming*, 225.

56. Ibid., 257.

57. Ibid.

58. Miranda, interview, 31 March 1998; Melendres, interview.

59. Compilation of statistics from *Yearbook(s) 1952–1959* (La Puente, Calif.: LABI, 1952–59), 13–18.

60. Miranda, interview, 31 March 1998.

61. LABI, *1975–79 Catalog(s)* (La Puente, Calif.: LABI, 1975–79), 15.

62. David Wilkerson, *The Cross and the Switchblade* (New York: Bernard Geis, 1963), 94–97.

63. Miranda, interview, 31 March 1998.

64. Ibid.

65. Robet V. Hine, *California's Utopian Colonies* (New Haven: Yale University Press, 1966), 169.

66. David Wilkerson, New York, to Theodoro Bueno, La Puente, March 1965, LABI Office Files, Box 2.

67. Theodoro Bueno, "Home Missions Schools Branch Out." *Pentecostal Evangel*, 25 May 1969, 13.

68. LABI, *1960 Yearbook* (La Puente, Calif.: LABI, 1960), 16.

69. Miranda, "A Study of LABI and Suggested Ways for Improvement" (M.R. thesis, Talbot Seminary, Biola University, June 1969), 10, 71.

70. LABI, *1975–79 Catalog(s)* (La Puente, Calif.: LABI, 1975–79), various pages.

71. Compilation from *1970–79 Yearbook(s)* (La Puente, Calif.: LABI, 1970–79), various pages.

72. Miranda, interview, 31 March 1998.

73. Compilation from *1980–82, 1988–89 Yearbook(s)* (La Puente, Calif.: LABI, 1980–82, 1988–89), various pages. No yearbooks were produced for 1983–87.

74. Miranda, "LABC," *El Eco Escolar* (1980?), 2.

75. Miranda, interview, 31 March 1998.

76. Melendres, interview.

77. LABI, *1992–97 Yearbook(s)* (La Puente, Calif.: LABI, 1992–97), various pages.

78. LABI, *1992–97 Catalog(s)* (La Puente, Calif.: LABI, 1992–97), various pages.

79. Berean Bible School (San Diego, 1926?; privately printed), various pages.

80. LABI, *1948–79 Catalog(s)* (La Puente, Calif.: LABI, 1948–79), various pages.

81. Ibid., 15.

82. Compilation derived from LABI yearbooks for the years 1950–59, 1960–64, 1966, and 1969, various pages.

83. LABI, *1976 Yearbook* (La Puente, Calif.: LABI, 1976), 6–7.

84. R. Marie Griffith, *God's Daughters: Evangelical Women and the Power of Submission* (Berkeley: University of California Press, 1997), 35.

85. Compilation from LABI/LABC yearbooks for the years 1980–82, various pages.

86. LABI, *Yearbook 1988* (La Puente, Calif.: LABI, 1988), 8–9.

87. LABI, *1993–94 Catalog* (La Puente, Calif.: LABI, 1993), 15.

88. LABI staff, personal conversation with author, 14 July 1997, La Puente, California, notes.

89. Toulis, *Believing Identity*, 164.

90. Ibid., 209.

91. Ibid., 164.

92. Clementina Chacón, interview by author, tape recording, La Puente, California, 10 October 1997.

93. Leonard Andrade, interview by author, tape recording, La Puente, California, 29 October 1997.

94. Xiuleth Santibenez, interview by author, tape recording, La Puente, California, 29 October 1997.

95. David S. Galindo, interview by author, tape recording, La Puente, California, 3 November 1997.

96. Adrian Muñoz, interview by author, tape recording, La Puente, California, 29 October 1997.

97. KC, interview by author, tape recording, La Puente, California, 29 October 1997.

98. James, interview by author, tape recording, La Puente, California, 8 October 1997.

99. Gabriel Martínez, interview by author, tape recording, La Puente, California, 3 November 1997.

100. Ibid.

101. Wacker, *Heaven Below*, 140.

102. Quotes from this section are from interviews of LABI students: Adrian Muñoz, Leonard Andrade, Clementina Chacón, James, Daniel S. Galindo, Xuileth Santibenez, October–November 1997, LABI, La Puente, California, tape recordings.

103. Ibid.

104. Toulis, *Believing Identity*, 105.

105. Information based on a compilation of interviews with LABI students conducted on campus from October to November 1997.

106. LABI, *1997 Catalog* (La Puente, California: LABI, 1997), various pages.

107. Cheryl Bridges Johns, *Pentecostal Formation: A Pedagogy among the Oppressed* (Sheffield: Sheffield Academic Press, 1993), 32.

108. Ibid., 62.

109. Ibid., 69.

110. Ibid., 122.

111. Ibid., 127–28.

112. Melendres, interview. Statistics on graduation completion compiled from LABI yearbooks for the years 1950–97.

113. Margaret Poloma, "The Assemblies of God at the Crossroads," in *Religion: North American Style*, ed. Thomas E. Dowdy and Patrick McNamara, 104–111, quote at 110 (New Brunswick, N.J.: Rutgers University Press, 1997).

114. Ibid.

115. Felipe E. Agredano Lozano, "The Apostolic Assembly at the Crossroads," unpublished paper delivered at the Society for Pentecostal Studies, Wheaton College, Wheaton, Illinois, 10–12 November 1994, 16.

116. Jesse Miranda, interview by author, tape recording, Azusa, California, 8 May 1997; Melendres, interview.

117. Chacón, interview.

118. Sara Evans, *Born for Liberty* (New York: Free Press, 1997), 57, 69.

119. Vicki Ruiz, *From Out of the Shadows* (New York: Oxford University Press, 1998), 51–52.

120. Ruiz argues persuasively that advertising alone did not popularize the use of cosmetics during the 1920s, but it was a combination of Madison Avenue advertising, barrio beauty pageants, neighborhood beauty patrols, and the idealization of glamour through various Spanish-language periodicals and magazines that captivated many Mexican and Mexican American women from the 1920s to the 1940s. See Ruiz, *From Out of the Shadows*, 55–58.

121. J. Gordon Melton, ed., *Encyclopedia of American Religions, Religious Creeds* (Chicago: Gale, 1988), 334–35, 341.

122. Stella Cantú, interview.

123. LABI, *1975–76 Catalog* (La Puente, Calif.: LABI, 1975), 11. Catalogs from the years 1964 to 1974 were not in the archival files.

124. Muñoz, interview.

125. Martínez, interview. That the devil disguises himself and appears as a positive force in the world is mentioned in the New Testament 2 Cor. 11:14–15.

126. Grant A. Wacker, "The Pentecostal Tradition," in *Caring and Curing: Health and Medicine in the Western Religious Tradition*, ed. Ronald L. Numbers and Darrell W. Amundsen, 514–38 (New York: Macmillan, 1986), 537.

3. *"Normal Church Can't Take Us"*:
Victory Outreach and the Re-Creating of a Latino Pentecostal Identity

1. Wilkerson, *The Cross*, 60.

2. Tena Katie Peters, "An Investigation into the Role of Religious Experience and Commitment as a Therapeutic Factor in the Treatment and Rehabilitation of Selected Drug Addicts from Teen Challenge: A Follow-up Study," (Ph.D. diss., New York University, 1980), 35.

3. Ibid., 129.

4. The rising bell was at 7:00 in the morning, breakfast was at 7:30, followed by cleanup and then devotions until 9:30, chapel from 9:30 to 11:30, lunch at noon, then cleanup and prayer until 2:00 in the afternoon, when Center residents went out for outreach or street evangelism until 7:30 in the evening. The day ended with evening service until midnight. See Wilkerson, *Cross*, 160.

5. Luther P. Gerlach, "Pentecostalism: Revolution or Counterrevolution?" in *Religious Movements in Contemporary America*, ed. Irving I. Zaretsky and Mark P. Leone, 669–98, quote at 682–83 (Princeton, N.J.: Princeton University Press, 1974).

6. Thomas Csordas, *Language, Charisma, and Creativity: The Ritual Life of a Religious Movement* (Berkeley: University of California Press, 1997), 72.

7. Wilkerson, *Cross*, 204.

8. Leon Gibson Hart and Carl D. Chambers, *The Heroin Epidemic* (New York: S. P. Books, 1976), 32; John M. Long, "Drug Use Patterns in Two Los Angeles Barrio Gangs," in *Drugs in the Hispanic Community*, ed. Ronald Glick and Joan Moore, 155–65, quote at 157–58 (New York: Rutgers University Press, 1990).

9. Wilkerson, "New Hope for Narcotic Addicts," *Teen Challenge Challenger* (spring 1965): 8.

10. Arlene M. Sánchez-Walsh, "Fieldnotes," La Puente Men's Home, May 11, 1998, notes.

11. Wilkerson, *Cross*, 143.

12. Sonny Arguinzoni, *God's Junkie* (Los Angeles: Victory Outreach, 1967), 7, 9, 23, 51.

13. Ibid., 65.

14. Csordas, *Language*, 55.

15. Arguinzoni, *God's Junkie*, 91; "Cruz Arguinzoni, " LABI lateral files, No. 3.

16. Miranda, interview, 22 May 1998.

17. Arguinzoni, *God's Junkie*, 90, 100.

18. Almaraz, interview.

19. Ibid.

20. Arguinzoni, *God's Junkie*, 100, 128.

21. *Teen Challenge Monthly Report* 2, no. 6 (August 1966): 1.

22. Arguinzoni, *God's Junkie*, 132, 204.

23. Prophecy, according to Csordas, is part of a larger genre of charismatic ritual and language. In his study of charismatic Catholics, Csordas found that prophecy was rarely used to foretell the future. "Its primary functions are usually listed as exhortation, encouragement, conviction, admonition, inspiration, correction, guidance, consolation, and revelation." See Csordas, *Language*, 170.

24. Arguinzoni, *Internalize the Vision* (La Puente, Calif.: Victory Outreach Publications, 1995), 35–36.

25. Nicky Cruz, *Give Me Back My Dignity* (La Puente, Calif.: Cruz Press, 1993), 135.

26. Arguinzoni, *God's Junkie*, 137–138.

27. Almaraz, interview.

28. Arguinzoni, *God's Junkie*, 137.

29. Ibid., 136–37.

30. Sánchez-Walsh, "Fieldnotes," Victory Outreach Headquarters, West Covina, California, 11 November 1998.

31. "Victory Temple Ex-Addict Church," Flyer 1960s? Personal papers of Roberto Almaraz, Box 1.

32. Almaraz, interview.

33. Arguinzoni, *God's Junkie*, 172.

34. Ibid., 152–53.

35. Ibid.

36. Almaraz, interview; Arguinzoni, *God's Junkie*, 120.

37. Griffith, *God's Daughters*, 38.

38. Martín Sánchez Jankowski, *Islands in the Street: Gangs and American Urban Society* (Berkeley: University of California Press, 1991), 22.

39. Ibid., 135.

40. Ibid., 27, 70.

41. Edward J. Escobar, *Race, Police, and the Making of a Political Identity: Mexican Americans and the Los Angeles Police Department* 1900–1945 (Berkeley: University of California Press, 1999), 174–75.

42. Ibid., 179, 185.

43. Ibid., 203.

44. Ibid., 256.

45. Joan Moore, *Homeboys: Gangs, Drugs, and Prison in the Barrios of Los Angeles* (Philadelphia: Temple University Press, 1978), 76.

46. Ibid., 78–79, 82–83.

47. Ibid., 84–88, 127–29.

48. Ibid., 139.

49. James Diego Vigil, *Barrio Gangs: Street Life and Identity in Southern California* (Austin: University of Texas Press, 1988), 58.

50. Daniel Ramírez, conversation with author, 10 October 1998.

51. Arguinzoni, *Treasures out of Darkness* (Green Forest, Ark.: New Leaf, 1991), 254.

52. Richard Grant, "Dial EmE for Murder," *Los Angeles Magazine*, May 1997, 37; Dirk Mathison, "Gunning for God?" *Los Angeles Magazine*, November 1997, 72–83.

53. Almaraz, interview.

54. Philip LaCrue, interview by author, tape recording, La Puente, California, 14 July 1998.

55. Julie Arguinzoni, "Remember Lot's Wife," speech at United Women in Ministry Convention, 1998, tape recording. Note: the conventions usually occur during the month of October, but the date was not mentioned on the tape or in the content of the speech.

56. Ibid.

57. Moore, *Homeboys*, 97.

58. Ed Morales and Mitzi Morales, *Defying the Odds* (Green Forest, Ark.: New Leaf, 1991), 32–33.

59. LaCrue, interview.

60. The "All-American" network is co-owned by Arguinzoni and Nicky Cruz. The network consists of a dozen low-wattage stations that carry both original Victory Outreach programming and programs from their partner, TBN.

61. Elaine J. Lawless, "Rescripting Their Lives and Narratives: Spiritual Life Stories of Pentecostal Women Preachers," in *Journal of Feminist Studies in Religion* (spring 1991): 2, 58–59.

62. Elaine J. Lawless, "The Night I Got the Holy Ghost: Holy Ghost Narratives

and the Pentecostal Conversion Process," in *Western Folklore* 47 (January 1988): 11–12.

63. Roxanne Rimstead, "Mediated Lives: Oral Histories and Cultural Memory," *Essays on Canadian Writing*, no. 60 (winter 1996): 141.

64. Patsy García, "Untitled," speech at United Women in Ministry Convention, 1998, tape recording.

65. Jeanne Alanis, "Untitled," speech at United Women in Ministry Convention, 1998, tape recording.

66. Jeannette Rodriguez, "Guadalupe: The Feminine Face of God," in *Goddess of the Americas: Writings on the Virgen de Guadalupe*, ed. Ana Castillo, 129–130 (New York: Riverhead Books, 1996).

67. Julie Arguinzoni, "Remember Lot's Wife."

68. Miriam, interview by author, tape recording, La Puente, California, 19 June 1997.

69. Griffith, *God's Daughters*, 183.

70. Mary Ann Lavayen, "Untitled," speech at United Women in Ministry Leadership Retreat, 1996, tape recording.

71. Ibid.

72. Faith Martínez, "Untitled," speech at United Women in Ministry Leadership Retreat, 1996, tape recording.

73. Gerlach, "Pentecostalism," 684–86.

74. Arguinzoni, *Internalize*, 49–50.

75. Ibid., 120.

76. Ibid., 172.

77. Gerlach, "Pentecostalism," 681.

78. *Victory Outreach Handbook 1998.*

79. Arguinzoni, *Internalize*, 19.

80. Cruz, *Give Me*, 204.

81. Arguinzoni, *Internalize*, 55.

82. Cruz, *Give Me*, 194.

83. Almaraz, interview.

84. Alanis, "Untitled," speech. The church eschews any ethnic identification that validates the demographics that the church is composed of English-speaking Latinos. I have heard church members refer to themselves as "Chicano" only in the sense that it is a descriptive term. For example, when Alanis used the term, it was within the context of saying that Victory Outreach, with its international focus, has outgrown that definition. Implicit in that statement is that Victory Outreach resists the term "Chicano" because it does not fit the larger goals of church growth, though I will argue that, in commitment, demographics, and style, Victory Outreach can indeed be called a "Chicano" church.

85. English-speaking men's homes, 136; Latino directors, 94. non-Latino directors, 42; English-speaking women's homes, 61; Latino/a directors, 37; non-Latino/a directors, 24; English-speaking men's reentry homes, 19; Latino direc-

tors, 14; non-Latino directors, 5; English-speaking women's reentry Homes, 2; Latino directors, 2; non-Latino directors, o. There were no non-Latino/a directors of Spanish-speaking homes. These numbers derived from the church's official website *www.victoryoutreach.org* and the 1998 *Victory Outreach Handbook*.

86. Averages were collected from a telephone survey. A membership of forty thousand was estimated by the Reverend Roy (a pseudonym) in a personal conversation, August 1998.

87. Jerry, personal conversation with author, July 1998.

88. Arguinzoni, *Internalize*, 201.

89. Cruz, *Give Me*, 152.

90. Miriam, interview.

91. Ibid.

92. Arguinzoni, "Countdown to Vision 2000, Victory Outreach Values Prepare for Vision 2000," in *Inner City Vision*, Thirtieth Anniversary Special Edition, 1997, 11.

93. Sánchez-Walsh, fieldnotes, La Puente Women's Home, 6 May 1998. On a personal note, my uncle failed to complete the first two weeks at a men's home. Insulted by the idea that the church was trying to convert him, he left, absconding with a few of the home staff's personal items in the process.

94. Cruz, *Give Me*, 58; Miriam, interview.

95. Sherry, interview by author, tape recording, La Puente, California, 2 December 1997.

96. Ibid. Unless otherwise noted, all quotations in this section are from the same interview.

97. Tex Sample, *Hard Living People and Mainstream Christians* (Nashville: Abingdon, 1993), 46.

98. Daniel E. Albrecht, "Pentecostal/Charismatic Spirituality: Looking Through the Lens of Ritual" (Ph.D. diss., Graduate Theological Seminary, 1993), 170.

99. Ibid., 212.

100. For an extended discussion of the liminal state and communitas, see Victor Turner, *The Ritual Process Structure and Anti-Structure* (Ithaca: Cornell University Press, 1977 [1969]).

101. Albrecht, "Pentecostal/Charismatic," 151–52.

102. Ibid., 269.

103. Ibid., 166.

104. Portes and Rumbaut, *Legacies*, 45–47.

105. Joe, interview by author, tape recording, La Puente, California, 22 May 1997.

106. Ibid.

107. Ibid.

108. Cruz, *Give Me*, 194.

109. Ibid.

110. Joan Moore and John Hagedorn, "What Happens to Girls in the Gang?" in *Gangs in America*, ed. C. Ronald Huff, 2nd ed., chap. 10, quote at 207 (Thousand Oaks, Calif.: Sage, 1996).

111. Ibid., 208. Moore's sample of adults were interviewed from 1986 to 1987. As teenagers, the women were active in gangs as far back as the 1950s and half the women were active in the 1970s.

112. Randall Balmer, *Blessed Assurance: A History of Evangelicalism in America* (Boston: Beacon, 1999), 72.

113. Peggy Pascoe, *Relations of Rescue: The Search for Female Moral Authority in the American West, 1874–1939* (New York: Oxford University Press, 1990), 37.

114. Julie Arguinzoni, "Remember."

115. Ibid.

116. Ibid.

117. Stacey Lewis, "Untitled," speech at United Women in Ministry Convention, 1998.

118. Josey Pineda, "Untitled," speech at United Women in Ministry Convention, 1998.

119. Griffith, *God's Daughters*, 38.

120. Miriam, interview.

121. Ibid.

122. Elizabeth Brusco, *Reforming Machismo* (Austin: University of Texas Press, 1995), chap. 7.

123. Ibid.

124. Ruth, interview by author, tape recording, Los Angeles, California, 11 August 1998.

125. Ibid.

126. Ibid.

127. Ibid.

128. Luís León, "Born Again in East LA: The Congregation as Border Space," in *Gatherings in Diaspora: Religious Communities and the New Immigration*, ed. R. Stephen Warner and Judith G. Wittner, 163–96 (Philadelphia: Temple University Press, 1998); see, especially, 181–87.

129. Martín García, personal correspondence with author, Wheaton, Illinois, 28 August 2002. García is a senior pastor of an Assemblies of God church in Southern California and a teacher at LABI.

130. Arguinzoni, *Internalize*, 12–13.

131. Miriam, interview.

132. Art Blajos, *Blood In, Blood Out* (Crowborough, East Sussex: Monarch, 1996), 24.

133. Blajos's relocation to Great Britain, although related to his mission, in all probability became a necessity when the former hitman was himself placed on a hit list by the Mafia. See Mathison, "Dial EmE," 72–83.

134. Del Castro, "Victory Outreach School of Ministry: Equipping the Saints to Fulfill Vision 2000," *Inner City Vision* Thirtieth Anniversary Special Edition, 1997, 29.

135. Del Castro, interview by author, tape recording, La Puente, California, 12 November 1997. Unless otherwise noted, all quotations in this section are from this interview.

4. *Slipping Into Darkness: "God's Anointed Now Generation" and the Making of a Latino Evangelical Youth Culture*

1. Sonny Arguinzoni Jr., interview by author, tape recording, La Puente, California, 13 July 1998. Unless otherwise noted, all quotations in the following section are from this interview.

2. Joel A. Carpenter, *Revive Us Again: The ReAwakening of American Fundamentalism* (New York: Oxford University Press, 1997), 45–46.

3. Art Lucero, personal conversation with author, 1 May 2000, Los Angeles, notes.

4. Todd Hahn, *Gen-Xer's After God: Helping a Generation Pursue Jesus* (Grand Rapids, Mich.: Baker, 1998), 112.

5. Robert Wuthnow, *After Heaven: Spirituality in America since the 1950s* (Berkeley: University of California Press, 1998), 7–8.

6. Sánchez-Walsh, fieldnotes, Victory Outreach, La Puente, 3–14 July 1998, notes.

7. Mando Gonzales Jr. interview by author, tape recording, La Puente, California, 5 May 1997. Unless otherwise noted, all the quotations in this section are from this interview.

8. Tricia Rose, *Black Noise: Rap Music and Black Culture in Contemporary America* (Boston: Wesleyan University Press, 1994), 21.

9. Ad for "Street Wisdom" clothing in *Underground Fire: Hip Hop/DJ/Dance Culture Magazine for the Faithful*, winter 1999.

10. Playbill, private papers of Roberto Almaraz.

11. LaCrue, interview.

12. Ibid.

13. Vigil, *Barrio Gangs*, 2–3.

14. Ibid., 33, 111.

15. Ibid., 120.

16. Duke of Earl, videocassette, Trinity Broadcasting Network, 1982.

17. Pam Carnline, "Christian Anti-Gang Play Draws 6,000," *Riverside Press Telegram*, 30 June 1997, B01.

18. Arguinzoni, *Internalize*, 213.

19. Ibid.

20. Ibid.

21. Leonard Sweet, *Soul Tsunami: Sink or Swim in the New Millennium Culture* (New York: Zondervan, 1999), 154.

22. Rose, *Black Noise*, 178.

23. Sánchez-Walsh, fieldnotes, Victory Outreach, La Puente, 26 July 1998.

24. Anonymous, "Untitled," *Underground Fire*, no. 4 (fall 1998): 5.

25. David Kelley, "Inland Gangs: Solutions," *Riverside Press Telegram*, 15 December 1998, B01.

26. David, interview by author, tape recording, Los Angeles, California, 8 August 1999. Unless otherwise noted, all quotations in this section are from this interview.

27. Sánchez-Walsh, fieldnotes, 26, July 1998.

5. Worlds Apart:
The Vineyard, La Viña, and the American Evangelical Subculture

1. Today there are more than five hundred U.S. Vineyards, and more than seventy in Great Britain and Ireland. In addition, the Vineyard has churches in Sweden, Australia, Costa Rica, Guatemala, Venezuela, Canada, Mexico, and Brazil.

2. John Wimber, *Power Evangelism* (San Francisco: Harper Collins, 1987), 35.

3. Ibid., 44.

4. Grant Wacker, "Wimber and Wonders—What about Miracles Today?" *Reformed Journal* 37 (April 1987): 18.

5. Donald E. Miller, *Reinventing American Protestantism* (Berkeley: University of California Press, 1998), 187.

6. In terms of the religious breakdown of the Latino population, estimates vary wildly on both the percentage of Latinos within the U.S. Catholic or Protestant population and the percentage of Latinos who identify themselves as either Catholic or Protestant. Such divergent projections suggest that the estimates are not very reliable. In part, this is the result of difficulties in estimating the undocumented Latino population. The Latino Catholic figures are based on the General Social Survey. The Latino Catholic population may be as high as 77 percent or as low as 66 percent, and the Protestant communities vary from 25 percent to 17 percent. See Edwin I. Hernandez, "Moving from the Cathedral to Storefront Churches: Understanding Religious Growth and Decline among Latino Protestants," in *Protestantes/Protestants: Hispanic Christianity within Mainline Traditions*, ed. David Maldonado Jr., 216–235, quote at 222 (Nashville, Tenn.: Abingdon, 1999).

7. Mark Fields, interview by author, tape recording, Pomona, California, 13 November 1998. Unless otherwise noted, all quotations in this section are from this interview.

8. Corwin Smidt and Lyman Kellstedt et al., "Spirit-Filled Movements in Contemporary America: A Survey Perspective," in *Pentecostal Currents in American Protestantism*, ed. Grant A. Wacker, Edith Blumhofer et al., 111–27, quote at 115 (Champaign: University of Illinois Press, 1999).

9. Ibid., 120–23.

10. *Harvest Bible College Catalog*, 1998, introduction.

11. Ibid.

12. Ibid.

13. Teresa Chávez Saucedo, "Race, Religion and La Raza: An Exploration of the Racialization of Latinos in the United States and the Role of the Protestant Church," in *Protestantes/Protestants*, chap. 9.

14. Christian Smith, *American Evangelicalism: Embattled and Thriving* (Chicago: University of Chicago Press, 1998), 185, 196, 210.

15. *Catalog*, 10

16. Ibid., 32.

17. Joe Castaños, interview by author, tape recording, Downey, California, 7 January 1999.

18. "Women in the Church," *Barna Reports*, March 2000, www.barna.com.

19. Smidt, "Spirit-Filled," 120–23.

20. Smith, *American Evangelicalism*, 39.

21. Ibid.

22. Castaños, interview.

23. Sánchez Walsh, fieldnotes, La Viña Downey, January–March 1999.

24. William Pinedo, interview by author, tape recording, Anaheim, California, 19 March 1999. Unless otherwise noted, all quotations in this section are from this interview.

25. Ryan De La Torre, interview by author, tape recording, Monrovia, California, 25 September 1998. Unless otherwise noted, all quotations in this section are from this interview.

26. Alex Vargas, interview by author, tape recording, San Francisco, California, 16 January 1999.

27. Ibid.

28. Bill Hernández, interview by author, tape recording, San Francisco, California, 17 January 1999. Unless otherwise noted, all quotations in this section are from this interview.

29. The scholarship on the growth of the Pentecostal movement is vast, but among the best is David Martin, *Pentecostalism: The World Their Parish* (London: Blackwell, 2002), quote at 1. Martin calls the Pentecostal movement the most dramatic development of Christianity in the century recently concluded: "On a fairly conservative estimate we are dealing with a quarter of a billion people. . . . Pentecostalism includes one in eight of the Christian 'constituency' of nearly two billion."

30. Richard Ochoa, interview by author, tape recording, Pico Rivera, California, 9 November 1998. Unless otherwise noted, all quotations in this section are from this interview.

31. The Word of Faith movement is a popular form of Pentecostalism characterized by teachings that stress prosperity and health for faithful followers. This

controversial movement has come under attack for its suggestion that good health and wealth are guaranteed only if the person "claims" by faith what he or she is seeking (health, wealth, or job success) before actually receiving it; if the person does not receive it, then a sufficient amount of faith is lacking.

32. Sánchez Walsh, fieldnotes, Lord's Vineyard, November 1998–March 1999.

33. Teresa Arce, interview by author, tape recording, Pico Rivera, California, 13 January 1999. Unless otherwise noted, all quotations in this section are from this interview.

34. Smith, *American Evangelicals*, 124.

35. Ibid., 140.

36. Hahn, *Gen-X*, 63.

37. John Luna, interview by author, tape recording, Pico Rivera, California, 27 November 1998.

38. Smith, *American Evangelicalism*, 100.

Bibliography

Agredano Lozano, Felipe E. "The Apostolic Assembly at the Crossroads." Paper presented at the annual Society for Pentecostal Studies, Wheaton College, Wheaton, Illinois, 10–12 November 1994.

Alanis, Jeanne. Untitled. Audiotape of speech. United Women in Ministry Convention, 1998.

Albrecht, Daniel E. "Pentecostal/Charismatic Spirituality: Looking Through the Lens of Ritual." Ph.D. dissertation, Graduate Theological Seminary, Berkeley, California, 1993.

Anderson, Robert M. *Vision of the Disinherited.* New York: Oxford University Press, 1979.

Anonymous, "Untitled." *Underground Fire* 4 (fall 1998): 5.

"The Apostolate of Women." *Weekly Evangel,* 18 March 1916, 6.

Apostolic Faith 1, no. 3 (March 1906): 1.

Apostolic Faith 1, no. 9 (September 1906): 3.

Arguinzoni, Julie. *Remember Lot's Wife.* Audiotape of speech. United Women in Ministry Convention, 1998.

Arguinzoni, Sonny. "Countdown to Vision 2000, Victory Outreach Values Prepare for Vision 2000." *Inner City Vision* (Special Thirtieth Anniversary Edition) (1997): 7–11.

——. *God's Junkie.* Los Angeles: Victory Outreach, 1967.

——. *Internalize the Vision.* La Puente, Calif.: Victory Outreach, 1995.

——. *Treasures out of Darkness.* Green Forest, Ark.: New Leaf Press, 1991.

Balderrama, Francisco, and Raymond Rodriguez. *Decade of Betrayal: Mexican Repatriation in the 1930s.* Albuquerque: University of New Mexico Press, 1995.

Baldwin, Deborah. *Protestants and the Mexican Revolution.* Urbana: University of Illinois Press, 1990.

Ball, Henry A. "A Call for More Laborers for the Mexican Work." *Weekly Evangel,* 24 March 1917, 13.

——. "Historia." *Luz Apostólica* (April–May 1966; September 1966; October 1966).

——. "Historia de La Luz Apostólica." *Luz Apostólica* (July 1972): 8.

——. "The Mission to the Mexicans." *Weekly Evangel,* 27 May 1916.

——. "Signs of Crumbling Walls." *Pentecostal Evangel,* 5 June 1943, 10.

——. "Writing from Ricardo, Texas." *Weekly Evangel,* 15 July 1916, 15.

Ball, Henry A., and Alice E. Luce. *Glimpses of Our Latin American Work in the*

United States and Mexico. Springfield, Mo.: Foreign Missions Department, 1940.

Balmer, Randall. *Blessed Assurance: A History of Evangelicalism in America.* Boston: Beacon, 1999.

Barton, Paul. "Inter-Ethnic Relations Between Mexican American and Anglo American Methodists." In *Protestantes/Protestants,* ed. David Maldonado, 60–84. Nashville: Abingdon, 1999.

Bax, Mable. "San Diego Bible School." *Pentecostal Evangel,* 13 July 1929, 11.

Bazán, Demetrio, and Nellie Bazán, with Elizabeth B. and Don Martínez Jr. *Enviados de Dios.* Miami, Fla.: Editorial Vida, 1987.

Bazán, Nellie. " '50 Años de Cristiana y De Ministerio Cristiana." *Luz Apostólica* (October 1967): 4.

——. "Conclusion." *Luz Apostólica* (June 1968): 9.

"Berean Bible Institute." *Pentecostal Evangel,* 21 July 1928, 13.

Berean Bible School. San Diego: Privately Printed, 1926?

"Bible School Opens in San Diego." *Pentecostal Evangel,* 13 November 1926, 4.

Billington, Ray Allen. *The Protestant Crusade.* Chicago: Quadrangle, 1964.

Bishop Putnam, Frank. "Teresa Urrea: The Saint of Cabora." In *Mystic Healers and Medicine Shows,* ed. Gene Fowler, 31–49. Santa Fe, N.M.: Ancient City, 1997.

Blajos, Art. *Blood In, Blood Out.* Crowborough, East Sussex: Monarch, 1996.

Blumhofer, Edith. *Restoring the Faith: The Assemblies of God, Pentecostalism, and American Culture.* Urbana: University of Illinois Press, 1993.

Brusco, Elizabeth. *Reforming Machismo.* Austin: University of Texas Press, 1995.

Bueno, Theodoro. "Home Missions Schools Branch Out." *Pentecostal Evangel,* 25 May 1969, 18.

Carnline, Pam. "Christian Anti-Gang Play Draws 6,000." *Riverside Press Telegram,* 30 June 1997.

Carpenter, Joel A. *Revive Us Again: The Reawakening of American Fundamentalism.* New York: Oxford University Press, 1997.

Castro, Del. "Victory Outreach School of Ministry: Equipping the Saints to Fulfill Vision 2000." *Inner City Vision* (Special Thirtieth Anniversary Edition) (1997): 28–29.

Chávez Saucedo, Teresa. "Race, Religion, and La Raza: An Exploration of the Racialization of Latinos in the United States and the Role of the Protestant Church." In *Protestantes/Protestants,* ed. David Maldonado, chap. 9 (Nashville: Abingdon, 1999).

Cox, Harvey. *Fire from Heaven.* New York: Addison Wesley, 1995.

Creech, Joe. "Visions of Glory: The Place of the Azusa Street Revival in Pentecostal History." *Church History* 65, no. 3 (September 1996): 405–25.

Cruz, Nicky. *Give Me Back My Dignity.* La Puente, Calif.: Cruz Press, 1993.

Csordas, Thomas. *Language, Charisma, and Creativity: The Ritual Life of a Religious Movement.* Berkeley: University of California Press, 1997.

Dayton, Donald W. *Theological Roots of Pentecostalism*. Peabody, Mass.: Hendrickson, 1987.

De Leon, Victor. *The Silent Pentecostals*. Taylors, S.C.: Faith Printing, 1979.

"Distribution of Missionary Funds." *Weekly Evangel*, 17 June 1916; 4 November 1916; 2 December 1916.

"Distribution of Missionary Funds," *Pentecostal Evangel*, 1926–28, various pages.

Duke of Earl. Videocassette Trinity Broadcasting Network, 1982.

Duryee, Spencer. "Great Aztec." *Christian Herald* (August 1936): 5.

Elwell, Walter A. "Revelation." In *Evangelical Commentary on the Bible*, 1197–1229, ed. Walter A. Elwell (Grand Rapids, Mich.: Baker, 1989).

Engh, Michael E. *Frontier Faiths: Church, Temple, and Synagogue in Los Angeles, 1846–1888*. Albuquerque: University of New Mexico Press, 1992.

Escobar, Edward J. *Race, Police, and the Making of a Political Identity: Mexican Americans and the Los Angeles Police Department, 1900–1945*. Berkeley: University of California Press, 1999.

Eskridge, Larry " 'One Way': Billy Graham, the Jesus Generation, and the Idea of an Evangelical Youth Culture." *Church History* 67, no. 1 (March 1998): 83–106.

Espinosa, Gastón. " 'El Azteca': Francisco Olazábal and Latino Pentecostal Charisma, Power, and Faith Healing in the Borderlands." *Journal of the American Academy of Religion* 67, no. 3 (September 1999): 597–616.

Evans, Sara. *Born for Liberty*. New York: Free Press, 1997.

Figueroa Deck, Allen. *The Challenge of Evangelical/Pentecostal Christianity to Hispanic Catholicism in the U.S. Working Paper Series: Cushwa Center for the Study of American Catholicism*. 1992.

"Flocking to See Mystic Santa Teresa." *Los Angeles Times*, 15 December 1902.

Flowers, J. R. "A Bible School for the Mexican Workers." *Pentecostal Evangel*, 6 January 1923, 13.

Fowler, Gene "Don Pedrito and Dr. Mud." In *Mystic Healers and Medicine Shows*, ed. Gene Fowler, 51–59. Santa Fe, N.M.: Ancient City, 1997.

García, Mario T. *Desert Immigrants: The Mexicans of El Paso, 1880–1920*. New Haven: Yale University Press, 1981.

García, Patsy. Untitled. Audiotape of speech. United Women in Ministry Convention, 1998.

Gaxiola-Gaxiola, Manuel. *El Serpiente y la Paloma*. South Pasadena: William Carey, 1970.

Gerlach, Luther P. "Pentecostalism: Revolution or Counterrevolution?" In *Religious Movements in Contemporary America*, ed. Irving I. Zaretsky and Mark P. Leone, 669–98. Princeton, N.J.: Princeton University Press, 1974.

Gohr, Glenn. "A Dedicated Ministry among Hispanics." *A/G Heritage* 9, no. 3 (fall 1989): 7–9, 17.

Grant, Richard. "Dial EmE for Murder." *Los Angeles Magazine*, May 1997, 34.

Griffith, R. Marie. *God's Daughters: Evangelical Women and the Power of Submission*. Berkeley: University of California Press, 1997.

Griswold del Castillo, Richard, and Arnoldo de León. *North to Aztlan: A History of Mexican Americans in the United States.* New York: Twayne, 1996.

Guillen, Miguel. *La Historia del Concilio Latino Americano de Iglesias Cristianas.* Brownsville, Tex.: Latin American Council of Christian Churches, 1982.

Hahn, Todd. *Gen-Xer's After God: Helping a Generation Pursue Jesus.* Grand Rapids, Mich.: Baker, 1998.

Hale, F. A. "Mexican Work at Ricardo, Tex." *Weekly Evangel,* 12 February 1916, 11.

Hart, Leon Gibson, and Carl D. Chambers. *The Heroin Epidemic.* New York: S. P. Books, 1976.

Harvest Bible College. Introduction to the catalogue. 1998.

Hernandez, Edwin I. "Moving from the Cathedral to Storefront Churches: Understanding Religious Growth and Decline among Latino Protestants." In *Protestantes/Protestants: Hispanic Christianity within Mainline Traditions,* ed. David Maldonado Jr., 216–35. Nashville, Tenn.: Abingdon, 1999.

Hine, Robert V. *California's Utopian Colonies.* New Haven: Yale University Press, 1966.

Holland, Clifton. "Appendice I." In *Hacia una Historia de la Iglesia Evangelica Hispana de California del Sur,* ed. Rodelo Wilson, 199–202. Montebello, Calif.: Hispanic Association for Theological Education, 1993.

——. *The Religious Dimension in Hispanic Los Angeles.* South Pasadena: William Carey Library, 1974.

"Hundreds Pray All Night at Unique Healing Service." *Cleveland Daily Banner,* 12 September 1936.

Johns, Cheryl Bridges. *Pentecostal Formation: A Pedagogy among the Oppressed.* Sheffield, England: Sheffield Academic Press, 1993.

Johns, Jackie D. "Pentecostalism and the Postmodern World View." *Journal of Pentecostal Theology* 7 (1995): 73–96.

Kelley, David. "Inland Gangs: Solutions." *Riverside Press Telegram,* 15 December 1998.

Kelty, H. May. "Needs of Bible Institute." *Pentecostal Evangel,* 27 August 1927, 11.

Kenney, L. V. "An Appeal." *Weekly Evangel,* 21 April 1917, 13.

Kessler-Harris, Alice. *Out to Work: A History of Wage-Earning Women in the United States.* Oxford: Oxford University Press, 1982.

LABI Catalogues. 1948–49; 1975–79; 1992–97.

LABI Yearbooks. 1952–59; 1970–79; 1980–82; 1988–89; 1992–97.

Land, Stephen J. *Pentecostal Spirituality: A Passion for the Kingdom.* Sheffield, England: Sheffield Press, 1993.

Laslett, John H. M. "Historical Perspectives: Immigration and the Rise of a Distinctive Urban Region, 1900–1970." In *Ethnic Los Angeles,* ed. Roger Waldinger and Mehdi Bozorguehr, 39–75. New York: Russell Sage, 1996.

Lavayen, Mary Ann. Untitled. Audiotape of speech. United Women in Ministry Leadership Retreat, 1996.

Lawless, Elaine J. "The Night I Got the Holy Ghost: Holy Ghost Narratives and the Pentecostal Conversion Process." In *Western Folklore* 47 (January 1988): 1–19.

——. "Rescripting Their Lives and Narratives: Spiritual Life Stories of Pentecostal Women Preachers." *Journal of Feminist Studies in Religion* 7 (spring 1991): 53–71.

"Latin American Bible Institute." *Pentecostal Evangel*, 13 December 1937, 7.

León, Luís. "Born Again in East LA: The Congregation as Border Space." In *Gatherings in Diaspora: Religious Communities and the New Immigration*, ed. R. Stephen Warner and Judith G. Wittner, 163–96 (Philadelphia: Temple University Press, 1998).

Lewis, Stacey. Untitled. Audiotape of speech. United Women in Ministry Convention, 1998.

Long, John M. "Drug Use Patterns in Two Los Angeles Barrio Gangs." In *Drugs in the Hispanic Community*, ed. Ronald Glick and Joan Moore, 155–65. New York: Rutgers University Press, 1990.

López, Abundio. "Spanish Receive the Pentecost." *Apostolic Faith* 1, no. 10 (October 1906): 4.

Los Angeles City Directory. Los Angeles: Los Angeles Public Library, microfilm, 1912, 1920.

Luce, Alice E. "Commencement at Latin American Bible Institute." *Pentecostal Evangel*, 6 June 1936, 9.

——. "Encouraging Report of Mexican Work." *Pentecostal Evangel*, 24 January 1920, 11.

——. "The Latin American Pentecostal Work." *Pentecostal Evangel*, 25 June 1927, 6.

——. "Latin American Bible Institute." *Latter Rain Evangel* (December 1930): 17–18.

——. "Latin American Bible Institute." *Pentecostal Evangel*, 6 June 1942, 7.

——. *El Mensajero y Su Mensaje: Manual Para Obreros Cristianos*. Rev. ed. Springfield, Mo.: Casa de Publicaciónes Evangelicas, 1953.

——. "Mexican Work in California." *Pentecostal Evangel*, 1 September 1923, 13.

——. "Mexican Work along the Border." *Christian Evangel*, 15 June 1918, 11.

——. *Missionary Report*. Assemblies of God Headquarters, Springfield, Missouri, 1920.

——. "Portions for Whom Nothing Is Prepared." *Pentecostal Evangel*, 9 December 1922, 6–7.

——. *Probad Los Espiritus*. San Antonio: Casa Evangelica de Publicaciónes, 1900.

——. "Scriptural Methods in Missionary Work." *Pentecostal Evangel*, 9 May 1931, 8–9.

——. "Strangers within our Gates." *Latter Rain Evangel* (December 1930): 22.

Maffly Kipp, Laura. *Society and Religion on the California Frontier*. Berkeley: University of California Press, 1994.

Martínez, Faith. Untitled. Audiotape of speech. United Women in Ministry Leadership Retreat, 1996.

Mathison, Dirk. "Gunning for God?" *Los Angeles Magazine*, November 1997, 72–83.

Matovina, Timothy M. *Tejano Religion and Ethnicity: San Antonio, 1821–1860.* Austin: University of Texas Press, 1995.

Melendres, Simón. Interview by author. Tape recording. La Puente, California, 9 July 1997.

Melton, J. Gordon. *Biographical Dictionary of American Cult and Sect Leaders.* New York: Garland, 1986.

——, ed. *Encyclopedia of American Religions and Religious Creeds.* Chicago: Gale Research, 1988.

Miller, Donald E. *Reinventing American Protestantism.* Berkeley: University of California Press, 1998.

Miranda, Jesse. Interview by author. Tape recording. Azusa, California, 6 May 1997; 31 March 1998; 22 May 1998.

——. "LABC." *El Eco Escolar* (1980?): 2–3.

——. "A Study of LABI and Suggested Ways for Improvement." M.R. thesis, Talbot Seminary, Biola University, June 1969.

Moore, Joan. *Homeboys: Gangs, Drugs, and Prison in the Barrios of Los Angeles.* Philadelphia: Temple University Press, 1978.

Moore, Joan, and John Hagedorn. "What Happens to Girls in the Gang?" In *Gangs in America*, ed. C. Ronald Huff, chap. 10. Thousand Oaks, Calif.: Sage, 1996.

Morales, Ed, and Mitzi Morales. *Defying the Odds.* Green Forest, Ark.: New Leaf, 1991.

"The Needs of Mexico." *Pentecostal Evangel*, 15 October 1921, 3.

Neimeyer, E. V. "Anticlericalism in the Mexican Constitutional Convention of 1916–17." *The Americas* 11 (July 1954): 31–49.

O'Brien, Gregory S. "A Short History of the Pacific Latin District of the Assemblies of God." Unpublished paper. Assemblies of God Theological Seminary, Springfield, Missouri, March 1994.

Olazábal, Francisco. "Carta Abierta al Hermano Richey." In *El Rdo. Francisco Olazábal*, 3. Brownsville, Tex.: Latin American Council of Christian Churches, 1986.

——. "Extracts from Missionary Letters." *Triumphs of Faith* 48 no. 6 (June 1920): 142.

——. "Preguntas y Repuestas." In *El Rdo. Francisco*, 207. Brownsville, Tex.: Latin American Council of Christian Churches, 1986.

——. "Speech to the Ninth Annual Convention of the Los Angeles District of the Epworth League." In *El Rdo. Olazábal*, 192–93. Brownsville, Tex.: Latin American Council of Christian Churches, 1986.

——. "Work among the Mexicans." *Triumphs of Faith* 38, no. 3 (March 1919): 71–72.

Ortegón, Samuel. "Mexican Religious Population of Los Angeles." Masters thesis, University of Southern California, 1932.

Pascoe, Peggy. *Relations of Rescue: The Search for Female Moral Authority in the American West, 1874–1939*. New York: Oxford University Press, 1990.

Peters, Tena Katie. *An Investigation into the Role of Religious Experience and Commitment as a Therapeutic Factor in the Treatment and Rehabilitation of Selected Drug Addicts from Teen Challenge: A Follow-up Study*. Ph.D. diss., New York University, 1980.

Pineda, Josey. Untitled. Audiotape of speech. United Women in Ministry Convention, 1998.

Pinson, M. M. "A Mexican Tent Meeting." *Weekly Evangel* 28 (July 1917): 12.

Poloma, Margaret. "The Assemblies of God at the Crossroads." In *Religion: North American Style*, ed. Thomas E. Dowdy and Patrick McNamara, 104–11. New Brunswick, N.J.: Rutgers University Press, 1997.

Portes, Alejandro, and Rubén G. Rumbaut. *Legacies: The Story of the Immigrant Second Generation*. Berkeley: University of California Press, 2001.

Preston, John. "Calexico, Calif." *Pentecostal Evangel*, 28 December 1918, 10.

Ramírez, Daniel. "Pentecostal Praxis: A History of Latino Immigrants and the Apostolic Assemblies." Paper presented at the annual meeting of the Society for Pentecostal Studies, Southeastern College, Lakeland, Florida, 5 September 1991.

"Report of Trip Through Texas." *Pentecostal Evangel*, 12 June 1920, 10.

Rimstead, Roxanne. "Mediated Lives: Oral Histories and Cultural Memory." *Essays on Canadian Writing*, no. 60 (winter 1996): 139–65.

Robeck, Cecil M., Jr. "Evangelization or Proselytism of Hispanics? A Pentecostal Perspective." Unpublished paper (1996): 5.

——, ed. *Witness to Pentecost: The Life of Frank Bartleman* (New York: Garland, 1985).

Rodriguez, Jeannette. "Guadalupe: The Feminine Face of God." In *Goddess of the Americas: Writings on the Virgen de Guadalupe*, ed. Ana Castillo, 25–33. New York: Riverhead, 1996.

Rose, Tricia. *Black Noise: Rap Music and Black Culture in Contemporary America*. Boston: Wesleyan University Press, 1994.

Ruiz, Vicki L. "Dead Ends or Gold Mines? Using Missionary Records in Mexican American Women's History." In *Unequal Sisters*, ed. Vicki L. Ruiz and Ellen Carol Dubois, 2nd ed., 298–313. New York: Routledge, 1994.

——. *From Out of the Shadows*. New York: Oxford University Press, 1998.

Sample, Tex. *Hard Living People and Mainstream Christians*. Nashville: Abingdon, 1993.

Sánchez, George. *Becoming Mexican American*. New York: Oxford University Press, 1993.

Sánchez, Josué. *Angels Without Wings*. Edited by Monte R. Madsen. New Braunfels, Tex.: Atwood, n.d.

Sánchez Jankowski, Martín. *Islands in the Street: Gangs and American Urban Society*. Berkeley: University of California Press, 1991.

Sánchez Korrol, Virginia. *From Colonia to Community: The History of Puerto Ricans in New York City*. Berkeley: University of California Press, 1983.

Seymour, William "Missionary Notes."*Apostolic Faith* 1, no. 10 (October 1906): 4.

——. "Missionary Notes." *Apostolic Faith* 1, no. 11 (November 1906): 3.

Singleton, Gregory. *Religion in the City of the Angels*. Ann Arbor, Mich.: University Microfilms Inc. Research, 1979.

Smidt, Corwin, and Lyman Kellstedt, et al. "Spirit-Filled Movements in Contemporary America: A Survey Perspective." In *Pentecostal Currents in American Protestantism*, ed. Grant A. Wacker, Edith Blumhofer, et al., 111–127 (Champaign: University of Illinois Press, 1999).

Smith, Christian. *American Evangelicalism: Embattled and Thriving*. Chicago: University of Chicago Press, 1998.

Stark, Rodney, and Roger Finke, *The Churching of America, 1776–1900*. New Brusnwick, N.J.: Rutgers University Press, 1992.

Stock, Jennifer, "George S. Montgomery: Businessman for the Gospel." *A/G Heritage* 9, No. 2 (summer 1989): 12–14, 20.

"A Sunday Service in Pisgah Tabernacle." *Word and Work* 28 (September 1918): 7.

Sweet, Leonard. *Soul Tsunami: Sink or Swim in the New Millennium Culture*. New York: Zondervan, 1999.

Synan, Vinson. *The Holiness Pentecostal Tradition*. Grand Rapids, Mich.: Eardmans, 1997.

Teen Challenge Monthly Report 2, no. 6 (August 1966): 1.

Thomas, G. H. "The Value of the Bible School in the Latin American Work." *Pentecostal Evangel*, 28 March 1931, 10.

Toulis, Nicole Rodriguez. *Believing Identity: Pentecostalism and the Mediation of Jamaican Ethnicity and Gender in England*. Oxford: Berg, 1997.

Turner, Victor. *The Ritual Process Structure and Anti-Structure*. Ithaca, N.Y.: Cornell University Press, 1977 [1969].

Underground Fire: Hip Hop/DJ/Dance Culture Magazine for the Faithful. Winter 1999.

Valdez, A. G. *Fire On Azusa Street*. Costa Mesa, Calif.: Gift, 1980.

Valdez, Lillian, and Berta García. "Historia." *Luz Apostólica* (June 1967), 3.

Vasquez, Jane Atkins. "La Iglesia Presbiteriana Unida." In *Hacia una Historia de la Iglesia Evangelica Hispana*, ed. Rodelo Wilson, 65–76. Montebello, Calif.: Hispanic Association for Theological Education. 1993.

"Veteran Missionary Dies." *Pentecostal Evangel*, 30 November 1955, 30.

Victory Outreach Handbook. 1998.

Vigil, James Diego. *Barrio Gangs: Street Life and Identity in Southern California*. Austin: University of Texas Press, 1988.

Villafañe, Eldin. *The Liberating Spirit*. Grand Rapids, Mich.: Eardmans, 1997.

Wacker, Grant A. *Heaven Below*. Boston, Mass.: Harvard University Press, 2001.

——."The Pentecostal Tradition." In *Caring and Curing: Health and Medicine in the Western Religious Tradition*, ed. Ronald L. Numbers and Darrell W. Amundsen, 514–38. New York: Macmillan, 1986.

——. "Travail of a Broken Family: Radical Evangelical Responses to the Emergence of Pentecostalism in America, 1906–1916." In *Pentecostal Currents in American Protestantism*, ed. Edith L. Blumhofer, Russell P. Spittler, and Grant A. Wacker, 23–49. Urbana: University of Illinois Press, 1999.

——. "Wimber and Wonders—What about Miracles Today?" *Reformed Journal* 37 (April 1987): 16–19.

Weber, Devra. *Dark Sweat, White Gold: California Farm Workers, Cotton, and the New Deal*. Berkeley: University of California Press, 1994.

Wilkerson, David, New York, to Theodoro Bueno, La Puente, March 1965, LABI Office Files, Box 2.

——. *The Cross and the Switchblade*. New York: Bernard Geis, 1963.

——. "New Hope for Narcotic Addicts." *Teen Challenge Challenger* (spring 1965): 8.

Wimber, John. *Power Evangelism*. San Francisco: Harper Collins, 1987.

"Women in the Church." *Barna Reports* (March 2000). *www.barna.com*.

Wuthnow Robert. *After Heaven: Spirituality in America since the 1950s*. Berkeley: University of California Press, 1998.

Yang, Hong Yeun-Cheng. "Formation of Pentecostal Spirituality through Theological Education Toward Effective Ministry." D.M. diss., Ashland Theological Seminary, 1992.

Index